FUNDAMENTALS
of
SUPPLY
CHAIN
MANAGEMENT

D1051672

To my wife, Brenda, and daughters, Ashley and Erin, who are always understanding when I am writing another book.

FUNDAMENTALS *of* SUPPLY CHAIN MANAGEMENT

Twelve Drivers of Competitive Advantage

John T. Mentzer

University of Tennessee, Knoxville

SAGE Publications
International Educational and Professional Publisher
Thousand Oaks ■ London ■ New Delhi

For information:

Sage Publications, Inc.
2455 Teller Road
Thousand Oaks, California 91320
E-mail: order@sagepub.com

Sage Publications Ltd.
1 Oliver's Yard
55 City Road
London EC1Y 1SP
United Kingdom

Sage Publications India Pvt. Ltd.
B-42, Panchsheel Enclave
Post Box 4109
New Delhi 110 017 India

Printed in the United States of America

Library of Congress Cataloging-in-Publication Data

Mentzer, John T.
Fundamentals of supply chain management: Twelve drivers of competitive advantage / John T. Mentzer.
    p. cm.
Includes bibliographical references and index.
  ISBN 0-7619-2908-8 (pbk.)
  1. Business logistics-Management. I. Title.
HD38.5.M463 2004
658.7—dc22   2003027866

This book is printed on acid-free paper.

04 05 06 07 10 9 8 7 6 5 4 3 2 1

Acquisitions Editor:	Al Bruckner
Editorial Assistant:	MaryAnn Vail
Production Editor:	Diane S. Foster
Copy Editor:	Robert Holm
Typesetter:	C&M Digitals (P) Ltd.
Proofreader:	Scott Oney
Indexer:	Will Ragsdale
Cover Designer:	Janet Foulger

Contents

1

Supply Chain Management

I t has been a true privilege to write this book—for the information necessary to write it came from many wonderful people: first, all the authors who wrote the more than 400 books, articles, and papers that went into the readings that were necessary to understand what supply chain management (SCM) is all about; second, the over 50 executives in major global companies who were generous enough with their time to be interviewed on their opinions of the scope and nature of SCM; third, the faculty, students, and practitioners who regularly participate in the meetings of the University of Tennessee's Supply Chain Management & Strategy Forum for their insights and critiques; and finally, the practitioners in the many companies that make up the examples and case studies in this book (my especial gratitude for their willingness to have their companies profiled, though disguised, in these pages). It is the in-depth experience we gained through working with these companies that led to the real purpose of the book: how to use supply chain management to drive competitive advantage.

Why Supply Chain Management as a Source of Competitive Advantage?

Why do so many people spend so much time thinking, writing, and doing SCM? The answer is that it is a considerable source of competitive advantage in the global marketplace. But why? The fierce competition in today's markets is led by advances in industrial technology, increased globalization, tremendous improvements in information availability, plentiful venture capital, and creative business designs (Bovet & Sheffi, 1998). In highly competitive markets, the simple pursuit of market share is no longer sufficient to ensure profitability and, thus, companies focus on redefining their competitive space or profit zone (Bovet & Sheffi, 1998). For example, companies pursue cooperative relationships to capture lifetime customer share rather than mass market share through systematic development and management of cooperative and collaborative partnerships (Gruen, 1997). Markets have been changed by such factors as power shifts from corporate buyers to end users, the requirement for mass customization, globalization, time, and quality-based competition, advances in technology, increasing knowledge intensity, and changing government policies.

Power in a broad spectrum of supply chains has shifted downstream toward the customer or end user (LaLonde, 1997) and, as a result, customer satisfaction becomes the ultimate goal of a company. As the customer increasingly is in charge in the marketplace, interfirm cooperation is critical to satisfy customers. Manufacturers and their intermediaries must be nimble and quick or face the prospect of losing market share and, thus, relationships and predictable performance become very important in a supply chain (LaLonde, 1997).

Mass customization provides a tremendous increase in variety and customization without sacrificing efficiency, effectiveness, or low costs (Pine, 1993). In other words, customers want low cost with high levels of service, and customization with availability (Bovet & Sheffi, 1998). Pine (1993), therefore, argues that mass customization can be achieved only through the committed involvement of employees, suppliers, distributors, retailers, and end customers.

Firms are competing in a global economy and, thus, the unit of business analysis is the world, not just a country or region. The communications revolution and globalization of consumer culture will not tolerate hand-me-down designs or excessive delivery times (Bovet & Sheffi, 1998). In this context, Kotler (1997) states, "As firms globalize, they realize that no matter how large they are, they lack the total resources and requisites for success. Viewing the complete supply chain for producing value, they recognize the necessity of partnering with other organizations."

Time- and quality-based competition focuses on eliminating waste in the form of time, effort, defective units, and inventory in manufacturing-distribution systems (Larson & Lusch, 1990; Schonberger & El-Ansary, 1984; Schultz, 1985). In addition, there has been a significant trend to emphasize quality, not only in the production of products or services, but also throughout all areas in a company (Coyle, Bardi, & Langley, 1996).

LaLonde and Powers (1993) suggest that the most profound and influential changes that directly affect companies are information technology and communications. With the advent of modern computers and communications, monolithic companies, which had become highly bureaucratic, started eroding. Fast communication that links all the members of a company decreased the need for multiple layers of people who were once the information channel and control mechanism. The decreased cost and ready availability of information resources allow easy linkages and eliminate time delays in the network (LaLonde & Powers, 1993).

In the new competitive landscape, knowledge (information, intelligence, and expertise) is a critical organizational resource and is increasingly a valuable source of competitive advantage (Hitt, Ireland, & Hoskisson, 1999). Similarly, LaLonde and Powers (1993) characterized the 1990s as the era of reassembly or reintegration after that of disintegration. Current reintegration is based not on position or prescribed roles in a hierarchy; it is based on knowledge and competence (LaLonde & Powers, 1993). Bringing together the knowledge and skills to effectively serve the market requires coordination (Malone & Rockart, 1991).

Finally, government policy may encourage cooperative strategies among firms. The U.S. *1996 Telecommunications Act* and subsequent court battles have created significant uncertainty for the firms involved, and consequently a significant number of alliances have emerged (Hitt et al., 1999). The enactment of the U.S. *National Cooperative Research Act of 1984,* as amended in 1993, eased the U.S. government's antitrust policy to encourage firms to cooperate with each other to foster increased competitiveness of American industries (Bowersox & Closs, 1996; Barlow, 1994).

Today's business environment puts stress on both relations with customers and the service provided such customers (Hitt et al., 1999). Kotler (1997) argued, "Customers are scarce; without them, the company ceases to exist. Plans must be laid to acquire and keep customers." The level of competition to capture customers in both domestic and international markets demands that organizations be quick, agile, and flexible to compete effectively (LaLonde, 1997; Fliedner & Vokurka, 1997). This quick, agile flexibility cannot be obtained without coordination of the companies in the supply chain.

Through all the sources mentioned earlier (the literature, executive interviews, and companies with which we have worked), we identified 12 drivers of competitive advantage that result from supply chain management, and these are the focus of this book. We will introduce these drivers later in this chapter, and each (with numerous examples) will be the subject of a subsequent chapter. However, first we need to explore the concept of supply chain management, starting with the discipline in which it originated—logistics.

Logistics and Supply Chain Management

The Council of Logistics Management, the "preeminent worldwide professional association of logistics personnel" (CLM, 2003), defines logistics as

> that part of the supply chain process that plans, implements, and controls the efficient, effective forward and reverse flow and storage of goods, services, and related information between the point of origin and the point of consumption in order to meet customers' requirements.

This definition tells us that logistics is managing all the movement and storage activities that are associated with product and service flows. It is focused on what we call the "focal organization," that is, on managing that organization's inbound and outbound flows of goods, services, and related information. We can imagine that "related information" encompasses inventory quantities and locations, order status, shipment status and location, transportation status and vehicle location, and so forth. But what about information that flows up and down a supply chain that is not related to the flow of goods and services? Information on marketing plans, advertising effectiveness, pricing structure, product management status, ownership and title, and financial status do not seem to be within the realm of logistics. For that matter, what about actual financial flows?

Arguably, SCM has risen to prominence from its beginnings in the logistics literature (Cooper, Lambert, & Pagh, 1997). For example, at the 1995 Annual Conference of the Council of Logistics Management, 13.5% of the concurrent session titles contained the words "supply chain." At the 1997 conference, just 2 years later, the number of sessions containing the term rose to 22.4%. However, there are clearly flows up and down the supply chain that are not part of the CLM definition of logistics. CLM acknowledges that SCM is something more than logistics by stating, "Logistics is that part of the supply chain process that. . . ." So, SCM must encompass logistics and these other flows mentioned above.

It was this realization that led the Supply Chain Research Group at the University of Tennessee (Mentzer, 2000) to define SCM as

> the systemic, strategic coordination of the traditional business functions within a particular company and across businesses within the supply chain, for the purposes of improving the long-term performance of the individual companies and the supply chain as a whole.

Unlike logistics, which focuses on the inbound and outbound flow of products, services, and related information from a focal organization's perspective, this definition leads us to the conclusion that SCM is a management process that deals with inbound and outbound flows, from the perspective of the focal organization, its suppliers, and its customers. This means a fundamental aspect of supply chain management is the consideration of not just the cost and profit goals of one company (the focal organization), but of all the companies involved in managing the supply chain.

This led the Supply Chain Research Group at the University of Tennessee (Mentzer, 2000) to define a supply chain as

> a set of three or more companies directly linked by one or more of the upstream and downstream flows of products, services, finances, and information from a source to a customer.

Since SCM involves managing inbound and outbound flows so that *all* companies involved benefit, it follows that a supply chain must entail three or more separate entities (companies). Further, the scope of SCM is much more than just inbound and outbound flows of products, services, and related information—it encompasses all the inbound and outbound flows between organizations in the supply chain. When we put together these definitions of supply chains and SCM, we realize that SCM is *the strategic management of all the traditional business functions that are involved in any flows, upstream or downstream, across any aspect of the supply chain system.*

Thus, SCM encompasses all the traditional business functions, their coordination within individual companies, and their coordination across companies in the supply chain. Mentzer (2000) illustrated this with Figure 1.1 (see page 23). First, supply chains today consist of all suppliers and customers, and they exist in a global environment. We know of no company that does not sell in a global market, source globally, or compete with a company that does. Second, all the traditional business functions must be coordinated within individual companies before they can be coordinated across companies in the supply chain (more on this in Chapter 2). Third, the intracompany concepts of trust, commitment, risk, and dependence must be managed with the intercompany concepts of functional shifting (more on this point in Chapter 3), third-party providers, relationship management, and supply chain structures, to efficiently and effectively manage the six flows of any supply chain. Finally, *efficiently* means with minimal commitment of financial resources, and *effectiveness* means providing customer satisfaction and value, which (combined with efficiency) leads to profitability, which leads to competitive advantage.

From this perspective, the members of the University of Tennessee Supply Chain Research Group (Mentzer, 2000) drew a number of fundamental conclusions regarding how to accomplish SCM. Although the purpose of this book is to discuss the utilization of SCM to achieve competitive advantage, the conclusions from the authors contributing to Mentzer (2000) are summarized here to provide a foundation for all our subsequent discussion of SCM.

Fundamental Conclusions About SCM

The members of the University of Tennessee Supply Chain Research Group (Mentzer, 2000) drew a number of managerial conclusions about SCM in 15 separate, but related, areas.

THE GLOBAL SUPPLY CHAIN MANAGEMENT ENVIRONMENT

Considering the globalization of the world economy, the diversity and environmental factors that influence a firm's global strategies and approach, drivers influencing firms to become increasingly global, and the different approaches to globalization that might be adopted by firms, Nix (2000a) concluded:

- Different approaches to globalization require different degrees of supply chain integration, and different supply chain strategies and structure.
- Whatever approach to globalization and global supply chain management is adopted, firms face the challenges of understanding and managing the greater complexity and risks inherent in the global environment.
- Global supply chain strategies must be developed in support of the strategic thrust of a firm's globalization initiatives, and must consider opportunities for global efficiency, management of risks, learning to enable innovation and adaptation, and the need to balance global efficiency and local responsiveness.
- Global supply chain processes should provide operating flexibility to respond to changes in the macroeconomic environment or government policies that adversely affect supply chain performance.
- Design and management of supply chain activities must consider the influence of differences in culture, industry structure, legal requirements, and infrastructure in different countries on customers, suppliers, competitors, and supply chain partners.
- The management of financial systems in a global supply chain must address differences in financial accounting systems, comparability of data, management of terms of sale and ownership transfer to minimize risk and optimize profits, optimization of transfer pricing to minimize taxes, the minimization of foreign exchange risks, and the use of countertrade.
- A much broader set of skills is required of supply chain professionals to successfully manage on a global basis, including operating knowledge of the global environment, understanding how to manage inherent risks, and the ability to deal with differences in language and culture.
- Compatibility of information technologies and standardization of systems and data are critical to a firm's ability to integrate supply chain operations on a global basis.
- Decision support tools that incorporate global variables and allow "what if" scenario analysis are important to enable managers to more effectively manage the complexities and uncertainties of the global environment.

Managerial Conclusion: No matter which approach to globalization is pursued, firms are faced with the challenges of understanding and managing the complexities and risks inherent in the global environment. Global supply chain managers must develop capabilities that allow them to understand the complexities in the global environment, anticipate significant changes, and adapt to those changes as needed. Systems and processes must be designed to address important environmental variables, and organizational skills and capabilities must be developed to deal with different languages, cultures, and business environments.

SCM OUTPUTS

Considering the overall objectives of supply chain management of creating value for customers, and competitive advantage and improved profitability for supply chain firms, the dimensions of value that may be important to customers, and the mechanisms whereby competitive advantage and improved profitability can be achieved for supply chain members, Nix (2000b) concluded:

- The objective of SCM is to increase the competitive advantage of the supply chain as a whole, rather than to increase the advantage of any single firm.
- The means to accomplish competitive advantage is through creating value for downstream customers greater than that offered by competitors.
- Customer value is created through collaboration and cooperation to improve efficiency (lower cost) or market effectiveness (added benefits) in ways that are most valuable to key customers.
- Value is not inherent in products or services, but rather is perceived or experienced by the customer.
- In order to compete through creating customer value, a firm must understand and deliver the value perceived as important by its customers.
- Since the value perceived as important will differ across customer segments, a firm must identify the customer segments important to its long-term success and match the capability of the firm to delivering the value important to those key customers.
- Value can be created at many points along the supply chain by making the customer firm at that point in the chain more effective in serving its markets, or more efficient and cost-effective in its operations.
- Delivering customer value in dimensions important to customers better than the competition leads to customer satisfaction and competitive advantage.
- By satisfying customers and achieving competitive advantage, firms in a supply chain influence customers to make choices and behave in ways that improve the financial performance of the supply chain and the firms within it.

Managerial Conclusion: The degree to which value is created for customers, and the customer's perception of the value received relative to that offered by the competition, are reflected in the customer's satisfaction with the offering. Customers who are satisfied with value created in areas important to them are expected to behave in ways that are beneficial to a firm's or a supply chain's success. Purchase behavior, customer loyalty, and positive communications about products and services result from customer satisfaction and, at the same time, contribute to a firm's or supply chain's success. In order to achieve these objectives, supply chain managers must work collaboratively with customers and suppliers to identify and deliver value considered important by critical downstream customers.

THE ROLE OF MARKETING IN SCM

Given the role of marketing in the implementation of supply chain management, suggested by a cause-and-effect relationship between the marketing concept, a market orientation, relationship marketing, and SCM, Min (2000a) concluded:

- The objective of marketing is creating exchanges, and the output of it is customer satisfaction.
- The marketing concept consists of three pillars: (1) customer focus, (2) coordinated marketing, and (3) profitability.
- The marketing concept is a business philosophy, guiding a firm toward customer satisfaction at a profit.
- A market orientation is the implementation of that philosophy, forcing the firm to generate, disseminate, and respond to market information.
- The marketing concept not only provides the philosophical foundation of a market orientation, but also plays an important role in the management of a firm, interfunctional relationships, and the implementation of SCM.
- A market orientation also affects the management of a firm, interfirm relationships, and a supply chain. That is, a market orientation leads a firm to focus on market information generation, dissemination, and responsiveness to satisfy customers, coordinate its marketing efforts, redefine the responsibilities of each function, restructure its organizational system, and achieve superior business performance. At the same time, a market orientation provides an environment that encourages a firm in its efforts to develop, maintain, and enhance close relationships with other firms, organizational learning from other firms, and building commitment, trust, and cooperative norms in the relationships with other firms.
- A market orientation is performed both inside and outside a firm to recognize and respond to customers' needs, and obtain experiences, products, skills, technologies, and knowledge from outside the firm that are not available to other competitors.
- A market orientation promotes the implementation of SCM.
- Relationship marketing aims at establishing, maintaining, and enhancing either dyadic relationships or multiple relationships in a supply chain to create better customer value.
- Relationship marketing helps achieve such objectives of SCM as efficiency (i.e., cost reduction) and effectiveness (i.e., customer service) through increased cooperation in close long-term interfirm relationships among the supply chain partners.
- With the help of the marketing concept, a market orientation, and relationship marketing, SCM achieves competitive advantage for the supply chain and its partners by reducing costs and investments, and improving customer service.

Managerial Conclusion: The role of marketing through the marketing concept, a market orientation, and relationship marketing is essential for the success of supply chain management.

THE ROLE OF SALES IN SCM

Given that the role of the contemporary salesperson is changing dramatically, and that in many situations, the old models of selling are simply outdated, ineffective, and counterproductive to supply chain management goals and objectives, Garver and Min (2000) concluded:

- While most sales organizations focus on prepurchase activities, supply chain partners focus on managing relationships and conducting postpurchase activities to enhance supply chain performance.
- The sales force is well positioned to implement, facilitate, and coordinate many supply chain management activities.
- In short, the supply chain sales force should be involved with any supply chain activity that goes beyond organizational boundaries.
- More specifically, the sales force should be an integral part of implementing cooperative behaviors (i.e., joint planning, evaluating, and forecasting), mutually sharing information, and nurturing supply chain relationships.
- To be effective at their new role, the supply chain sales force must gain new expertise in logistics and supply chain management. Salesperson logistics expertise is defined as a customer's perception of a salesperson's knowledge, experience, or skills relevant to logistics issues. Salesperson logistics expertise concerns the seller's and supply chain partners' logistics operations, systems, and processes at both tactical and strategic levels. Thus, salesperson logistics expertise includes internal (company) logistics expertise, external (supply chain partner) logistics expertise, tactical logistics expertise, and strategic logistics expertise.
- While the logistics manager may be the primary person designing logistics solutions, the salesperson is likely to be the primary person representing the supply chain partner's needs and requirements.
- For effective teamwork and innovative solutions, salespeople and logistics managers need to be able to communicate effectively and work together on supply chain management issues.

Managerial Conclusion: To support the sales force in their new supply chain management roles, sales managers need to train, support, and encourage supply chain activities and logistics expertise. To achieve this goal, sales managers must also adopt a new orientation and embrace new management techniques to enhance supply chain performance. Specifically, sales managers must become *change agents* in the sales organization and lead the sales force in a new direction. Traditional training programs, performance objectives, and compensation packages need to be adapted and better aligned with supply chain management.

THE ROLE OF RESEARCH AND DEVELOPMENT IN SCM

Considering the role of research and development (R&D) within the firm, and with suppliers, customers, and the supply chain, Zacharia (2000a) concluded:

- Supply chain activities have a major impact on the capabilities and profitability of the supply chain and its member firms in new product development.
- Innovative and effective new-product development is important in the turbulent, highly uncertain business environment of the future.
- By collaborating with immediate customers and suppliers, R&D can significantly improve the new-product development process.
- By collaborating with customers' customers and suppliers' suppliers along the supply chain, R&D improves the new-product development process.
- Companies that are multinational in scope can benefit through globalization of the R&D process and collaborating with global supply chain partners.
- The concept of postponement, delaying final product configuration as close to the end consumer as possible, benefits greatly from collaborating R&D with supply chain partners.
- Speed to market or reducing the cycle time to develop new products can be improved significantly through supply chain R&D involvement.
- Flexible new-product development enables companies to incorporate rapidly changing customer requirements and evolving technologies through supply chain R&D involvement.

Managerial Conclusion: Broadening the knowledge base involved in a firm's R&D process better enables managers to design and develop effective and efficient new-product development systems. This suggests that developing a supply chain orientation for R&D leads to opportunities for lower costs, improved customer value, and competitive advantages for the long term.

THE ROLE OF FORECASTING IN SCM

Given the increasingly important contribution to supply chain performance offered through effective sales forecasting management, Smith (2000) concluded:

- Supply chain sales forecasting management can significantly influence operating performance within each member, and across members, of a supply chain.
- To affect supply chain operations in a positive manner, organizations working together in a supply chain must improve forecasting management performance (an internally directed measure) as well as supply chain forecasting management performance (a cross-company measure).
- The four dimensions of sales forecasting management—functional integration, approach, systems, and performance measurement—can be extended to incorporate a supply chain orientation.
- Initiatives such as Collaborative Planning, Forecasting, and Replenishment (CPFR) reflect the four forecasting management dimensions and provide an approach to forecasting that addresses factors that influence forecasting management performance and supply chain forecasting management performance.

Managerial Conclusion: In order to contribute to improved supply chain performance, supply chain managers must go beyond traditional measures of forecast accuracy to understand the overall supply chain demand-planning process and influence the behaviors of individuals and organizations involved in the development and application of sales forecasts.

THE ROLE OF PRODUCTION IN SCM

Considering the role of production within the firm, with suppliers, customers, and the supply chain, Zacharia (2000b) concluded:

- Functional products in stable markets need a supply chain production system that focuses on reducing volume cost and increasing production efficiency.
- Highly innovative products in uncertain, constantly changing environments need a supply chain production system that focuses on strategic flexibility and speed to market.
- Dispersed production is a supply chain production system of great value in a globally competitive market that focuses on cost efficiency.
- Build to order production and postponement are useful supply chain production systems in markets with quickly obsolete existing products, rapidly changing customer requirements, and shrinking product life cycles.

Managerial Conclusion: Understanding the different types of production systems better enables managers to design and develop the production system that is most suitable for the specific supply chain market environment.

THE ROLE OF PURCHASING IN SCM

Given the evolution of the role of purchasing and the purchasing role in support of a firm's SCM strategies and objectives, as well as the objectives and role of purchasing in a supply chain management context versus historical approaches, Nix (2000c) concluded:

- Purchasing plays a critical, boundary-spanning role in the supply chain management activities of a firm.
- In order to achieve the potential benefits of SCM, the role of purchasing must be viewed in a systemwide context, and must be focused beyond managing the buyer-seller relationship.
- Managers must understand the potential benefits to be achieved through SCM relationships, based on environmental conditions and specific resource or performance requirements.
- It is important for managers to understand the potential benefits, as well as the costs, of developing such relationships so that appropriate business decisions can be made.
- In order to be successful in achieving SCM objectives, purchasing requirements must be understood within the context of the overall strategy of the firm,

supply chain partners must be selected to meet the strategic requirements, and the relationships must be managed appropriately over the long term.

- Cost and quality improvements must be understood and implemented from a systemwide perspective to achieve optimum results.
- To achieve the objectives of improved quality and reliability, reduced inventories, and lower total system cost associated with an operational approach to SCM, an emphasis on the integration of purchasing and logistics is required.
- To achieve the objectives of speed, flexibility, and competitive advantage associated with a strategic approach to SCM, collaboration with strategic supply chain partners focused on redesigning products and business processes to deliver value to customers is required.
- In a strategic context, the role of purchasing is to understand the capability of suppliers and identify ways to match that capability to the needs of strategic customers.
- Purchasing can enhance the effectiveness of product and process design by ensuring reliability and quality of supply of materials, components and services, managing supplier involvement in the process, and providing insights about the competitive supply environment.
- Organizational structure and communications processes must be designed to support the requirements and objectives of the purchasing organization in support of the firm's supply chain management activities.
- Information technology is critical to manage the increasing complexity of the purchasing function, facilitate the integration of processes across firms in a supply chain context, and provide decision support tools to enable systemwide optimization.

Managerial Conclusion: To date, researchers and managers alike have primarily focused on supplier partnerships, or building stronger relationships between the buyer and seller firm. In order to achieve the potential of SCM, managers and researchers alike must adopt a broader, systemwide approach to understand and achieve the contribution that purchasing can make in a SCM context.

THE ROLE OF LOGISTICS IN SCM

Considering the role of logistics in the supply chain, including the major functions comprising logistics, emerging logistics strategies, and logistics competencies that drive competitive advantage for the firm, Min and Keebler (2000) concluded:

- Logistics activities have a major impact on the capabilities and profitability of the supply chain and its member firms.
- Logistics functions are key operating components of an organization that require design and management consistent with corporate strategy and changing competitive environments.
- Logistics strategies need to be implemented that support corporate strategies and that are based on the needs of the marketplace and the distinct capabilities of the firm.

- Corporate leaders who can understand and shape logistics competencies can dramatically enhance firm competitiveness.

Managerial Conclusion: Capitalizing on these opportunities requires the ability to build alliances within and between firms, a commitment to planning and integrating information flows, and the ability to measure performance to guide the improved design of the logistics system and supply chain processes. The importance of the supply chain manager's ability to leverage logistics competencies will increase in the future.

THE ROLE OF INFORMATION SYSTEMS IN SCM

Given the role of information systems within the firm and the role of information systems with suppliers, customers, and the supply chain, Zacharia (2000c) concluded:

- As the business environment continues to emphasize more variety and quicker response to a dynamic customer driven marketplace, better and more effective information systems need to be developed.
- One of the best ways to serve a demanding marketplace is to develop effective intrafirm information systems.
- Intrafirm information systems such as enterprise resource planning systems are an important precursor to improve the flow of information between firms.
- Managers need to determine if the benefits of effective and efficient information flow mitigate the risks associated with developing partnerships with either suppliers or customers.
- By developing relationships with members of their supply chains, firms can develop more efficient and effective information systems that facilitate better supply chain integration utilizing the enabling capabilities of the Internet.
- In the future, the Internet will allow true supply chain management through the transparent, real-time connection of all supply chain links.

Managerial Conclusion: Managers have little choice but to embark on the path to develop supply chain enhancing and integrating information systems. This augments the competitiveness of firms in terms of lower costs, improved customer value, and maintaining long-term competitive advantages in the rapidly changing, customer driven, Internet-enabled, e-commerce business environment.

THE ROLE OF FINANCE IN SCM

Considering the financial implications of supply chain decisions, trends in supply chain costs, a financial model for evaluating investments, and concerns for financial and supply chain management, Keebler (2000a) concluded:

- Supply chain activities affect profit and loss statements, balance sheets, and the costs of capital.
- Significant opportunities exist for the competent supply chain manager to reduce expenses, generate better returns on invested capital, and improve cash flows.
- By controlling supply chain expenses, profit margins are improved.
- By continuing to shorten cycle times, cash flows are enhanced.
- Superior supply chain performance can also produce the leverage and competitive advantage to increase revenues and the supply chain's share of market.
- Traditional accounting techniques do not provide accurate and timely information that informs the financial aspects of supply chain trade-off decisions.
- Activity-based costing is not widely employed.
- The potential benefits of improved supply chain management are stymied by the absence of activity-based financial data and the inability to link performance measurement with cost.
- Improved collaboration between finance and other business and supply chain functions is necessary to facilitate the process to develop Activity Based Costing.
- This collaboration should help to overcome the seemingly widespread inability of supply chain managers to articulate the costs and benefits of supply chain activities.

Managerial Conclusion: Capitalizing on these opportunities requires the ability to plan for and measure supply chain performance and to effectively communicate performance implications in financial terms. The supply chain manager's ability to articulate the financial implications of exchanges between firms will continue to increase in importance.

THE ROLE OF CUSTOMER SERVICE IN SCM

Considering the elements of customer service management important to supply chain management, performance outcomes associated with customer service activities and their contribution to supply chain objectives, and customer responses to the outcomes of a firm's customer service activities, Nix (2000d) concluded:

- To achieve supply chain objectives, customer service activities must be strategic in nature and must be designed based on an understanding of the service levels important to critical customers.
- Important customer segments must be identified and the requirements of those segments understood for both immediate and downstream customers.
- The impact of service levels on customers should be understood and internal capabilities designed to deliver service levels that optimize the overall performance of the supply chain.
- The quality of the customer interface is likely to influence the level of trust and openness of information exchange between firms, which can contribute to a better understanding of the customer's needs and improved performance of supply chain management activities.

- It is important to measure customer service outcomes as perceived by the customer and understand which performance outcomes are most valued by customers at various levels of the supply chain.
- Customer service requirements and performance, as well as the influence of customer service levels on customer behavior, should be understood and monitored for both immediate and downstream customers in a supply chain.
- Customer service is not the ultimate objective of supply chain management but rather an outcome of supply chain management that can create value for customers through improved efficiency or effectiveness.
- Creating value for customers superior to that created by competition is expected to result in greater customer satisfaction and competitive advantage and influence customers to behave in ways that improve the performance of the supply chain as a whole.

Managerial Conclusion: Customer service is often cited as a key objective of supply chain management. However, only if service offerings create value for customers will they lead to behaviors that improve supply chain performance. To achieve this objective, it is important for supply chain managers to manage customer service strategically and develop supply chain capabilities to deliver services viewed as important by critical downstream customers.

INTERFUNCTIONAL COORDINATION IN SCM

Highlighting the importance of interfunctional coordination within individual supply chain members to successfully implement supply chain management, Min (2000b) concluded:

- Concurrent management in supply chain management requires a balance between specialization through division of labor and cross-functional coordination.
- Interfunctional coordination within a particular firm is the coordinated efforts across functions to accomplish common goals, such as creating customer value and responsiveness to market changes, under close relationships among the functions and tight management control.
- The various ways of implementing interfunctional coordination include
  o Cooperative arrangements through which personnel from different functional areas perform interaction and collaboration
  o Managerial control, especially integrating managers who are essentially liaison personnel with formal authority over something important across functions (such as budgets)
  o Standardization to guide the processes of coordination so that the coordinated work is ensured
  o Functional expertise necessary for participation in cooperative arrangements
  o Organizational structure that integrates the flows of products, services, finance, and information within an organization

- No organization can rely on a single mechanism or organizational structure and, as a result, organizations must be flexible to utilize a proper combination of these mechanisms to achieve a high level of coordination.
- Common goals, trust and commitment among personnel from different functional areas, and top management support are the factors that promote cooperative efforts within a firm.
- Well-executed, interfunctional coordination brings competitive advantage, in terms of reduced cycle time, new-product success, and finally profitability.

Managerial Conclusion: Individual firms within a supply chain need expertise in key functional areas and, at the same time, must achieve functional integration as a precursor to supply chain management.

INTERCORPORATE COORDINATION IN SCM

Considering the importance of interfirm cooperation in supply chain management, and suggesting a model of interfirm cooperation from drivers, to prerequisites, to the outcomes of successful cooperative relationships in a supply chain context, Min (2000c) concluded:

- The demand for flexibility in today's turbulent business environment requires supply chain management, rather than the vertical integration or arm's length relationships of the past.
- Supply chain management (SCM) extends the concept of functional integration beyond a firm to all the firms in the supply chain and, therefore, the members of a supply chain need to help each other to improve the competitiveness of the supply chain.
- Implementing SCM inherently requires cooperation, which is defined as a set of joint actions of firms in a close relationship to accomplish a common set of goals that bring mutual benefits.

Managerial Conclusion: The supply chain manager's ability to build, maintain, and enhance cooperative interfirm relationships is essential for supply chain management.

PERFORMANCE MEASUREMENT IN SCM

Given the role of performance measurement in the supply chain, Keebler (2000b) concluded:

- Supply chain activities are not adequately defined, measured, or improved.
- Supply chain measurement research is largely single-firm focused.
- Research has emphasized internal efficiency over external effectiveness.
- There is an absence of multifirm performance measurement, or measures across the supply chain.

- Interdependent planning and governance structures do not appear to exist across firms.
- Supply chain members still appear to act largely as independent supply chain members, focused on self-interest.
- Vertical conflicts exist within supply chains that could be resolved with joint planning and measurement.
- Activity Based Costing, a critical performance measurement capability, is not widely employed.
- Potential benefits of improved supply chain management are stymied by the absence of activity-based financial data and the inability to link performance measurement with cost.

Managerial Conclusion: Capitalizing on the opportunities to plan and measure key supply chain processes improves both single-firm performance and supply chain outcomes. Supply chain performance measurement is in its infancy but will increase in importance.

From the foundation of these managerial conclusions, we can begin to discuss SCM as a source of competitive advantage. Our first example illustrates how this all-encompassing approach to a "*systemic, strategic orientation*" can lead to competitive advantage, especially when we realize that the final consumer can be considered one of the "*three or more companies (entities) directly linked by the supply chain flows.*"

Company A—Consumer
Supply Chain Competitive Advantage

Company A is a major manufacturer of snack foods that sells through many outlets, the most prominent of which are the many stores of a mass merchandiser we will call Retailer B. Retailer B represents a major percentage of sales for Company A and clearly is an important customer. One of the drivers we will discuss later is "Not all customers are created equal," and Company A certainly recognized Retailer B as key to their success. Thus, Company A wanted to look for ways to compete and create value for Retailer B.

Company A realized that Retailer B was driven by the same two values that drive many retailers: traffic and vendor float. Traffic is the means by which retailers get their customers, the final consumer, into their store. Many retailers recognize that a significant percentage of their sales are unplanned purchases (i.e., the customer came in the store to buy certain things, but also impulse bought other items). One clothing retailer we have worked with estimates that 60% of their sales are unplanned purchases! So anything that helps the retailer get more customers walking through their stores is a value to the retailer. Later in this book, we will examine how another company (Company R) used this retailer value to gain market share (that is, to help the retailer increase traffic), but this option did not seem feasible to Company A—after all, how many people shop in a particular retail store just for the snack food? Snack food brands are usually carried in a multitude of retail chains, and few people go to a mass merchandise store just to buy snack food. In fact, snack foods are often the products that are impulse bought after the customer is in the store.

So Company A decided to concentrate on improving the vendor float of Retailer B. Vendor float is a retail calculation of the effectiveness of their working capital, where

$$\text{Working Capital} = \text{Inventory} + \text{Accounts Receivable.}$$

More specifically, vendor float is the percentage of working capital that is paid for by the vendors:

$$\text{Vendor Float} = \text{Accounts Payable/Working Capital.}$$

For instance, if Retailer B has 25 days inventory on hand, 35 days accounts receivables (AR), and has to pay vendors in 30 days (accounts payable, or AP), then

$$\text{Vendor Float} = 30/(25 + 35) = 50\%.$$

This means vendors are financing 50% of Retailer B's working capital.

If Retailer B could push their vendors to accept 45 day payment terms, reduce inventory by 5 days, and get customers to pay 10 days sooner, then Retailer B's vendor float would be 100%, which means Retailer B would have none of its own money invested in its own working capital—the vendors are financing it (vendors do not have to be paid until the money is received from Retailer B's customers).

Company A would be foolish to simply offer to allow Retailer B more time to pay Company A, since this would hurt their own vendor float, but other supply chain options must be available. This is precisely what Company A sought—a SCM solution to provide more value (in the form of better vendor float) to Retailer B that did not hurt their own financial viability.

Company A originally considered the basic premise for competing for share of final consumers' business to be solely their products. Product design, a quality product, advertising, and promotion create brand equity. However, the strength of their brands is not much different from the strength of any other snack food manufacturer. Market share does not shift very much in this particular supply chain. So Company A approached the problem by not asking the question, "How do we compete based on the product?" but instead, "How do we innovate the services we offer, not to the final customer, but to the retailer?"

What they developed was a forecasting and demand planning process to manage the supply chain flows we discussed earlier: the flow of the product, the flow of services, the flow of information, the flow of financial resources, and the flow of demand and forecasts. What they discovered was an interesting fact about many supply chains: the average time between a customer buying a Company A product in Retailer B and Company A finding out about it was 23 days! In this world of electronic data interchange (EDI), how could this be so? In fact, Company A and Retailer B were both proud of the EDI interface between the two companies—when Retailer B placed an order with Company A, it was instantaneously received by Company A.

To answer this question, let's look at how traditional, logistics-oriented inventory management systems work. When the customer in Retailer B buys one of Company A's products, what immediately happens in a traditional logistics system? The answer is—nothing. That is, nothing happens until inventory decreases enough to hit the reorder point (ROP). When the ROP is hit, the store automatically orders its order quantity to replenish inventory from its Retailer B regional distribution center (RDC). When the RDC finally hits its ROP, it looks for excess inventory at any of Retailer B's other RDCs (this is done to keep inventory from sitting too long in any one RDC and thus hurting shelf life freshness). Eventually, all the RDCs have inventory levels low enough that Retailer B finally sends an order to Company A, and yes, that order is instantaneously electronically transmitted and received. However, on average, it has been 23 days since the customer bought the Company A product in the store.

This traditional system affects shelf life of the product, average days of inventory that Retailer B carries in its stores and RDCs, inventory levels Company A carries to meet the sudden large order it eventually receives from Retailer B, and Company A production costs to meet this "lumpy" demand (i.e., sudden large orders from a major retailer, with no demand from this retailer in between the large orders). All of these are supply chain costs that could be reduced through supply chain management.

After examining all these flows, Company A devised an offer for Retailer B that could not be refused. Company A told the retailer, "First of all, we're better at forecasting demand for our products in your stores than you are. Give us real-time, point-of-sale (POS) demand data—which includes sales of the product, promotions, merchandising activities, co-op ads, and so forth—and we'll forecast individual demand. We're so certain we can do this well, we'll offer to directly manage the inventory of each of our stock keeping units (SKUs) in each of your stores (a concept today called VMI, or vendor-managed inventory). We're so sure we can do this well, if we stock out of any of our products in any of your stores, we'll pay you a per day stock out penalty. Further, we are so sure we can do this well, we won't ask you to pay for any inventory of our product until it sells in your store."

Now, the benefits of the offer to Retailer B were obvious. As one supply chain executive in Retailer B put it, "You're offering to put us in the consignment business." Retailer B now has the ability to sell Company A products in all their stores and have no investment in inventory. All the inventory in their regional distribution centers and in their stores belongs to Company A, up to the instant when it sells. When it is rung up on the cash register, and the customer is taking it away, Retailer B now owes the purchase price of that product to Company A.

This creates some interesting changes in typical financial measures. What's the return on working capital for Retailer B on their Company A business? The answer is that the inventory component of working capital just dropped to zero. In our earlier example, vendor float for Retailer B is

$$\text{Vendor Float }_{\text{Retailer B}} = 30 \text{ days AP}/(0 \text{ days inventory} + 35 \text{ days AR}) = 85.7\%.$$

This is an incredibly high vendor float, made possible because no Retailer B dollars are invested in the inventory component of Retailer B's working capital of Company A products. This creates a motivation for Retailer B to sell more of this product, to give it better merchandising, better shelf location, and better store placement because the more of this product Retailer B sells, the more money Retailer B is making on a zero investment in inventory.

The supply chain management system that was put in place allows Company A to monitor sales of each of their products real time in each Retailer B store. So rather than Retailer B selling the product until it hits a reorder point, then ordering from the regional distribution center, then ordering from the corporate headquarters, and eventually ordering from Company A, Company A can, first, forecast the independent demand (that is, individual customers walking into the store and buying the product—a concept we will discuss further in Chapter 7), and then plan the derived demand, back through the RDCs, and eventually back to the distribution centers and production facilities at Company A.

The demand information cycle in this case has been taken from 23 days to 0 days. The effect on Retailer B was, again, obvious. They now have the same sales or higher sales of Company A products, and they have no money invested in inventory. They do not have to forecast or manage Company A products. Any orders that come into the Company A distribution centers, or the Retailer B RDCs, look like Retailer B orders. They look like they came off the Retailer B computer but, in fact, they were initiated by Company A, either to order from Company A and ship to the RDCs, or for the RDCs to ship to individual stores. The inventory is entirely managed by the vendor.

The effect for Company A is equally profound, but a little less obvious. Because they took those 23 days out of the information cycle (which means they have continuous demand information, real time, rather than the old, lumpy, occasional demand information), their inventory levels through the entire system actually went down, even though now they own the inventory in the Retailer B RDCs and retail stores. Because the demand affecting Company A is no longer lumpy and unexpected, production costs also significantly decreased.

We have left one piece out of this story, by the way. Once Retailer B was excited about this idea of having zero inventory in working capital, Company A put one last piece to the puzzle on the table: "If we're going to manage your inventory for you and we're not going to ask you to pay for it until the instant it sells, then we want you to instantly pay us."

"Wait a minute," said the Retailer B CFO. "We have a standard policy that says all of our sales are 2/10, net 30, which means that we'll pay you in 30 days, or if we pay you in 10 days we'll take a 2% discount."

Company A's answer was, "Unless you agree to this final part of the deal, then we cannot make money and the deal is off." Visions of zero investment in inventory with Company A were suddenly flying out the window for Retailer B.

"Okay," reluctantly they said, "we'll agree to it."

Well, let's look at what we have now done to the flows in the supply chain. We have already talked about Retailer B. We talked about the fact that Company A's inventory went down. But what happened to all the flows under the old system? Company A had to carry enough inventory in their own distribution centers to anticipate potential orders coming in, on average, 23 days in the future from Retailer B. Once they received that order, the product had to be moved to Retailer B and eventually would be distributed to various stores. When it hit the Retailer B system, Retailer B then issued a process that would pay Company A in 30 days. The 23-day inventory Company A carried, plus 30 days accounts receivable, add up to Company A working capital invested in Retailer B of 53 days. Working capital, remember, is accounts receivable plus all inventory. What happened when we took the 23 days out? Now, of course, the whole 23 days of inventory did not go away for Company A because there is uncertainty, but under the new system of better, more timely information, Company A now only carries 15 days of inventory. More important, when the order actually happens, they get paid 30 days earlier. So their working capital, systemwide to support Retailer B, went from 23 plus 30, or 53 days, down to 15 days. Their total investment in working capital to support Retailer B sales dropped by more than two thirds!

This example illustrates managing the supply chain flows and having profound effects on the bottom line profitability of not just one company, but several companies in the supply chain. Company A now sells more products

Table 1.1   Twelve Drivers of SCM Competitive Advantage

Chapter	Driver Number	Driver
Two	One	Coordinate the traditional business functions across the company and across the supply chain.
Three	Two	Collaborate with supply chain partners on noncore competency functions.
Four	Three	Look for supply chain synergies.
Five	Four	Not all customers are created equal.
Six	Five	Identify and manage the supply chain flow cycles.
Seven	Six	Manage demand (not just the forecast) in the supply chain.
Eight	Seven	Substitute information for assets.
Nine	Eight	Systems are templates to be laid over processes.
Ten	Nine	Not all products are created equal.
Eleven	Ten	Make yourself easy to do business with.
Twelve	Eleven	Do not let tactics overshadow strategies.
Thirteen	Twelve	Align your supply chain strategies and your reward structures.

through the Retailer B supply chain, at considerably greater margins for both. This, of course, leads to a greater willingness on the part of Retailer B to work closely with Company A, which is an ongoing source of competitive advantage for Company A.

Twelve Drivers of SCM Competitive Advantage

The Company A example tells us that competitive advantage can be obtained not just through the products sold, but also through the way in which we manage the flows in a supply chain. In fact, our work with many companies like Company A has led to what we call the "Twelve Drivers of SCM Competitive Advantage." Each of these drivers (illustrated in Table 1.1) is briefly presented here, and each is discussed in greater detail (with real examples) in the following chapters.

COORDINATE THE TRADITIONAL BUSINESS FUNCTIONS

Much of supply chain management involves coordinating the various business functions listed in Figure 1.1. Functional shifting is a term commonly

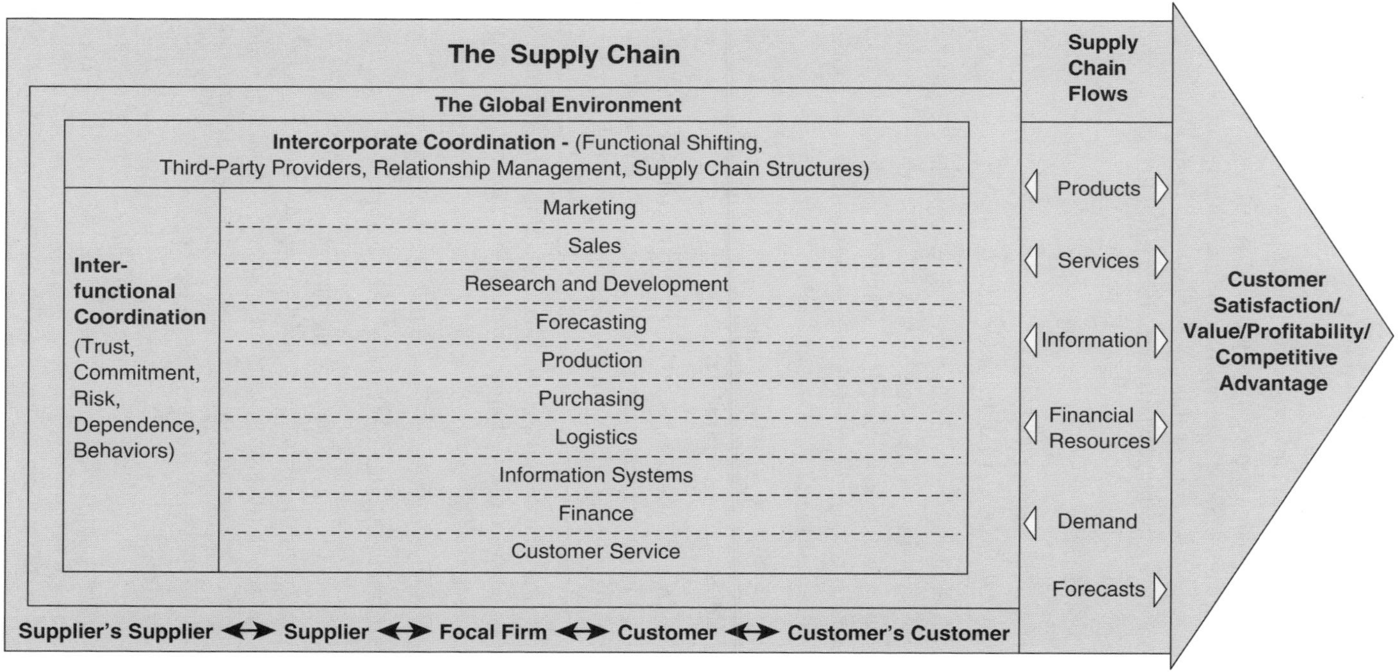

The Supply Chain

The Global Environment

Intercorporate Coordination - (Functional Shifting, Third-Party Providers, Relationship Management, Supply Chain Structures)

Inter-functional Coordination (Trust, Commitment, Risk, Dependence, Behaviors)

- Marketing
- Sales
- Research and Development
- Forecasting
- Production
- Purchasing
- Logistics
- Information Systems
- Finance
- Customer Service

Supply Chain Flows

- Products
- Services
- Information
- Financial Resources
- Demand
- Forecasts

Customer Satisfaction/ Value/Profitability/ Competitive Advantage

Supplier's Supplier ◄► Supplier ◄► Focal Firm ◄► Customer ◄► Customer's Customer

Figure 1.1 A Model of Supply Chain Management

Adapted from Mentzer (2000)

used to refer to two or more companies in a supply chain deciding who best performs a certain function and allowing them to perform this function for the supply chain as a whole.

However, it is a fundamental concept of supply chain management that you cannot coordinate business functions across companies within the supply chain if you cannot do this coordination first within your own company. There is a reason we present this driver first—the remaining 11 SCM Drivers of Competitive Advantage will come to little if this first one cannot be accomplished.

COLLABORATE WITH SUPPLY CHAIN PARTNERS ON NONCORE COMPETENCY FUNCTIONS

How companies identify and manage their core competencies, and out-source noncore competencies, is the focus of this SCM Driver of Competitive Advantage. We will examine how companies identify core competencies and noncore competencies and decide on which ones to outsource to (and cooperate with as), supply chain partners.

LOOK FOR SUPPLY CHAIN SYNERGIES

SCM Drivers One and Two, respectively, encourage companies to coordinate the traditional business functions within the company and across supply chain partners, while keeping core competencies under internal control and outsourcing noncore competencies. The result of these two drivers is that synergistic effects (the whole is greater than the sum of the parts) can result. However, these synergies seldom happen unless they are actively sought, identified, and managed.

NOT ALL CUSTOMERS ARE CREATED EQUAL

To achieve competitive advantage, companies must realize that not all customers are created equal—some are critical to our success, some are less important and should be treated as such, and some are distracting us from serving the first two groups and should not be served at all. To understand these segments of customers, companies first need to answer several questions about their supply chains:

- Who is our customer?
- How do we reach our customer?
- How do we reach competitive advantage with our customer? (Hint: It is not always the product.)

As the first question indicates, identifying the relevant customer is the first step. Once we identify who the customer is, we must identify what the customer values, choose the customer values that we will emphasize, provide that value to the customer, communicate to the customer the fact that we are providing that value, and finally (and continuously) assess the customer's satisfaction with the value we are delivering.

IDENTIFY AND MANAGE THE SUPPLY CHAIN FLOW CYCLES

There are numerous flows in supply chain management. Products and services flow from suppliers through manufacturers through distributors through retailers to final customers. Services that accompany product flows in supply chains also flow both ways. Information about product/service availability, inventory location, transportation options, customer values, finances—in fact, information about any aspect of supply chain management—flows up and down the supply chain. Although financial flows are ultimately up the supply chain from the final customer to all supply chain participants, the timing of those flows (as Company A illustrated) is a critical aspect of supply chain management. Finally, demand for products and services flows up the supply chain, and the ability to forecast, anticipate, and plan for those demand flows has a huge impact on the viability of the supply chain.

MANAGE DEMAND (NOT JUST THE FORECAST) IN THE SUPPLY CHAIN

Little attention has been paid to the role of sales forecasting and demand management in the supply chain, or how that role might change depending upon the position in the supply chain that a company occupies. From a SCM perspective, the question arises, "Do all members of the supply chain need to forecast demand?" In fact, taking a SCM perspective reveals that any supply chain has only one point of *independent demand*—or *the amount of product demanded (by time and location) by the end-use customer of the supply chain.* Whether this end-use customer is a consumer shopping in a retail establishment or online (B2C), or a business buying products for consumption in the process of conducting their business operations (B2B), these end-use customers determine the true demand for the product that will flow through the supply chain.

The company in the supply chain that directly serves this end-use customer directly experiences this independent demand. All subsequent companies in the supply chain experience a demand that is tempered by the order fulfillment and purchasing policies of other companies in the supply chain. This second type of supply chain demand is called *derived demand,* because it is not the independent demand of the end-use customer but rather a *demand that is derived from what other companies in the supply chain do to meet their demand from their immediate customer (i.e., the company that orders from them).* It is important to note that only one company in any given supply chain is affected by independent demand. The rest are affected by derived demand. Equally important, the techniques, systems, and processes necessary to deal with derived demand are quite different from those of independent demand. In fact, many companies develop elaborate sales forecasting techniques, systems, and processes when, in fact, *they do not even need to forecast!*

Recognizing the differences between independent and derived demand, recognizing which type of demand affects a particular company, and developing techniques, systems, and processes to deal with that company's particular type of demand can have a profound impact on supply chain costs and customer service levels.

SUBSTITUTE INFORMATION FOR ASSETS

Information technology is changing at an incredible rate of speed. The cost of obtaining that information is also becoming cheaper and cheaper. At the same time, the costs of assets to run a supply chain are not decreasing rapidly. The cost of inventory, plants, equipment, people, and storage facilities, to name a few, is not becoming cheaper. Thus, the key to SCM Driver Seven is how we use increasingly available and inexpensive information and information technology to eliminate other, more expensive supply chain assets.

SYSTEMS ARE TEMPLATES TO BE LAID OVER PROCESSES

It is easy to become enamored with the technology implied in Chapter 8, and companies often do. They become convinced that supply chain management is solely an information systems problem. However, no system or computer package exists today that can overcome poorly thought out processes. Processes are the procedures, rules, steps, and personnel involved in accomplishing any task or tasks. Systems are the computer and communications devices, equipment, and software brought to bear to augment accomplishment of those processes. Thus, systems are templates to be laid over processes.

NOT ALL PRODUCTS ARE CREATED EQUAL

Not all products contribute equally to the profitability of a company or a supply chain. In fact, many supply chains keep in stock a multitude of products that should be discontinued for lack of sales. As one supply executive put it, "We are great at introducing new products, but terrible at killing off loser products." SCM Driver Nine is about understanding when we put too much attention into products that do not make money for the company or the supply chain.

MAKE YOURSELF EASY TO DO BUSINESS WITH

Companies that are able to create value for their customers by satisfying their needs and wants generally increase their market share and their profitability. Thus, an important part of any business, and certainly of any supply chain, is making it easy for customers to do business with us.

DO NOT LET TACTICS OVERSHADOW STRATEGIES

Letting attention to short-term tactics overshadow the accomplishment of long-term strategies can hurt the profitability and competitive viability of a company or a supply chain as a whole. Setting and meeting quarterly goals is no more important than setting and meeting the long-term goals of the supply chain. These long-term goals include the types of relationships to have with various supply chain partners to achieve profitability and competitive advantage.

ARE YOUR SUPPLY CHAIN STRATEGIES
AND YOUR REWARD STRUCTURES ALIGNED?

There is a basic principle of organizational behavior (Mentzer & Bienstock, 1998a): "What gets measured gets rewarded, and what gets rewarded gets done." But what happens when we pay our people to do the wrong things? The key to this SCM Driver is to reward (and, thus, motivate) company employees and supply chain partners to act in ways consistent with our supply chain management strategies.

Summary

From the foundations of what has been written before, and our experience with numerous companies, 12 Supply Chain Management Drivers of Competitive Advantage emerge. In each of the following chapters, we will address one of these SCM Drivers, illustrating its strategic impact by bringing to bear what others have said before and examples of real companies that have succeeded or failed by heeding or ignoring that driver. The purpose in each case is to stimulate the reader to think about how that particular driver can be applied in his or her company and supply chains.

2

Coordinate the Traditional Business Functions Across the Company and Across the Supply Chain

Much of supply chain management involves coordinating the various business functions listed in Figure 1.1. Functional shifting is a term commonly used to refer to two or more companies in a supply chain deciding who best performs a certain function and allowing them to perform this function for the supply chain as a whole.

However, it is a fundamental concept of supply chain management that you cannot coordinate business functions across companies within the supply chain if you cannot do this coordination first within your own company. There is a reason we present this driver first—the remaining 11 SCM Drivers of Competitive Advantage will come to little if this first one cannot be accomplished. Before looking at examples of this driver, however, we first examine the nature of functional coordination and supply chain relationships.

Functional Coordination

Min (2000b) proposed five dimensions of functional coordination: cooperative arrangements, management control, standardization, functional expertise, and organizational structure. Before exploring this SCM Driver further, and the nature of supply chain relationships, each of these dimensions is discussed.

COOPERATIVE ARRANGEMENTS

Min (2000b) proposed that cooperative arrangements consist of interaction and collaboration. Specific examples of interaction include committee meetings, teleconferencing, conference calls, hall talk, memoranda, and the exchange of standard documents (Jaworski & Kohli, 1993; Galbraith, 1977; Van de Ven & Ferry, 1980). In this way, managers in particular departments rely on activities to structure relationships between the department and other departments through the diffusion of market information (Kahn & Mentzer, 1998). In the same context, information flows or updates within a firm and across the firms within a supply chain are essential elements of supply chain management (Cooper & Ellram, 1993; Cooper, Ellram, Gardner, & Hanks, 1997).

Coordination is a collaborative process in which "teams" and "resource sharing" typify interdepartmental relationships. The importance of cross-functional teams seems to have increased. For example, in the 1993 report on cross-functional sourcing teams by the Center for Advanced Purchasing Studies (CAPS), 80% of U.S. companies surveyed said they planned to emphasize the use of such groups over the next 3 years to support procurement and sourcing decisions (Hyman, 1996). Another example is Procter & Gamble's (P&G) Multifunctional Account Teams that bring product and sales managers together. P&G staff teams with salespeople from different divisions and brand people assigned to a large account. Team members spend 1 to 2 years at customer sites and learn what is involved in executing brand programs through the distribution channel (Cespedes, 1996). Finally, customer-focused teams (CFT), which consist of people from sales, manufacturing, shipping, finance, purchasing, and engineering, assure interfunctional communication by removing formal communication barriers and require communication at the point of need (Dwyer & Tanner, 1999).

MANAGEMENT CONTROLS

In a traditional functional silo structure with a narrow functional view, decision making that involves several different functional areas is pushed up the organizational hierarchy to top management (Hodge, Anthony, & Gales, 1996). However, slow decision making by overloaded top management is not appropriate for successful supply chain management that requires coordination of expertise of different functions and time- and quality-based competition. Instead, integrating managers—essentially liaison personnel with formal authority—provide stronger coordination (Mintzberg, 1996). These managers are given authority, not over the units they link but over something important to those units, like budgets (Mintzberg, 1996). The processes by which strategic decisions are made (i.e., the way in which team leaders elicit, receive, and respond to team members' input) have a significant impact on team members' coordination (Korsgaard, Schweiger, & Sapienza, 1995). This is true especially when team leaders show strong consideration of members' input, and team members see the decision-making process as fair and, consequently, have greater commitment to the decision, attachment to the team, and trust in the leader.

STANDARDIZATION

Coordination can be achieved through standardization because standards predetermine what people do and, thus, ensure that their work is coordinated (Mintzberg, 1996). The standardization of work processes is accomplished by behavioral formalization that imposes operating instructions, job descriptions, rules, and regulations. Unlike functional silo structures, people involved in supply chain processes should be given job descriptions, operating instructions, and behavioral norms for seamless, efficient flows of products, services, information, and finances in addition to those within a particular functional area. Therefore, standardization becomes a useful mechanism of supply chain management coordination.

FUNCTIONAL EXPERTISE

Although cross-functional coordination is a must, the need for functional in-depth expertise should not be ignored. Each management discipline has seen increasing sophistication in its concepts and methods and requires mastery of this knowledge (Wind & Mahajan, 1997; Cespedes, 1996). To form a cross-functional team, firms should look for people who work effectively with other multidisciplinary team members in addition to mastering their functional expertise (Wind & Mahajan, 1997).

ORGANIZATIONAL STRUCTURE

An ideal organizational structure for coordination within a firm is an integrated supply chain process for seamless flows of information, products, services, and finances.

In other words, supply chain management requires a structure beyond a functional silo structure in which people are not able to go between the functions. As supply chain organizations become more complicated, the preferred means of coordination shifts from mutual adjustment to direct supervision, then to standardization, finally reverting back to mutual adjustment.

Supply Chain Relationships

A large part of managing supply chains consists of managing multiple relationships among the member organizations (Cooper, Ellran, et al., 1997; Mentzer, 2000; Mentzer, DeWitt, et al., 2001). Connections among these organizations range from single transactions to complex interdependent relationships. As the business environment becomes more complex, organizations within supply chains realize that many benefits can be obtained from long-term relationships

(Ganesan, 1994). Building interdependent or closer relationships with customers is thought to increase customer satisfaction (Berry & Parasuraman, 1991). Day (2000) even goes so far as to say that committed relationships are among the most durable of advantages because of their inherent barriers to competition. Thus, many firms are moving away from adversarial exchanges toward closer and more long-term relationships (Holmlund & Kock, 1993; Kalwani & Narayandas, 1995).

Much has been written about the drivers and expected benefits from various supply chain relationships, such as alliances, partnerships, collaborative relationships, and supply chain management. However, a high level of ambiguity still exists among the different definitions and descriptors of relationships (Cravens, Shipp, & Cravens, 1993; Lambert, Emmelhainz, & Gardner, 1996; Rinehart, Eckert, Hanfield, Page, & Atkin, 2002). The terms to describe these various relationships are often used interchangeably, creating confusion for all. For relationships to be as effective and efficient as possible, a mutual understanding of expectations is necessary. Therefore, the purpose of this section is to understand the effect of relationship intensity and relationship structure types on supply chain relationships.

RELATIONSHIP STRUCTURE

Personal relationships are structured based on needs and the level of attraction or intimacy between two or more people. The attributes of trust and commitment often describe the intimacy or level of closeness of the relationship as opposed to the type of relationship (e.g., friendship, marriage) (Golicic, Foggin, & Mentzer, 2003). Analogous to this, the structure of supply chain relationships is composed of relationship type, but with relationship intensity also influencing the nature of the relationship.

RELATIONSHIP TYPE

Supply chain relationships have historically been categorized by where they fall on a governance spectrum. The channels literature was the first to propose a range of relationships from arm's-length transactions (or market governance) to vertical integration (or hierarchical governance). More recently, it has been recognized that integration of more than one firm may be more appropriate for the latter end of this range, because one firm cannot effectively accomplish the control and management of the whole channel (or supply chain). Several authors have since acknowledged these two end points, arm's length and integration, and placed interfirm cooperative relationships (types of relationships where there is cooperation between or among the firms involved) in the middle (for example, Contractor & Lorange, 1988; Heide, 1994; Landeros & Monczka, 1989; Nevin, 1995; Webster, 1992).

The different cooperative relationships have been identified as partnerships, alliances, joint ventures, network organizations, franchises, license agreements, contractual relationships, service agreements, and administered relationships, to name a few. Some authors have proposed where these relationships fall in relation to each other ranging from arm's length to integration (Contractor & Lorange, 1988; Webster, 1992). These studies attempted to categorize the relationships under a particular type based on the relationship characteristics. Thus, type is defined here as the group or class of relationships that share common traits or characteristics.

Different types of relationships have received a great deal of attention in the literature; however, there is little consensus about the terminology and typology to describe them (Cravens, Shipp, & Cravens, 1993; Rinehart et al., 2002; Webster, 1992). For example, Cannon and Perreault (1997) conducted an empirical study in which they classified eight different types of relationships displaying different combinations of five characteristics. The authors called the eight types basic buying and selling, bare bones, contractual transaction, customer supply, cooperative systems, collaborative, mutually adaptive, and customer is king. A similar study by Rinehart et al. (2002) used different characteristics and had practitioners name the types rather than naming the types themselves. This resulted in seven relationship types (non-strategic transactions, administered relationships, contractual relationships, specialty contract relationships, partnerships, joint ventures, and strategic alliances), which reflected those often represented in the literature and used by managers.

Based on the literature, the most commonly discussed categories of relationship structure types are arm's length, cooperative relationships (which include those that are administered or governed by contracts), and integration. There seems to be no disagreement about the categories on the ends—arm's length consists of discrete transactions (Contractor & Lorange, 1988; Heide, 1994; Webster, 1992), and integration is one firm (vertical integration), or several firms acting as one (supply chain management), performing all channel functions (Harland, 1996; Heide, 1994; Landeros & Monczka, 1989; Webster, 1992).

Cooperative relationships are not as clearly defined. Partnerships and alliances are the descriptors most often used for these types in the logistics literature. While there is some agreement in the literature that these terms mean working together toward common goals and sharing investments, the definitions presented vary (the reader is referred to a representative sample of literature for these definitions—Boddy, Macbeth, & Wagner, 2000; Cooper, Ellran, et al., 1997; Cravens et al., 1993; Das & Teng, 1998; Ellram, 1991; Hoyt & Huq, 2000; Lambe & Spekman, 1997; Lambert, Emmelhainz, & Gardner, 1996; Lorange, Roose, & Bronn, 1992; Monczka, Trent, & Handfield, 1998; Stern, El-Ansary, & Coughlan, 1996; Webster, 1992). Although there is confusion as to the distinction among the different types of cooperative relationships (i.e., a continuum), relationship structure can be broken out into these three main types—arm's-length, cooperative relationships and integration—which differ based on certain characteristics.

Mentzer, DeWitt, et al. (2001) state that relationships vary on their levels of trust, commitment, mutual dependence, organizational compatibility, vision, leadership, and top management support; the higher the levels of these, the closer the firms are to an integrated relationship. Cannon and Perreault (1997) differentiated their types based on the characteristics of expectations of information sharing, degree to which operations are linked, contractual agreements, expectations about working together, and relationship-specific adaptations by the seller or buyer. Rinehart et al. (2002) used trust, commitment, and the frequency of interaction. Dabholkar and Neeley (1998) categorize business-to-business relationships on temporal perspective (long-term versus short-term), goal orientation (individual gain versus joint gain), and power (balanced versus unbalanced). According to Boyle, Dwyer, Robicheaux, and Simpson (1992, p. 464), types "vary in the inclusiveness of goals, the locus of decision-making, the scope of supervision and control, commitment to the system, and the formality of roles and division of labor"; and these characteristics are thought to be highest in corporate systems or integrated relationships. Landeros and Monczka (1989) described cooperative relationships as differing from the relationship spectrum ends based on five attributes—the supply pool, a credible commitment, joint problem solving, an exchange of information, and joint adjustment to marketplace conditions.

Although authors consider different combinations of differentiating characteristics, there are similarities in some of the concepts. For example, some refer to actions by one or more parties, some are expectations, and some are affective or social aspects. The social aspects or affective aspects have received some attention but deserve closer examination as a possible component of relationship structure.

RELATIONSHIP INTENSITY

Relationships between people, although different, are analogous to those between firms—they have different levels of intimacy or intensity. The psychology literature provides some examples of the variation in intimacy as personal relationships progress through different types (often referred to as stages in the psychology literature). For example, McCall (1970) uses the idea of social bonding to investigate friendships. Collins, Kennedy, and Francis (1976) confirm this idea when they discuss the variation of intimacy through the stages of courtship—casual dating, going steady, and engagement. Guerrero and Andersen (1994) discuss the evolution of relationship types through casual dating, serious dating, and marriage—each relationship having varying levels of intimacy. In an article on communication, Aune, Buller, and Aune (1996) discuss initial interactions taking place on an impersonal level and over time becoming more personal and progressing toward greater intimacy. This occurs even if the type of relationship (e.g., a friendship) remains the same. Although the formation and maintenance of interpersonal relationships are different than supply chain relationships, the notion of differing levels of intimacy within one type of relationship provides support to the concept of supply chain relationship intensity.

Santoro (2000) conducted research on the link between relationship intensity and outcomes in industry-university ventures. The research was based on the notion that firms and universities cooperate through different types of relationships with varying levels of personal interaction. Intensity has been indirectly studied through a few similar concepts in marketing, management, and sociology. Rindfleisch and Moorman (2001) discuss the concept of relational embeddedness as the degree of reciprocity and closeness among new-product alliance participants. This concept is based on the strength-of-ties literature, which is primarily concerned with the nature of the relational bond between two or more social actors. Tie-strength researchers typically classify the relation as linked by a strong or a weak tie. Strong ties are viewed as having higher levels of closeness, reciprocity, and indebtedness than weak ties (Granovetter, 1973). Similar to the notion of strength-of-ties, coupling research looks at the relationships among elements or variables and their variation from loose to tight. Both strength-of-ties and coupling may be applied to relations between organizations as well as individuals. Thus, relationship intensity, defined as the level of closeness or strength of the relationship between or among organizations, is a component of supply chain relationship structure.

Terms such as collaboration, cooperation, and coordination are commonly used to refer to closeness in relationships. Santoro (2000) referred to collaboration as a powerful linkage between firms and universities, and said that firms and universities cooperate through different relationships. In his work on social networks, Gulati (1998) suggests that alliances characterized by a high degree of relational embeddedness (i.e., the companies in the alliance are strongly tied to each other) display high levels of cooperation. Spekman, Kamauff, and Myhr (1998) propose that relationships get closer as companies move from open market transactions to collaboration—trading parties can cooperate and coordinate certain activities but still not behave as close trading partners, which requires high levels of trust and commitment.

Some interorganizational research has discussed variation within relationship types, typically indirectly describing different intensities within one type of relationship. Birnbirg (1998) proposed that strategic alliances take a variety of differing forms depending on factors such as degree of commitment, symmetry of rewards, and degree of mutual trust. In their research on partnerships, Lambert et al. (1996) distinguish among three different levels based on the interactions and closeness between the partners. Within the type of partnership, the authors distinguish among coordination between the partners (what the authors term Type I), integration (Type II), and significant integration (Type III). Barringer and Harrison present several types of interorganizational relationships with varying degrees of linkages or coupling (2000).

Golicic et al. (2003) conducted an exploratory study to develop an understanding of how company executives view close supply chain relationships. Initial interviews with selected individuals were conducted to clarify terms and pretest a protocol for the focus groups. Focus-group interviews with executives from various industries were then conducted. The focus-group participants discussed various aspects of interorganizational relationships. They spoke of relationship characteristics—what would make one relationship different from another. They used terms for relationship types (e.g., alliance, partnership) that support what is used in the literature. They discussed different levels of closeness in relationships—using the common metaphor of marriage—and they discussed different levels of intensity within a single type of relationship.

SUPPLY CHAIN RELATIONSHIP TYPE AND INTENSITY

The above discussion demonstrates how a relationship type takes a particular form based on the intensity between the firms. Relationship intensity has always existed; it just has not been recognized as such. Relationship type and intensity are distinct components of relationship structure. The intensity between two or more organizations helps determine the type of relationship they will pursue.

Because there are so many different combinations of type and intensity that firms can implement within their supply chains, the lack of a common understanding of what a particular relationship with another company entails can lead to problems. For example, firms may experience unmet expectations, wasted resources, relationship failure, and/or lawsuits, which could all lead to lost business. A common understanding by both parties of what is expected from a specific type, given a particular level of intensity, can help prevent these types of problems from occurring.

The concept of intensity is an important one for practitioners. Firms must realize that within a particular type of relationship, there can be different intensities depending on the time and effort put into the relationship. Thus, firms can better match their various suppliers and customers with different relationship intensities as appropriate. For example, a firm may have multiple supplier alliances but may not wish to expend the resources needed to make all of them very strong, close relationships. Based on the time and effort (or costs) spent, different benefits will be achieved from different intensities. Firms need to be aware of the possible costs and benefits from different relationship intensities in order to subsequently measure the value (i.e., benefits/costs) of their relationships.

Many executives have commented that terms for closer, committed relationships are overused, and that most existing relationships are not that close. Because of the investment required for achieving higher intensities, there are very few truly collaborative relationships. However, relationships at lower levels of intensity may be perfectly appropriate for firms in certain situations. Managers need to be able to determine which combination is best for their portfolio of supply chain relationships. Many may already be where they need to be. For others, and whenever a firm obtains a new supplier or customer, companies need to understand the differences in order to determine which relationship to pursue. This is based on the importance of the supplier and/or customer and other characteristics important to a firm, the business objectives the firms have together, and the costs and benefits of achieving the particular relationship level. For example, if a company engages a new supplier that provides a critical component and is operationally and culturally similar to the firm, and the firms decide they want to jointly develop new products and services, then a highly intense partnership may be the appropriate relationship to pursue.

Managers should examine their existing portfolio of relationships and try to determine the type and level of intensity of each. They should then begin to track the resources spent to maintain the current level of intensity and to measure the benefits the company realizes from this investment. Only then can managers determine if they are getting value from their existing interorganizational relationships or if changes need to be made.

FUNCTIONAL INTEGRATION
AND SUPPLY CHAIN RELATIONSHIPS IN PRACTICE

There are a number of examples of functional integration and supply chain relationships succeeding (and failing) in supply chain management. Several of each are now presented.

Company C—Failing to Coordinate
the Sales Function With Supply Chain Capacity

Company C is a long-established manufacturer of clothing—clothing that was functional and fairly resistant to fashion fads. As a result, Company C demand patterns from their retail customers were reasonably stable and predictable, which led Company C to tightly plan their capacity (i.e., plants were run fairly close to optimal capacity).

This situation allowed a smooth and well-planned supply chain from Company C suppliers, through Company C production operations, to retailers, and finally, to customers. The supply chain was complicated by a large number of SKUs, since each style of clothing had multiple colors and sizes (after all, the perfect shirt in the perfect color in the wrong size is not going to satisfy the customer), but this problem was dealt with (though not satisfactorily) by carrying a considerable amount of inventory in various styles, sizes, and colors at various points in the supply chain.

The complication came when the teenage market, which had never bought Company C's products in the past, suddenly decided Company C's products were "in style." Teen magazines and movies were full of celebrities wearing products with the Company C logo. This wreaked havoc with Company C's supply chains. Where demand had been fairly stable, it was now volatile. Where production operations had been run at optimal capacity, they were now capacity constrained. Where inventory had been high and expensive, but manageable, it was now out of control. Where smooth relations had existed with suppliers, Company C was now pushing suppliers to the limits of their capacity to supply cloth. Where traditional retailers had always been able to obtain adequate supplies of Company C products (admittedly, at considerable Company C inventory cost), they were now in a constant backorder situation (after all, Company C was making higher margins on the new teen market retailers, so they were given priority).

Company C's traditional functional silo organization did the best it could in this situation. Production tried to optimize production runs. Purchasing tried to force suppliers to give their cloth needs priorities. Inventory management tried to keep the right combinations of style, size, and color in stock at numerous distribution centers to meet erratic demand. Capacity planning tried to balance the immediate need to expand production capacity for the fad demand, while not expanding capacity too much in case the fad demand went away and Company C would be left with excess capacity. Trade relations tried to give the higher-margin teen retailers priority while still maintaining relations with the traditional retailers that, Company C hoped, would still be there when the fad demand went away.

All of this seemed a reasonable attempt to meet SCM Competitive Driver One, until it was discovered that the sales area was paying salespeople a bonus to open new retail accounts. This had always been the policy of the company and was considered a good way to expand retail coverage. However, think through the logic of having no capacity to meet present demand, all retail customers are dissatisfied because they cannot get enough of the product to sell, long-range planning is reluctant to take the risk of expanding capacity because there is a pervasive belief that the teen fad demand will not last, and the sales force is being rewarded for opening new accounts, accounts that we know—before they are even signed up—we will not be able to satisfy. Further, these new accounts will take product away from our already dissatisfied existing accounts.

How could an otherwise well-run company make such a seemingly obvious mistake? The answer is simple—they failed to follow the principle behind SCM Competitive Driver One. While all the problems listed above were occurring in production, inventory management, purchasing, and trade relations, no one was coordinating these problems with the sales force. Sales managers were doing what they had always done, rewarding their salespeople for opening new accounts. Thus, we can see that ignoring SCM Competitive Driver One can lead to deleterious effects on the supply chain.

Company D—Failing to Coordinate an Industrial Service Supply Chain

Company D is a major North American railroad. As such, this company is in the business of providing a service—transportation—to other companies. Unfortunately, when upper management in this company was asked, "What business are you in?" they invariably answered, "the railroad business" despite the fact that they have seen increasing competition from the trucking industry for over 70 years! Competition is so effective that the U.S. trucking industry's *growth* in 2001 was more than the *entire size* of the U.S. Class One railroad industry!

This philosophy of "we only compete with other railroads" led to a very fragmented and isolated organization structure—a structure aimed more at operating efficiencies than serving the customer. The operations side of the railroad was run with efficiency parameters that had nothing do to with the needs of specific customers, regardless of their importance to the railroad. For example, engines were routinely pulled off trains that had shipments from customers that represented hundreds of millions of dollars in annual revenues for the railroad to move trains that the operating department had decided needed (for operating efficiency reasons) to be moved sooner. Further, this was done with no information on the decision provided to the sales department, the marketing department, or the major customers. The result was huge customers not getting their shipments on time, calling their sales representative, and being told the sales representative did not even know where the railcar was! At the same time, the marketing department was developing a marketing campaign aimed at this customer that touted the impeccable service Company D offered the customer!

We interviewed one such customer that made a product that was perfectly suited to travel on rail. The product came in single units that weighed over six tons, was of low value on a per pound basis, and was shipped to a customer over 1,500 miles away—a near-perfect definition of a product to move efficiently on rail. However, 80% of all outbound shipments from this customer went by truck! Why, when it is perfectly suited for economical rail movement, would the customer use the far more expensive truck option? The answer from the customer was simple. "We cannot trust the railroad to get the product to our customer when they promised, and when they do not get it there, no one at Company D knows anything about its status. You call Company D with a tracking question, and get transferred to five different people before you are finally told they just do not know where the car is, but they are sure it's on the way." Company D was losing huge amounts of volume to the trucking industry because the operations, information systems, marketing, sales, pricing, and demurrage departments were not coordinated.

The last department mentioned (demurrage) deserves particular attention here as an illustration of the implications of not following SCM Competitive Driver One. Another customer of Company D represents over $100 million in annual sales for Company D. As a result, this customer is the focus of considerable Company D marketing efforts, with sales representatives who focus on nothing but selling to this customer. However, a separate function in Company D is charged with making certain the customer empties railcars delivered to it and, in a timely fashion, gives the empty railcars back to Company D so they can be reused. After all, a major measure of operating efficiency in the railroad industry is "railcar turns," or how many times each railcar is used to ship something per year. (A railcar turn of 8 means a particular railcar was used to move 8 revenue-producing loads in a given year; the rest of the time it was empty and unproductive.)

The department in Company D that is in charge of getting these railcars back from customers is called demurrage. The way demurrage works is a certain railcar is delivered to a customer, and the customer has a certain amount of time (the time is usually negotiated with the customer) to return the railcar without any charge. For example, if the customer keeps the railcar 1 day past this "grace period," they are charged a demurrage fee. If they keep it another day, the demurrage fee rises, often doubling the daily charge for each additional day. Company D views this as a penalty for customers not efficiently unloading and returning their railcars and, thus, aggressively tries to collect the demurrage fees. Demurrage personnel are evaluated on how much money they collect, and upper management views this "penalty" as a revenue center for Company D.

However, many Company D customers see demurrage as a service. After all, for a negotiated number of days, the customer gets free storage. The customer sees the job of their inbound materials manager as managing the cost of stocking out, against the cost of storing the inventory in a building, against the cost of storing it in a railcar. Lack of coordination of functions in Company D led them to miss the fact that demurrage was not actually a penalty in the customers' eyes, but rather a potential marketing service.

Back now to the $100 million Company D customer. We interviewed Company D demurrage employees who were proud of the fact that they had just settled a lawsuit against this customer for $5,000 worth of demurrage. Company D claimed this customer owed them $20,000 in demurrage, and the customer claimed they did not, so Company D sued for the demurrage. After an acrimonious lawsuit involving charges and countercharges, the customer agreed to pay $5,000 just to get rid of the nuisance. The demurrage managers at Company D were delighted because, in their own words, "We actually only thought they owed us $5,000. Our records showed they owed us $20,000, but we were not certain they (Company D's own records) were correct, because of errors in recording when the railcar was actually delivered to the customer. So we sued them for the larger, inaccurate amount in hopes of getting what we thought they actually owed us." When we pointed out to the demurrage managers the incongruence of suing a $100 million customer over a $5,000 fee (a suit that might lose Company D a valuable customer), the manager's response was, "My bonus is based on collecting demurrage fees, so that is what we do."

A final example of lack of functional coordination between Company D and one of its customers further illustrates the supply chain costs that can occur. A major customer of Company D is an auto manufacturer that ships thousands of cars by rail every year. The research and development (R&D) function of this manufacturer launched a several-year project to redesign one of their popular models of cars—a project that would keep the car model sporty and fuel-efficient, yet give it a roomier interior. The redesign was successful, resulting in a very popular version of the car. However, in this entire redesign, the R&D group of the manufacturer never thought to coordinate this redesign with Company D, who has many railcars specially designed to haul this model of car. In fact, R&D never got around to telling Company D that the new version of the car was *three inches taller* than the old model.

You can guess what happened—the first three newly redesigned cars that Company D tried to load onto the rail cars were spontaneously turned into convertibles! The drivers took the roofs right off the cars! Of course, the question immediately comes to mind, "Why did it take *three cars* before Company D figured out something was wrong?" In fairness to Company D, it was one car at each of three different loading points. But the point to be made here is the entire problem could have been avoided if the auto manufacturer's R&D function had coordinated their redesign with Company D. The solution, which could have been developed ahead of time without any damage to any cars, was to simply let some of the air out of the tires for shipment (thus lowering the height three inches) and reinflating the tires upon delivery.

Company E—Coordinate
Retail Functions for Market Expansion

After several examples of what happens when companies do not coordinate the traditional business functions, let's look at what happens when they do. Company E is a large chain of auto parts retail stores. After attending an executive development program, the CEO of Company E became convinced (correctly so) that the distribution cost per unit in each store could be reduced considerably if all products were delivered to a central distribution center for mixed shipment to each store, rather than the present supply chain of direct store delivery by each vendor. Transportation costs would be considerably less (volume load rates into and out of the distribution center, instead of less-than-volume rates to each store), and inventory could be held at the central distribution center, rather than at each store, significantly lowering systemwide inventory levels.

When a supply chain network analysis was conducted, however, it was determined that the 245-store chain did not generate enough flow-through volume to justify the cost of a distribution center. Distribution centers (DCs) are high fixed-cost operations, and a high volume of product flow-through is necessary to generate the economies of scale to bring the fixed cost per unit down to a competitive level. In other words, if it costs $1,000,000 per year to run the DC (regardless of unit throughput), and the company ships 100,000 units per year through the DC, the fixed DC cost per unit (which has to be covered in the retail price) is $10. However, if 1,000,000 units can be run through the same DC, the fixed DC cost per unit drops to $1. Imagine running 10,000,000 units through the DC—the fixed DC cost per unit is now $0.10!

The conclusion from the supply chain network analysis was that Company E would need to expand its number of stores to over 400 to generate greater supply chain flow-through volume before the DC was feasible. Thus, Company E launched a 3-year campaign to open new stores in new geographic markets, at the same time that it was building the DC and developing the supplier relations to serve the new DC. With the promise of greater sales of their products through a larger Company E, vendors (through Company E purchasing managers) were willing to work with Company E logistics personnel and trucking companies (through Company E transportation managers) to coordinate inbound and outbound shipments to the new DC to allow for maximum cross docking—coordinating inbound, from-vendor shipments with outbound, to-store shipments so products from a number of vendors arrive at the same time to simply be off-loaded from the trucks, sorted on the loading docks into the mixture that is going to the stores, and reloaded onto the trucks without ever taking up DC storage space. This resulted in considerably lower DC costs, inventory costs, transportation costs, and purchasing prices.

However, none of this would have worked if the expansion had not been coordinated with the Company E marketing group that was responsible for the research to find new potential geographic markets. This, in turn, had to be coordinated with the real estate staff who located and bought the new store sites, and with the merchandising staff who decided how to stock them (based on the marketing group's research).

The result was a smooth, 3-year plan of coordination of marketing, merchandising, real estate, logistics, purchasing, and vendors to expand from a 245-store chain to a 415-store chain with expanded geographic coverage and lower delivered-to-store unit costs.

Company F—Coordinating the Traditional Retail Functions for Supply Chain Economics

In a time where many clothing store chains are having financial problems and going bankrupt, Company F maintained a steady growth in earnings by coordinating traditional functions across its supply chains. Traditionally, retailers are organized around three functions for each department: buying, logistics, and merchandising. The independence, and often competitiveness, of these functions is considered "healthy" in many retailers, but causes a great deal of supply chain problems. Buyers travel the world looking for, and buying, products they think will sell well in their departments in the store—often without communicating with their logistics and merchandising counterparts.

The result often takes the form of shipments arriving at the retail chain's distribution center with the logistics manager having no advance notice that the shipment is coming or any information on what to do with the product other than place it in storage (which costs money in terms of inventory investment and storage capacity utilization). The merchandise managers are told the product is available for sales, again without any advance notice so plans of how to merchandise (display and price) the product can be made. This, of course, causes uncoordinated store displays and marked down pricing on items that cannot be moved.

Company F attacked this problem with a simple organizational change— each department in their chain was given an office in the central headquarters, and in that office was located the buyer, the logistics manager, and the merchandise manager for that department. Further, bonuses for these three managers were based upon the *combined* impact of their decisions on purchasing price, logistics costs, and store markdowns. Thus, by office location and rewards, these three traditional functions of a retail chain were encouraged to coordinate, rather than compete. As a result, Company F drastically improved the earnings from the same level of retail sales. In a year when sales growth was flat, earnings increased by 8%, caused by cost improvements in buying, logistics, and merchandising. Improved merchandising meant less product sold at marked down (lower profit) prices. Logistics cost savings took several forms. A reduction in inbound and outbound transportation costs at the distribution center resulted from a dramatic increase in cross-docking. Again, this meant arrivals of purchased product could be coordinated with shipments to stores so trucks were unloaded, the product was remixed to fill store orders, and the products were placed back on the same trucks for delivery to the stores. Since the trucking companies were receiving inbound and outbound shipments, their rates went down. Since 27% of all inbound product was now cross-docked, this product did not take up expensive DC storage space. Finally, limited storage space at the individual stores was not used for product that was not ready to go immediately onto the shelves for sale.

Company G—Coordinating R&D, Order Processing, and Inventory Management

Company D and its auto manufacturer customer incurred the costs of not coordinating R&D with other SCM functions. Now, let's look at an example of a company that used the coordination of R&D with order management and inventory management to achieve a considerable competitive advantage.

Although many companies complete the production function in their manufacturing facilities, some "postpone" the commitment to the final version of the product until an actual order is received from a customer. However, this strategy of postponement requires close coordination between both the order management and inventory management functions of the manufacturer and their supply chain partners, and the R&D function to design a product whose final form can be postponed. This postponement concept was pursued by a manufacturer of home appliances (Company G) when one of its retail customers (Retailer H) decided not to carry inventory—Retailer H wanted Company G to carry the inventory for them. Since this would put an unacceptable financial burden on Company G, Company G proposed redesigning the product and the supply chain so both companies would sell the same amount of product with less systemwide inventory.

Company G now designs its products and creates a production environment so the product is actually made in components. The final assembly of those components is not done at a manufacturing plant but is completed at

Company G RDCs (located close to Retailer H stores) when a final order is in hand. So a customer walks into a Retailer H store and orders a particular product in a particular color. The order is entered into the cash register, which electronically sends that order directly and immediately to the Company G RDC, where the component parts are pulled from stock and assembled into a product that is shipped to the customer the same day. So when a customer buys it, they assume they are buying a product that already is in inventory when, in fact, the product does not even exist.

The supply chain standard for this manufacturer is that the product components are pulled from inventory and the product is in the process of being assembled at the RDC in the time it takes the customer to leave the store and walk to his or her car. The result is the only inventory Retailer H now carries are the floor display models. However, since any components can be assembled into any product, Company G no longer has high levels of inventory in every model they market. The result is less systemwide inventory for Company G, as well—a fact that could not have been accomplished if Company G and Retailer H had not coordinated their order management, information management, and inventory management functions with Company G's R&D function.

Summary

What all these examples illustrate is the profound impact on supply chain performance of not first coordinating the traditional business functions within the company, and then across the supply chain as a whole. But which functions should be coordinated internal to the company, and which should be shifted to supply chain partners to be performed? In fact, what are the basic supply chain functions that someone in the supply chain has to perform? It is these questions that are addressed by SCM Competitive Driver Two in the next chapter.

3

Collaborate With Supply Chain Partners on Noncore Competency Functions

When you think of the things a supply chain has to accomplish, there are several basic functions that have to be done no matter who does them (see Figure 3.1). Someone has to design the product. That design is typically based on input from research and development and from marketing's information gathering about customers, competitors, and the general marketplace. So the design function involves not only engineering and production and logistics, but also the marketing function of gathering market information.

- Design
- Make
- Brand
- Price
- Promote
- Buy

- Sell
- Stock
- Display
- Deliver
- Finance
- Risk

Figure 3.1   Supply Chain Functions

Someone has to make the product. Someone has to do the production—taking raw materials from the ground, producing component parts, and assembling the final product. This production is not always done by what we typically consider a manufacturer, but somewhere that process has to happen. In many supply chains, the principle of postponement is applied, and the final version of the product is not committed (produced) until a confirmed order comes from the customer. One example of postponement was presented in Chapter 2 as Company G. Company G does not complete the final assembly of those components at a manufacturing plant but rather at RDCs when a final order is in hand from Retailer H.

Someone in the supply chain has to create identification with a particular product and a particular company (branding). This is a core competency for many companies, particularly in the consumer products goods industries. If you talk to executives at such companies as Anheuser-Busch, Kraft, Procter & Gamble, or a legion of others, they will tell you their core competency is the brand recognition and equity that they have built up in various brands and the loyalty customers have to those brands. In many cases that brand equity has little or nothing to do with the production, logistics, or many other supply chain processes, but someone in the supply chain has to create that brand identification.

Someone in the supply chain has to determine the sensitivity of final customers to prices. Combining this market-based price information with the cost of making and distributing the product, and a cogent structure of pricing—from suppliers, through manufacturers, through distributors, down to the final customer—can be determined.

Related to price (a visible manifestation of the value of the product) and branding is the promotion effort. Someone has to inform, communicate, and persuade people on which products to buy.

In every supply chain, there are companies buying and there are companies selling, so these two functions are inseparable. The buying function is typically called purchasing or procurement in companies and is the process of not just buying the lowest-cost product but buying the product that is a combination of low price, high quality, and a dependable supplier. Sales is convincing customers that the salesperson's company is the best combination of low price, high quality, and dependable supplier.

For several reasons, someone has to carry inventory in the supply chain. One reason is that the rate of production often, and in fact usually, does not match the rate of consumption, so the products are produced at a different rate, at a different time, at a different place, and in different quantities than they are consumed. The buffer between those two rates—production and consumption—is inventory, or the stocking function.

Inventory is also carried in the supply chain because of seasonality. Consumers may buy the product in a repetitive pattern when production is at a steady pattern, so inventory continually goes through a process of building up and then being bought down.

Products are often carried in inventory because they have to age to reach a salable state. Certain types of fruits have to ripen before they are salable. Different types of wines take on more value as they age. Certain types of meat products have to "cure" before they are marketable. All these aging processes require the storage of inventory.

A particular form of inventory or stocking is called display. Display is making the product available in an attractive and salable form for the final customers. Whether it is Wal-Mart putting the product on display so customers can find it and make the decision, or whether it is putting it in a display in an industrial distribution center so customers can easily find the product, display is an important part of supply chain management.

The timing, coordination, and expense of delivering a product from Point A to Point B in a condition and at a time that the customer wants is a critical supply chain function.

The final two functions, finance and risk, go hand in hand. From raw materials through component parts to final product to final delivery, someone has to own the product. Someone has to finance the cost of making, moving, and storing the product. It is perhaps the most important aspect of supply chain management to remember—*the last thing that happens in any supply chain is the final customer actually provides any money.* Up to that point, every SCM activity is conducted in anticipation of selling that product, which carries with it risk. What if the customer does not buy it? What if the customer does not want the product as much as we thought and is not willing to pay as much as we thought? What if, in the process of moving the product to the customer, it becomes obsolete or damaged or less valuable than it was when it was originally produced? All those aspects of financial risk have to be assumed by someone in the supply chain.

It is not the purpose of this book to discuss these functions in great detail but to stimulate the reader to think about who performs these functions in their particular supply chains. An important point is that no one company has to perform all these functions. In the early 1900s, Ford Motor Company, under the leadership of Henry Ford, attempted to perform all the supply chain functions for the purpose of keeping control of all operations. Ford Motor Company owned the iron mines to mine the iron ore that was moved on Ford Company ships to Ford steel mills to make Ford steel that was made into Ford automobiles that were moved to Ford dealerships. It was not long before Henry Ford and the directors of the company realized that too much capital was required for Ford to have the luxury of controlling the entire supply chain. What evolved then is what has evolved in many modern supply chains: a struggle to balance the need to control operations with the need to manage risk. Companies are constantly evaluating the question, "What should we do ourselves, and what should we allow someone else to do for us?"

The answer to that question is often, "Can we do it cheaper than someone else?" If the answer is no, we must ask ourselves if the function is a core competency. *A core competency is something we do well that gives us a competitive advantage in the marketplace.* Not everything we do well is a core competency. For instance, what if your company is really good at running your company cafeteria? Even though your company does it well, it does not give you a competitive advantage and, thus, it is not a core competency. For functions that are core competencies, however, even though they may cost us more money to do them ourselves, we still should keep control over them.

Several examples of how companies identify and manage their core competencies and outsource noncore competencies should help. However, to fully understand this SCM Driver of Competitive Advantage, let us first examine what others have said about cooperating to shift noncore competencies to supply chain partners.

Supply Chain Cooperation

Cooperation has been defined as the joint striving toward a common object or goal (Stern, 1971; Day & Klein, 1987). In other words, cooperation is the process of coalescing with others for a good, goal, or value of mutual benefit (Stern & Reve, 1980). Cooperation is an activity in which the potential collaborators are viewed as providing the means by which a divisible goal or object desired by the parties may be obtained and shared (Stern & Reve, 1980).

Alliances give shape to cooperative behaviors in an interfirm context. Lambe and Spekman (1997) define an alliance as a collaborative relationship among firms to achieve a common goal that each firm could not easily accomplish alone. Alliances encompass a variety of agreements, whereby two or more firms agree to pool their resources to pursue specific market opportunities (Gulati, 1995). Perhaps the most significant manifestation of the rise in interfirm cooperation has been the dramatic increase in interfirm strategic alliances (Gulati, 1995). A strategic partnership between any two firms, whether it is between buyer and seller or manufacturer and carrier, could be a segment of an extended supply chain (Gentry, 1996). This is so because each partner in a strategic alliance, which is a primary cooperative strategy, brings knowledge or resources to the partnership (Lyles & Salk, 1996). In other words, a supply chain is a set of firms among which cooperation should take place.

CHARACTERISTICS OF COOPERATION
IN SUPPLY CHAIN MANAGEMENT

A powerful means of enhancing the likelihood of achieving cooperative action among firms is the selection of partners based on some good predictors of relevant cooperative behaviors (Grandori & Soda, 1995). It is impossible for a buyer to develop and maintain close relationships with thousands of suppliers and, as a result, each purchased item or family of items has only a limited number of suppliers (Monczka, Trent, & Handfield, 1998). For example, Siemens Telecom Networks reduced its number of suppliers and now tightly works together with that limited set of suppliers to achieve its quality and cost-reduction targets. In return, the remaining suppliers benefit by getting more business volume (Schwalbe, 1998).

In a complex relationship where performance is difficult to measure, profit or income sharing based upon incentive schemes is an important cooperation mechanism (Grandori & Soda, 1995). By the same token, Monczka et al. (1998) proposed that a win-win approach to share the rewards of the business between both parties is required. Procter and Gamble (P&G), for example, rewarded customers who adopted highly efficient logistics practices such as 2-hour carrier turnaround, on-time customer pickup, electronic purchase orders and invoicing, use of a pallet pool, and ordering in unit-load quantities, all of which brought P&G significant economic benefits (Drayer, 1999). Chrysler also expected its suppliers to submit cost-reduction suggestions that resulted in savings equal to 5% of their annual sales to Chrysler. Chrysler, in turn, rewarded them for continually improving Chrysler (Stallkamp, 1998).

A joint effort is driven by a desire to improve supplier performance in all critical performance areas, including cost reduction, quality improvement, delivery improvement, and supplier design and production capabilities (Monczka et al., 1998). For example, Toyota, with its Toyota Production System that assumes the development of close cooperative relationships between Toyota and its supplier network, performs objective and accurate assessments of each supplier's performance and provides direct assistance to improve each supplier's quality and reliability (Langfield-Smith & Greenwood, 1998). Similarly, Siemens Telecom Networks sends a team to a supplier's facility for about 3 days to work with the supplier's team to identify where waste could be eliminated (Schwalbe, 1998).

Participating firms work together to resolve disputes through mechanisms that support joint problem solving (Monczka et al., 1998; Salmond & Spekman, 1986). Dant and Schul (1992) found that, in a franchise context, if the relational properties of solidarity, mutuality, or role integrity are high, franchisers are likely to use mechanisms such as problem solving and persuasion. Useful mechanisms include interfunctional teams working across firms and co-location, both of which allow exchange of personnel. For example, both Chrysler employees and supplier employees co-locate at the Chrysler Technology Center to develop new Chrysler cars and trucks (Stallkamp, 1998). Presumably, the participants grow to appreciate the other's point of view and carry more understanding when they return to their original positions (Kotler, 1997).

Participating firms practice an open exchange of information (Monczka et al., 1998). For example, in order to minimize inventory in the supply chain, information systems must be able to track and communicate production and customer requirements at different levels in the chain (Cooper, Lambert, & Pagh, 1997). In addition, information about new products, supplier cost data, and production schedules and forecasts for purchased items should be shared among supply chain members (Monczka et al., 1998). As such, information sharing is an essential enabler of synchronization of the supply chain through cooperative design (Anderson & Lee, 1999). Wal-Mart is open and willing to work with its vendors and shares point-of-sale data with suppliers, and its employees communicate with the supplier employees on a regular basis (Gill & Abend, 1996). Shared information between supply chain partners can only be fully leveraged through process integration, collaboration between buyers and suppliers, joint product development, and common systems (Christopher, 1999).

Participating firms maintain a credible commitment to work together during difficult times (Monczka et al., 1998). For example, a buyer does not eliminate a supplier who experiences short-term production problems. Cooperative relationships require joint action to resolve concerns about the market environment affecting both parties. When Chrysler expected future cost hikes in purchasing headliners used inside Dodge Intrepid and Chrysler Concorde sedans, instead of traditional competitive bidding among multiple suppliers, Chrysler and its key suppliers worked together to realize cost savings that far exceeded those expected from traditional competitive bidding (Stallkamp, 1998).

Finally, participating firms are deeply involved in supply chain activities. For example, in the upstream flows in a supply chain, Chrysler invited suppliers to a "teardown" program, in which it took competitors' products apart, piece by piece, to learn how they build them, and actively asked the suppliers to submit proposals to improve the Chrysler minivan (Stallkamp, 1998). Siemens Telecom Networks also looked for suppliers' improvement ideas in such areas as purchasing efficiency, make/buy, design, specification, packaging, lead time, and quality via the Internet, fax, or file transfer (Schwalbe, 1998). In the downstream flows in a supply chain, P&G let its customers participate in its project to simplify pricing, standardize ordering, and reduce invoices and system errors (Drayer, 1999). In addition, helping distributors set quotas for customers, studying the market potential for distributors, forecasting a member's sales volume, and inventory planning and protection are all examples of involvement of a firm in the downstream flows in a supply chain (Mallen, 1963). Anderson and Lee (1999) also propose cooperative demand planning, order fulfillment, and capacity planning among supply chain partners to send a more accurate demand signal throughout the supply chain, which minimizes waste and maximizes responsiveness.

PRECURSORS TO SUPPLY CHAIN COOPERATION

There are several characteristics that must be in place (precursors) before supply chain cooperative behavior will take place: (1) trust and commitment, (2) cooperative norms, (3) interdependence, (4) compatibility, (5) managers' perceptions of environmental uncertainty, and (6) extendedness of a relationship.

Trust and Commitment

Morgan and Hunt (1994) propose that cooperation arises directly from both trust and commitment. Kumar, Scheer, and Steenkamp (1995) propose that trust has two dimensions: honesty and benevolence. Honesty is the belief that a partner stands by its word (Anderson & Narus, 1990; Schurr & Ozanne, 1985), fulfills promised role obligations, and is sincere (Dwyer & Oh, 1987). Benevolence is the belief that a partner is interested in the firm's welfare (Deutsch, 1958; Larzelere & Huston, 1980; Remple, Holmes, & Zanna, 1985), is willing to accept short-term dislocations (Anderson, Lodish, & Weitz, 1987), and will not take unexpected actions that have a negative impact on the firm (Anderson & Narus, 1990). Moorman, Deshpande, and Zaltman (1993) define trust as a willingness to rely on an exchange partner in whom one has confidence. Thus, trust represents honesty, benevolence, and willingness.

Dwyer, Schurr, and Oh (1987) define commitment as an implicit or explicit pledge of relational continuity between exchange partners. Committed partners are willing to invest in valuable assets specific to an exchange, demonstrating they can be relied upon to perform essential functions in the future (Anderson & Weitz, 1992). Gundlach, Achrol, and Mentzer (1995) conceptualized commitment as (1) an input dimension of the credibility and proportionality of resources committed to the relationship, (2) an attitudinal dimension of long-term commitment intentions, and (3) a temporal dimension of the consistency of inputs and attitudes brought to the relationship over time. Kumar, Scheer, and Steenkamp (1995) see commitment as two-dimensional: (1) the desire to stay in the relationship because of the positive affect toward the other party (Meyer, Allen, & Smith, 1993), and (2) incorporating continuity expectations and willingness to invest (e.g., Anderson & Weitz, 1992). Thus, commitment consists of (1) inputs of credible and proportional resources,

(2) attitudes (e.g., intentions and desires) toward commitment, (3) continuity expectations and willingness to invest, and (4) consistent inputs and attitudes toward commitment over time.

There are several impacts of trust and commitment on cooperation. Trust works to overcome mutual difficulties such as power, conflict, and lower profitability (Dwyer, Schurr, & Oh, 1987). Trust significantly stimulates favorable attitudes and behaviors, including communication and bargaining with respect for the current supplier (Schurr & Ozanne, 1985). Mutual trust in a relationship reduces the development of opportunistic intentions and, thus, may eliminate the need for structural mechanisms of control (Granovetter, 1985). Thus, trust and a desire to coordinate with another party are closely related (Pruitt, 1981). Finally, commitment is an essential ingredient for successful long-term relationships that are required for cooperation (cf. Gundlach, Achrol, & Mentzer, 1995). In summary, commitment and trust are key because they encourage supply chain partners to (1) work at preserving relationship investments by cooperating with exchange partners, (2) resist attractive short-term alternatives in favor of the expected long-term benefits of staying with existing partners, and (3) view potentially high-risk actions as being prudent because of the belief that their partners will not act opportunistically (Morgan & Hunt, 1994).

Cooperative Norms

Cooperative norms reflect the belief that both parties in a relationship must combine their efforts and cooperate to be successful (Cannon & Perreault, 1997). In this context, Siguaw, Simpson, and Baker (1998, p. 102) defined cooperative norms as "the perception of the joint efforts of both the supplier and distributor to achieve mutual and individual goals successfully (Cannon & Perreault, 1997; Stern & Reve, 1980) while refraining from opportunistic actions."

Interdependence

Interdependence or mutual dependence has a positive impact on cooperation (Aiken & Hage, 1968; Heide & Miner, 1992; Pfeffer & Salancik, 1978; Rogers & Whetten, 1982; Williamson, 1985). Dependence of a firm on its partner refers to the firm's need to maintain a relationship with the partner to achieve its goals (Frazier, 1983). Dependence of a firm on its partner is increased when (1) outcomes obtained by the focal firm from the partner are important and highly valued and the magnitude of the exchange is high, (2) outcomes obtained by the focal firm exceed outcomes available to the focal firm from the best alternative partner, and (3) the focal firm has few alternative sources or potential sources of exchange (Heide & John, 1988).

Interdependence is related to cooperation in several ways. First, Lusch and Brown (1996) found that high bilateral dependence between a supplier and a wholesaler-distributor increases relational behavior. Buchanan (1992) argued that when mutual dependence between a wholesaler-distributor and its supplier is high, both parties have a high stake in ensuring the relationship's success. In such cases, both parties have invested time, effort, and money in the relationship and are committed to the relationship (Anderson & Weitz, 1992). On the contrary, in channels with low levels of mutual dependency, neither party has many stakes in the relationship and, therefore, relational behavior will not develop to a significant degree.

Second, acknowledged dependence is a prime force in the development of supply chain solidarity (Bowersox & Closs, 1996). In addition, this dependence is what motivates willingness to negotiate functional transfer, share key information, and participate in joint operational planning (Bowersox & Closs, 1996). Finally, the dependence of a firm on another firm is positively related to the firm's long-term relationship orientation (Ganesan, 1994).

Compatibility

Organizational compatibility is defined as having complementary goals and objectives, as well as similarity in operating philosophies and corporate cultures (Bucklin & Sengupta, 1993). Organizational compatibility between firms in an alliance, a form of cooperation, has strong positive impact on the effectiveness of the relationship (i.e., the perception that the relationship is productive and worthwhile) (Bucklin & Sengupta, 1993). By the same token, cooperation involves a combination of object- and collaborator-centered activities that are based on compatibility of goals, aims, or values (Stern & Reve, 1980). Though meshing cultures and individuals' attitudes is time-consuming, it is necessary at some level for the channel to perform as a chain (Cooper, Ellran, et al., 1997).

Managers' Perceptions of Environmental Uncertainty

The development of alliances, which are many forms of interfirm cooperation (Nooteboom, Berger, & Noorderhaven, 1997), is positively associated with key managers' perceptions of environmental uncertainty (Dickson & Weaver, 1997). Managers' perceived environmental uncertainty is posited as a multidimensional construct that includes (1) high general uncertainty, (2) high technological volatility and demand, (3) low predictability of customer demands and competitor actions, and (4) demands for internationalization (Dickson & Weaver, 1997).

Dickson and Weaver (1997) also found a significant three-way interaction among perceived uncertainty, entrepreneurial/conservative orientation, and individualism/collectivism. For example, the probability of the increasing use of alliances with greater perceived general uncertainty is higher for collectivist managers than for individualistic managers, and the probability is the greatest for collectivist managers with low entrepreneurial orientations and lowest for individualistic managers with high entrepreneurial orientations (Dickson & Weaver, 1997). Dickson and Weaver's findings may be explained by the fact that managers with an entrepreneurial orientation are more likely to take risks in the face of uncertainty (e.g., Covin & Slevin, 1991; Palich & Bagby, 1995) and that managers with collectivist orientations emphasize the importance of belonging to a stable, select in-group, value cooperation with the in-group, and expect the group to help provide for the welfare of group members (cf. Hofstede, 1980, 1984; Hui, 1988; Hui & Triandis, 1986; Hui & Villareal, 1989). As such, alliance formation may be contingent upon taken-for-granted orientations and cultural norms of the management team (e.g., perceived uncertainty, entrepreneurial orientation, and individual culture) who want to hedge against risk and uncertainty.

Extendedness of a Relationship

Heide and Miner (1992) define the extendedness of a relationship as the degree to which the parties anticipate that the relationship will continue into the future with an indeterminate end point. Based on their observations of the Prisoner's Dilemma game, Heide and Miner (1992) argued that, although antic-ipated open-ended interaction does not require cooperation, it does make it possible—even when neither party has altruism or concern about the other party's well-being. The first implication of the iterated game framework of Heide and Miner (1992) is that, in a Prisoner's Dilemma situation, extendedness in a relationship increases the probability of a pattern of cooperation. Thus, extend-edness in a relationship, or open-ended interaction, has a positive effect on the level of cooperation between two interacting firms (Heide & Miner, 1992).

NONCORE COMPETENCY COOPERATION IN PRACTICE

There are a number of examples of companies successfully (and unsuc-cessfully) cooperating in the supply chain on noncore competency functional shifting. Several examples of each are now presented.

Company I—Outsourcing Too Much

In the words of the CEO of Company I, a major chemical manufacturer, "We have outsourced so many things, we no longer have control over the things that are our core competency in the marketplace." This company had taken outsourcing too far. They had outsourced things that other companies could do cheaper for them—often a good decision. However, they had also outsourced various activities that other companies could do cheaper for them, but were the basis on which they competed in the marketplace. Under no circumstances should they have allowed those critical functions in the supply chain outside their control. A 2-year project was initiated to determine what activities this company should outsource and what activities this company should pull back in and take control over because it gave them their unique advantage in the marketplace.

The question then became "What is it that gives a chemical company a competitive advantage?" It was not branding, nor promotions, nor stocking, nor display, nor delivery. In fact, after much discussion, Company I management realized the true competitive advantage of a chemical company is in the design and make components listed in Figure 3.1. Truly successful chemical companies have world-class R&D groups that develop products to do certain things well, and not inadvertently do other things.

Take, for example, the plastic in the bottle of water you drink. This chemical formula creates a product that a chemical company makes in little plastic pellets that can be sold cheaply to the water bottlers, who in turn melt the plastic pellets and form them into the distinctive shape of their bottles. These bottles have to hold that shape, not leak, and be clear enough that you can see the liquid (water) inside the bottle. The bottle also has to be able to hold the label for the water bottler's branding function. What the plastic has to not do, is give off any harmful chemicals into the water so that the customer drinking the water (you) gets sick. Thus, chemical manufacturers who make this product must design a chemical formula so that the product does certain things well (hold its shape, not leak, and be clear), does not do other things (give off harmful chemicals), and can be made inexpensively and exclusively.

This last point (the make function) is how the chemical company makes money and achieves competitive advantage. Designing the product so that the chemical company can inexpensively make the product provides the ability to sell it cheaply to bottlers and, thus, make a reasonable profit margin. By designing the product so that the chemical company has a unique manufacturing process that few, if any, can copy creates a barrier to entry into the business that gives the chemical company an advantage over potential competitors.

Through the application of this logic to its own products and supply chain processes, Company I gradually pulled all functions related to the make and design functions back under their direct control and allowed other noncore competency functions to be performed by supply chain partners.

Company J—Outsourcing the Noncore Logistics Function

Another chemical industry went through the same analysis, but started at the point of asking the question, "What should we be outsourcing?" instead of the Company I question, "What should we stop outsourcing?" As discussed in the Company I example, although it sounds facetious, large chemical companies are large chemical companies because they are large chemical companies. That seemingly nonsensical statement actually has a lot of logic behind it.

One of the great driving economies of scale of chemical supply chains is production size. If a chemical company is large enough to afford the cost of building a billion-dollar facility and to run the kind of volume through that billion-dollar facility to get the fixed cost per unit down to a small number, that chemical company is going to be more cost competitive in the marketplace. So a core competency in the chemical industry is production size. It is not to the advantage of a big chemical company to outsource production operations. It is unlikely we will see examples around the world of three large chemical companies getting together and saying, "Hey, let's build a big production facility together in Argentina, and we'll share our technology and the production cost." They should not let go of that core competency of their business.

As we discussed with Company I, another core competency in the chemical industry is R&D. Companies have competitive advantages in the marketplace because they develop unique chemicals with specific characteristics for which a patent can be obtained and, thus, cannot be immediately copied by their competition. It gives them an advantage in the marketplace for specific applications. Chemical companies should not share that design function of the supply chain with their competitors.

When you think about the chemical industry from a logistics point of view, it is a unique industry. Chemical companies move products that generally are high bulk, sometimes high in weight, often low in value, and very often high in risk. When a cookie truck has a wreck on the side of the road and you turn all the kids within a mile of the wreck loose on the cookie truck, the problem is completely cleaned up. If a chemical truck wrecks, we may have to evacuate a several-mile area because of the deleterious effects of the chemical. So we are moving a product that has unique delivery characteristics—heavy, bulky, low value, and potentially harmful. That does not mean it is a core competency. It is simply a problem of the industry—getting a difficult-to-handle product cheaply and safely from Point A to Point B without hurting the product or hurting anyone or the environment along the way.

As a result, we have a function within the chemical industry, the delivery function in Figure 3.1, that takes unique expertise but is not the basis on which chemical companies compete with each other in the marketplace. Therein lies the example of Company J, and that is outsourcing and achieving economies of scale on items that are noncore competencies.

Company J is an example of a company taking advantage of that particular economy in a particular industry. Company J was formed as a spin-off company from a large global chemical company. The concept behind this spin-off was, "We will create a company that specializes strictly in the delivery function of chemicals on a global basis."

Since Company J has the logistics economies of scale of a large chemical company (the parent company agreed to ship all its chemicals through Company J), every small chemical company in the world wanted to use Company J services and achieve the same economies of scale. As a result, Company J quickly grew from a start-up to a billion-dollar company because it provided a basic fundamental value driver in the supply chain—any small chemical company could join Company J and achieve the same economies of scale that other large companies achieve. Large chemical companies could join the Company J operation and also maintain their economies of scale, and because they combined the economies of scale of shipping across numerous companies, they, in fact, achieved greater economies of scale of delivery than they had experienced in the past. Even the parent company achieved lower logistics costs, because the economies of scale of the larger Company J were greater than those of the parent chemical company alone.

Why would otherwise competitive companies cooperate on this function? The answer is that two chemical companies could help each other both lower their cost per pound of shipping a particular product and still not hurt the core competency on which they compete in the marketplace. None of the chemical companies were going together with Company J saying, "Let's combine our research and development functions." None of the companies went together and said, "Let's combine our production facilities." But many companies in effect said, "Let's go together and lower our cost per pound of the delivery function, especially since it's not our core competency." In other words, "It's not the basis on which we're going to compete with each other, so let's cooperate."

Outsourcing the Noncore Procurement Function

Another example of this cooperation on noncore competencies is in the consumer package goods industry. A number of "commerce exchanges" have arisen in recent years to consolidate the purchasing function. In particular, the automobile industry and the consumer package goods industry have begun—under various names—to "non-compete" on noncore competency issues. To examine these two particular industries, we must again ask the question, "What are their core competencies?" What gives Toyota, General Motors, Ford,

Chrysler, and other automobile companies their competitive advantage? What gives companies in the consumer package goods industry their competitive advantage? What gives Procter & Gamble or Kraft or Frito-Lay or any of a number of other consumer package goods companies their competitive advantage?

The answer in both of these industries is brand equity. The branding function, the promotion of that brand, the creation of an image of quality, the advertising that goes around creating the name recognition, these are the bases on which companies in both these industries compete with each other.

What they do not compete on in the supply chain is the purchasing function. No company in either industry will say, "My basis of succeeding in this industry is I'm better at purchasing raw materials than any of the other companies." In fact, in both of these industries, otherwise fierce competitors have gotten together and said, "Let's form a company that will perform the purchasing functions for various different ingredients and supplies and equipment that we need to run our operations, and let's combine our buying power. And in the process, we'll reduce our purchasing costs in many cases as much as 40%." The fact that all the competitors in the market are now purchasing at a lower cost does not necessarily give anyone a competitive advantage over the other, but it certainly gives them a lower cost structure, a lower cost of goods sold, and as a result, higher earnings on the same level of sales.

Company K—The Virtual Corporation

This SCM Driver can be carried to its ultimate conclusion, that of a virtual corporation. The virtual corporation is one in which most of the functions, except for one or two core competencies, are outsourced to other supply chain partners. For an example we turn to Company K in the electronics industry (Figure 3.2). Company K is the number two manufacturer of a particular type of electronics product, a curious statement since this company does not make a single solitary product. Let's repeat that—the number two manufacturer of this product in the world does not make any products.

It used to. Five years ago it had a large manufacturing plant where products were made and shipped all over the world to various customers (distributors). However, in examining their supply chain and going through an examination of their core competencies, Company K management started asking the question, "What is it that gives us a basis of competitive advantage in the marketplace?" Is it manufacturing expertise? Well, no. When Company K management benchmarked themselves against other companies in their industry, they determined that their production operations were no lower in cost per product than any other company in the global marketplace. Their quality was

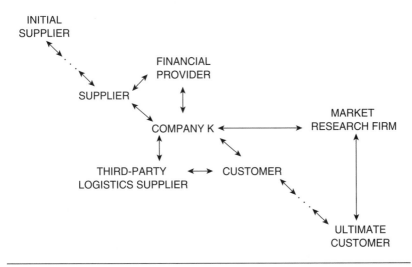

Figure 3.2   An Ultimate Supply Chain

no better, but no worse. In fact, they were just as good as and no worse than any other manufacturer of this particular product worldwide.

What about logistics? Were they better at distributing the product and moving it around the world? Actually, when Company K started benchmarking against other companies, they found out that this was a particular source of problems for them. Remember, this is an electronic product. During transit and storage, the temperature cannot be too hot, the temperature cannot be too cold, the humidity has to be maintained within a certain range, and the product cannot be subjected to too much bouncing around. If any of these occur, and they often did, the product will invariably be damaged. Company K discovered that historically 20% of its products arrived at their final distributor DOA, "dead on arrival," which meant that one out of five products that were made had to be sent back to the manufacturer to be repaired simply because in the process of distributing they had gotten too hot or too cold or too moist or been bounced around too much. Although Company K logistics costs—their cost per unit of moving the product to the final demand location—were a little bit higher than the benchmark norm for their industry, their damage rate was out of control.

How about market research? They actually were not very good at market research—they did not have the internal staff to go out and gather information from their customers. They did find a source of advantage related to the market research function though. Once the information was gathered by an independent market research company, Company K was excellent at taking insights from customers about what they valued and turning those value ideas into features in the products they designed (more on this in Chapter 5).

In other words, Company K is excellent at R&D. They are excellent at taking market research information, turning it into the design for the product to be built, and then—based on that combination of market information and product characteristics—they are superlative at estimating the demand for that product on a global basis, and the phase-in and phase-out timing of that product. As is true of much of the electronics industry, the product life cycle for this company's products is relatively short. On average, from introduction to obsolescence, a particular product model lasts only about 9 months. This company was excellent at estimating for each of their world markets—for North America, South America, Europe, Africa, Asia, and Australia—what the demand was going to be per month from the introduction of the product until it became obsolete.

Let's look at what a reconfigured supply chain for this particular company looks like. Company K decided that because they had no particular expertise in production and it was not a source of competitive advantage for them (it was not a core competency), they should look elsewhere for the production function. As a result, Company K picked five manufacturing subcontractors in Southeast Asia. The 5-year contract with each subcontractor guarantees each subcontractor will annually receive orders for 20% of Company K's production requirements.

In each case, Company K develops a new product. They take market information, design the new product, and—based on this information—develop a monthly production schedule for the 9-month life of the product. Company K then goes to each of the five manufacturing subcontractors, gives them the product design and production schedule, and asks them for their quote on the per unit price they will charge to produce the product.

The general idea of the agreement is that the low-cost supplier will get the contract. However, remember that Company K has agreements with each of the five suppliers that over a 5-year period, each of the five is guaranteed to get 20% of the production contracts from Company K. So even if subcontractors 1, 2, 3, and 4 are traditionally the low-cost bidders, 1 out of every 5 contracts still goes to subcontractor 5 to support their operations. This provides each of the contractors with a 5-year window of guaranteed production levels so they can build capacity and capabilities to that 5-year production plan. However, the understanding is that, after 5 years, if any one of those five contractors is habitually a higher-cost supplier, it will be eliminated in the 5-year review. This means that long-term stability is guaranteed for each subcontractor, but there is an ongoing motivation to drive costs down, while still maintaining rigorous quality standards. The result for Company K was a 23% reduction in per-unit production costs.

Where do we get the market information to design the products? The company turned to a professional market research company to continually conduct what is called "value-based research" with customers around the world to identify not just features, but the general value they get from this product in the customers' operations (more about value determination in Chapter 5). The research company is not asked to interpret that information. It simply performs the function of gathering the information, compiling it, and turning it over to the company's marketing operations, who interpret this information to develop new products and product features, and estimate their demand.

What about that logistics damage situation? The company, again, acknowledged that their core competency, the basis on which they compete, is interpreting marketing information, product design, and turning those two pieces of information into market-based schedules of demand for particular products. What they were not good at was the delivery function in Figure 3.1. The company then turned to three global third-party logistics providers (3PLs) and signed long-term contracts with each for particular global regions. The contracts specified that Company K would provide each 3PL with their production schedule for each product and the schedule of expected demand at each of Company K's demand points around the world. Each 3PL's job was to pick up the product at the plants in Southeast Asia and deliver them on time to the various global demand points. In other words, Company K let logistics professionals take over the professional logistics (or delivery) function.

Finally, Company K addressed the finance and risk functions in Figure 3.1. As we discussed, Company K was superlative at forecasting and managing demand, which reduced risk. However, their internal cost of money was 25%, which was how Company K financed their inventory and internal operations. Company K put together an international consortium of banks to provide a line of credit in the hundreds of millions of dollars to finance their inventory and operations.

Financing their inventory is a fairly straight-forward statement, but operations needs some elaboration. One of the drawbacks of using outsourced manufacturers was that these manufacturers all ran their companies on a cash basis. As soon as Company K awarded a contract to one of these subcontractors, the subcontractor immediately asked for all the money they would be paid for the contract up front (in fact, this provision was in all the contracts). Since the subcontractors operated on a cash basis, they needed money up front to finance direct labor and direct materials (from their second-tier suppliers) for the production schedule.

The banking consortium provided Company K with a line of credit at several points over Prime (at the time of this example, this meant a line of credit financed at 9%). This meant that, by going outside the company to a third-party financial provider, Company K turned their cost of money for inventory and operations from 25% to 9%, a 16% per year savings in the financial function. Sixteen percent a year spread over, on average, $300 to $400 million in financing is a considerable bottom line impact!

The result of all this outsourcing of noncore competencies is that over a 2-year period the company not only lowered their cost of production by 23% per unit and financing cost by 16% per year; logistics costs have gone down 2% for Company K. This is because Company K turned to companies who are professionals at the delivery function of electronics. More important for Company K, the rate of DOA (dead on arrival) products went from 20% before outsourcing this function, to less than 1%.

The result is the number two global manufacturer of this particular electronic product does not make a single solitary product. What they still do is design products their customers desire. They deliver those products on time at a higher delivered quality than they did before, at a lower production and financial cost than they did before, with a much lower capital base than they did before. The company no longer has production facilities. As a matter of fact, one of the largest challenges to management was selling the production facilities they no longer needed. Inventory levels have gone down, so working capital has gone down. The company is still a major player in the market at its core competency, the thing that it does better than anyone else and which is the basis of their competitive advantage, but it had significantly lowered its supporting function costs of finance, production, market research, and logistics.

Summary

These examples provide us with an insight into the advantages that can be obtained from recognizing and emphasizing our core competencies. When a company combines the insights from the first two SCM Drivers of Competitive Advantage, the core competencies of a company, and of its supply chain partners, can lead to synergies in the supply chain. Synergies occur when the combined efforts of two or more supply chain partners produce results greater than each supply chain partner could produce acting independently. Or "One plus one equals three!" It is the search for these synergies that SCM Competitive Driver Three addresses.

4

Look for Supply Chain Synergies

S CM Drivers One and Two, respectively, encourage companies to coordinate the traditional business functions within the company and across supply chain partners, while keeping core competencies under internal control and outsourcing noncore competencies. The result of these two drivers is that synergistic effects (the whole is greater than the sum of the parts) can result. However, these synergies seldom happen unless they are actively sought, identified, and managed collaboratively. It is the purpose of this chapter, after a brief discussion of supply chain collaboration, to provide several examples of supply chain synergies.

Supply Chain Collaboration

Collaboration between supply chain members is becoming more and more common. Many believe it brings competitive advantage for their particular supply chain. But what allows collaboration to occur? What are the obstacles that must be overcome to achieve this? Is it really worth the effort? To address these issues, Mentzer, Foggin, and Golicic (2000) interviewed (individually or in focus groups) 20 supply chain executives from various companies. Their purpose was to understand what supply chain collaboration is, how much is taking place, how it can be achieved, and the benefits obtained. Specifically, they explored the enablers of supply chain collaboration (Table 4.1), its impediments (Table 4.2), and its benefits (Table 4.3). This understanding can guide companies to accomplish collaboration in their own supply chains.

Many of the enablers, impediments, and benefits identified by the participants were expected by the authors. However, they were surprised by how many of them were related to people and relationships, as opposed to technology and infrastructure. The focus groups compared collaboration to marriage, saying that both had similar characteristics. According to the participants, companies

Table 4.1   Supply Chain Collaboration Enablers

- Common interest in the relationship
- Openness with the other party
- Recognizing who and what are important
- Helping each other
- Clear expectations
- Leadership (champions)
- Working together and adjusting to one another
- Problem solving, not punishing
- Trust
- Sharing benefits
- Technology
- Longevity

Table 4.2   Supply Chain Collaboration Impediments

- Doing things the old way
- Conventional accounting practices
- Tax laws
- Antitrust laws
- Limited view of the entire supply chain
- Annual negotiation process
- Time investment
- Betrayal
- Inadequate communications
- Inability to consistently meet requirements

that collaborate are expected to benefit from better supply chain relationships, reduced costs, increased sales and returns, improved customer service, and a competitive advantage. These benefits can be achieved if there are enablers in place such as trust and openness between supply chain members, leadership that is committed to collaboration, a common interest in actually collaborating, and, yes, the technology to assist in the sharing of information. Impediments such as inadequate communication, betrayal, and the time investment required must be controlled or removed for collaboration to be successful.

Table 4.3   Supply Chain Collaboration Benefits

- Reductions in inventory
- Reductions in personnel
- Improved customer service
- Better delivery through reduced cycle times
- Increased speed to market of new products
- Focus on core competencies
- Public image
- Strengthened trust and interdependence
- Increased sharing of information, ideas, and technology
- Working toward the goals of the supply chain and not the individual companies
- Increased shareholder value
- Competitive advantage over other supply chains

Participants provided a couple of additional impediments that were not obvious and, therefore, not expected. Tax and antitrust laws were considered impediments to collaboration. An interesting benefit identified was the positive impact on the public image of the companies that were collaborating. It was also surprising to note how candid executives were about how little collaboration is actually taking place in supply chains today.

SUPPLY CHAIN COLLABORATION DEFINED

In order to discuss the enablers, impediments, and benefits of supply chain collaboration, it was necessary to gain an understanding of how the interview and focus group participants viewed collaboration. As defined by the participants, supply chain collaboration is all companies in the supply chain actively *working together as one* with common objectives. One participant stated that collaboration is like all of the companies being under common ownership. Participants also felt that collaboration is characterized by *sharing*, the sharing of information, knowledge, risk, and profits. It incorporates an understanding of how other companies operate and make decisions. It is considered much more than cooperation or negotiation and is a step beyond partnerships: "*Cooperation is how I think a lot of companies have [operated] in the past and that's basically a successful negotiation. In collaboration, you're really moving to a whole different level.*"

Many of the participants agreed that supply chain collaboration was first started by Japanese automobile companies practicing a philosophy of harmony in their business relationships. A specific example of one company's philosophy was provided by one respondent: *"Toyota fundamentally believes that if they show you what they do, then you get better, you will push them to get better, and it just keeps going back and forth."* Another participant described working with another Japanese company who sent their own employees in at no cost to teach die exchange, paid all of their own expenses, and did not ask for anything in return when finished. The participants agreed this is how collaboration should work.

Two metaphors were used by participants to describe supply chain collaboration. The first, cooperation and negotiations are like dating, but collaboration is marriage. *"It's like being married . . . It takes a lot of work to build a relationship and keep it going and keep it active and keep it vibrant."* Also, *"Once the commitment is made, you don't throw it away after a couple of years."* The other metaphor is that supply chain collaboration is a crew race. *"We're going to get to the finish line if we somehow figure out a way to row together."* Both of these metaphors incorporate the ideas of working together and sharing, but with a long-term perspective.

Due to the commitment necessary for true collaboration to occur, implementation of this type of relationship is not widespread. Supply chain executives vary on their estimations—ranging from 10% to 30%—of supply chains that are collaborating in some fashion. The view is that it is fragmented, and much of what is considered by some companies to be collaboration is, in fact, not. *"It's almost the difference between an older or adult child versus having a 4-year-old that you are going to tell what to do . . . that child will cooperate with you so they don't get paddled, but that's not collaboration."*

Part of the problem is deciding with whom to collaborate. The consensus was that it is not possible to collaborate with everyone. So where do you focus your resources? According to the participants, you look for the key suppliers or customers, those that are a large portion of your business. One participant stated, *"Because of the time and effort, you might as well not go after the guy that's doing $1,000 a year with you."* Several of the participants said they focused on suppliers or customers that provided over 70% of their business.

Another factor to consider is whether or not the key supplier or customer is willing to participate in this effort. The process that emerged from the focus groups was to pick key suppliers or customers, work with them, get them on board, work out the problems, and move on to the next set of suppliers and customers. The opinion is that as collaboration begins taking place with some of these key supply chain members, it eventually becomes routine and the focus can turn to new relationships. *"You only do 8 or 10 this year, but then they're running. Now less resources are needed to manage that going forward, so you can embark on the next 8, then the next 8."* The participants agreed that you cannot begin to embark on these collaborative relationships unless there are some enablers in place first.

SUPPLY CHAIN COLLABORATION ENABLERS

As stated above, several of the executives compared collaborative relationships to the state of marriage. A number of things can cause marriages to fail, such as being an adversarial partner, having unrealistic expectations, failure to communicate, and, of course, betrayal. Maintaining a marital relationship under stress requires a great deal of time and effort. But many things help marriages, and some of these are the same things that help collaborative supply chain relationships.

Some of these things are involved in building the relationship to begin with, such as a common interest in the relationship. For example, one of the executives said, *"It's a lot easier to get a date with somebody who wants to date you than it is to go after the beauty queen that tells you to drop dead. So, you need somebody that's . . . important to you, somebody that you're important to also."* He went on to say, *"I really think it's sort of like personal relationships to the degree that the other party's got to be as interested and as committed. . . . I think it's the same here that you need . . . somebody who is committed and has that staying power to keep working through the details to truly make the difference."*

Another behavior that helps to build a relationship is being open with the other party. *"You have to be very open about what you know and what you have done in the past. This is not standard industry mode of operation."* But, of course, there are risks associated with this. *"Being absolutely open and putting all of your cards on the table is a leap in vulnerability because it can be used against you."*

Starting anew may be a way to build a relationship. In describing an effort to build collaboration within an organization, one executive said *"We started from scratch, so the people we hired were hired with the object in mind that this is a collaborative effort. Everybody's going to work together as a team. Nobody is hired by somebody else. There are no preferred parking places or anything like that. And, this was a big operation, but it was that way from the beginning. We didn't have to retrain anybody."*

Building relationships takes a great deal of effort. The company seeking a relationship must first focus on *who* is important. *"Really understanding who are the players you need in developing the supply chain is as critical as defining who's in the supply chain."* And it is just as critical to identify and focus on *what* is important. Everything is not equally important. *"There are some very key components, key commodities, key subsystems, and until you define what those are, you don't know what to collaborate on. . . . Once you start seeing success and build excitement in your supply base around the collaboration work, that's how you fuel it."*

Successful relationships are fostered when partners help each other. Sometimes companies ask the other party for help. For example, some customers ask suppliers to help design the process or the product. *"If you will invite them in and you show them your process and you make them a partner in the process in making it leaner and quicker, then I think you can make significant break-throughs.*" Another executive said, "*We are absolutely dependent on our suppli-ers for new designs. . . . That means we are dependent. There has to be a lot of cooperation on product design and that implies a lot of things. It implies sharing of new technology, it implies security, and not sharing it with competition, even though they may be supplying it . . . There's a degree of ethics that's involved.*" The savings from this arrangement were described as "huge."

The executives spoke more frequently of offering help rather than asking for help. Several had examples of their companies helping their suppliers. Said one, "*We have as part of our supply chain strategy to be able to bring our suppli-ers up to speed where they need to be in lean manufacturing. Lean manufactur-ing is about the fourth or fifth item in a series of steps to get them where they need to be.*" Another executive described working for a Baldrige winner in a former job. He stated that once they decided that a company "*was going to be their A-supplier, not only would they go in there and help them with Six Sigma tech-niques and remanufacturing, they would also funnel the demand from all of their divisions to that supplier to make sure that supplier had enough volume to make sure they had the lowest cost. . . . Not many corporations [ask] 'How do I make that supplier better so he can make me better?'*" Another executive described how a well-known Japanese manufacturer helps their suppliers solve problems. "*They will come into your facility and they will work with you to solve it. They believe that you are their supplier for life and they stand up to that. If you get kicked out of [their] supply chain, it's because you deserve to be kicked out. They are not punitive in any nature. It's total collaboration.*"

Clear expectations are required in any lasting relationship. Several of the executives described different situations involving people on the manufactur-ing floor, or with third-party logistics providers (3PLs), and the need for them to know what they could expect from their partners, and what was expected of them. They described how, for example, standards are made visible, how responsibilities and ownership have been clearly defined, and how processes are clear, visible, and rewarded. Expectations are also helped when each party is consistent. As one participant said, "*You do what you say you can do reli-giously.*" Another said, "*You build for the consistent relationship with the consis-tent messages coming down from all over the organization, from the chairman right on down. That makes it work.*"

Leadership is absolutely required to build these relationships. "*Each com-pany has got to have a leader or a champion or somebody who's got a personal stake in it, who wants to work beyond the details and make something happen. The easiest thing to do is to say, 'This is going to take too much time. I've got bottom-line things to worry about. I've got day-to-day pressing stuff.' If you don't have that champion who's going to move this thing forward, it's not going to go.*" Another panelist stated that a company needs a champion with staying power. Others said, *"If a company doesn't have leaders with a passion to make it work, it won't."*

Like marriage, however, much more effort is needed to keep the collaborative relationships alive than to start them. For example, the partners need to learn to work together, to compromise, and to adjust to one another. This does not come naturally. As one executive said, *"There's no legal entity that constitutes a supply chain. There's no president or CEO of the supply chain that can basically dictate what happens. The whole thing depends upon cooperation and collaboration within all the parties and partnerships in it."* Firms in the supply chain have to *"be able to make individual compromises to achieve the greater good for the whole supply chain."* That may even involve changing your own company. Another participant stated, *"Before you try to change your supply chain, you've really got to change what you are doing internally or you will never get there."*

Several of the participants commented on the need to not punish suppliers when problems occur. One participant said when things are not going well, *"You talk about it. You really work through issues. And you get over those things. And those things [relationships] don't dissolve unless there's some real betrayal that takes place between those two companies. And until you reach that betrayal level, you work through issues. That's where you've got to get to if you really want to move forward."* Another pointed out that when companies are talking to one another, they discover where they have problems. Yet another said that it was necessary for each party to be willing to bring up problems in a way that was not disrespectful, nor adversarial.

It has already been pointed out that betrayal will destroy relationships. Trust is required to build and maintain them. Panel members said things like *"You better be a trustworthy person"* and *"The first thing you've got to have is integrity, and if you don't have that, none of this stuff is worth anything."* But trust must go beyond the individual. It must extend to the organization, because no matter whom you deal with in either company, be it purchasing, engineering, sales, or marketing, it does not matter, because the company itself must have the ethical integrity that you can always rely on.

Sharing is part of any relationship, and this is true of supply chain relationships as well. Although one panelist pointed out how difficult sharing could be, several pointed out that sharing of benefits was necessary. A good job should be rewarded with more business, and a way of doing that is to ensure that performance measurements are in place to identify who is performing well. Another panelist described a cost avoidance initiative where suppliers are asked to save a certain percentage for the customer, and are allowed to keep anything in excess of that percentage. Documented performance measures and scorecards are also necessary to show senior management and gain credibility for the collaboration efforts.

Advanced technology is essential to the success of collaborative relationships. Several panelists described the following as some of the benefits of technology:

- Technology links together a worldwide enterprise and its supply chain. A firm cannot build worldwide collaborative relationships without it.
- Technology links together the multiple tiers of a supply chain. It allows a firm to communicate with its suppliers at all levels.
- Technology speeds up information flows. Problems can be identified quickly and solutions developed proactively, rather than by responding to the problem too late.
- Technology can help break down barriers between companies. Technology in the hands of 3PLs can identify opportunities for firms to collaborate that would not be apparent to either one individually.
- Technology is necessary to convert the very large amounts of data flowing in a supply chain into useful collaborative information. One panelist described the newest planning systems as "*monsters waiting to be fed*" with data.

The panelists agreed, however, that technology by itself is not enough: "*If you don't add intelligence to it [technology], you can screw up quicker. If you don't analyze and have intelligence to take that raw data and turn it into good information, then the information is going to be worse. You will continue to use it the wrong way and screw it up.*" Even in the area of technology, the human factor is essential.

Finally, and not surprisingly, longevity of the relationship was also viewed as an enabler. One panelist recounted, "*What made the relationship successful in this case was the longevity of it and the trust between the companies. They never let us down, and we never let them down.*"

IMPEDIMENTS

Many of the impediments that must be overcome are the result of behaviors carried over from the past, such things as the existence of functional silos in some firms. Some are simply the fact that old habits get in the way.

Various kinds of rules often cause the continuation of doing things the old way. For instance, some of the practices associated with supply chain management "*and extended enterprises, are the kinds of things that . . . tend to fly against conventional accounting practice.*" Accountants have the responsibility to determine the value of dealing with other firms and how to protect the company against a partner passing cost on to them. Supply chain managers need to learn how to overcome these problems to really have an impact. Tax departments, reacting to tax laws, may dictate how products flow in the supply chain, limiting the opportunities to develop collaborative relationships. Finally, antitrust laws may prevent two competing companies from collaborating to find supply chain efficiencies.

Another form of the old way may be the result of not being able to see the big picture. Several of the executives described how many managers still have only a limited view of the entire supply chain. Sometimes potential supply chain partners do not understand total system costs. Other times, managers within the organization focus only on their functions and fail to recognize how the functions both inside and outside the organization benefit from collaboration.

For another example, the practice of annual negotiation runs counter to collaborative efforts. They are often adversarial. Said one executive, *"We have been involved in negotiations with these guys and you go in, negotiate, beat them down as bad as you can, and then report back to management that 'I have beat Tom up and got two cents a pound from him.' We don't think that's the way to do it in the future. We still need the two cents or whatever, but we need to do it in a way that we involve him and involve his supply chain."* Even when annual negotiations are not adversarial, they are not cooperative either.

Annual negotiations also cause one or more of the parties to hold something back. Suppliers know *"They've got to come to the table the following year. Why would you want to put everything that you've got up on the table then because what's left for a year from now?"* Said another executive, *"It seemed like we were spending 3 to 4 months every year on annual contracts and negotiations. . . . We were just so tired of all of the issues that we had to deal with every single year. And they took out a lot of the time. And as a result of that now there really truly is a partnership."* That company has now signed a 5-year contract with one of its service providers.

Speaking of time, one set of impediments to developing truly collaborative relationships is the amount of time involved. For example, several of the executive participants discussed the amount of time it took to create one: *"One of the biggest impediments is it takes time, and time for people like us is even more critical than the money,"* and *"The investment of time is huge."* Furthermore, because of the amount of time, companies can only manage a few collaborative relationships. *"We're not going to do 20 of these things. We just don't have the horsepower or the time."*

The time needed to establish these relationships often exceeds the time employees stay with a company. One executive described an example. *"They've had four bosses in 4 years. Why would I bother to invest a bunch of effort in that company, because who knows what the message is going to be next year?"* Another said, *"In Silicone Valley, 5 years ago, the average longevity of an employee was 3½ years. Today, it's a year and a half out there. Now, what can you implement in a year?"*

A very serious impediment is when one partner betrays another. Betrayal can be as simple as lying, which may result in a partner refusing to deal with another firm in the future. It may be in the form of stringing along a potential partner. One executive told how his company met with another, and at the end of the meeting, the leader of the other team stated on leaving, *"We'll go away and let's think about this for about 18 months or 2 years or so, and then we'll get back together and see what we can do."* Or it may be in the form of sharing concepts developed for a partner with the partner's competitors. One executive told how trust was lost when its supplier began selling an idea to his competitor. Another described how a very large customer asked that the vendor develop a patented technology, then insisted that the supplier give the technology to a competitor. The supplier would have to do so if it wished to protect its other business with the customer.

Other factors that may impede the development of collaborative relationships include an inability to consistently meet requirements. For example, one panelist described how a potential partner's inconsistent behavior from top to bottom caused a relationship to break down. *"A lack of vision or commitment or creativity internally can kill these things very, very quickly."* While some in the firm are trying to build the alliances, others say, *"Well, we can't do that. We can't change loading hours. We can't change this practice."* Another described how his relationship with a supplier's national account representative was very good, but at the operational level, people in his company described how poor the service actually was.

Last, a lack of communications may result in behaviors that break down collaboration efforts. A panelist described how a promotion was *"never communicated with us, and it just put us through the roof. Customers were screaming at us. It took us 3 months to recover and refresh the supply chain."* There may even be poor communications, such as the situation described by one where *"the more data we have the more we are confused, because there's no apparent rhyme or reason for what the data shows."*

BENEFITS

Once impediments are overcome and collaboration is enabled, executives expect to see benefits from collaborating within the supply chain. The biggest benefit they expect is financial. Several of the participants anticipated reduced costs and increased sales from reductions in inventory, reductions in personnel, improved customer service, better delivery through reduced cycle times, and increased speed to market of new products. It was also expected that improvements occur within each company, such as the breaking down of functional barriers and less fire fighting. Collaboration should allow a company to eliminate waste both internally and externally and to focus on their core competencies. Participants believe that collaboration also positively influences the public image of the companies involved. When companies work together, they are seen as humanitarian, striving for the good of all, not just themselves.

The end result of these benefits is expected to be improved returns, increased shareholder value, and, thus, a competitive advantage over other supply chains.

There are other benefits that participants expect which do not directly lead to financial improvements. These are related to the relationships between supply chain members. As companies collaborate, trust and interdependence are further developed and strengthened. With the increased trust comes more sharing of information, ideas, and technology. This sharing pushes the companies in the supply chain to act increasingly as if they were one enterprise, working toward the goals of the supply chain and not the individual companies. This, in turn, fuels the success of the collaborative effort.

The executives that participated in this study also gave several examples of the benefits they were achieving or had achieved due to collaborative relationships in their supply chains. Many of these resulted in reduced costs due to collaborative efforts to improve the efficiency of the supply chain.

- A supplier offered a manufacturer an incentive (reduced price) to obtain the manufacturer's business in a certain geographic location. The manufacturer got the product at a lower price, and the supplier was able to maximize their output at the particular location and ship the product a shorter distance, which reduced their overall costs as well.
- One manufacturer works with several suppliers to develop costs savings in the supply of their products. The incentive is that any costs savings incurred are split between the two parties.
- A supplier went beyond providing product to a manufacturer. They worked with their own supplier to develop better ways to cut the material, which reduced waste, damage, and loss of the product while improving the cycle time of delivering the product. This reduced costs for all the parties involved.
- In order to eliminate processing steps, a chocolate supplier offered to ship chocolate liquor rather than the finished chocolate. The liquor had a richer flavor, could be used immediately, and in liquid form was much cheaper to ship. The manufacturer had no way of knowing this was possible prior to collaborating with the supplier.
- An electrical supplier wanted to help reduce warranty costs for a manufacturer. They put people in the manufacturer's call center to identify better ways of investigating problems related to their products. They were able to get to the root cause and better correct the problems identified, which reduced warranty claims.
- One manufacturer works with suppliers on new technology and product designs. Due to these relationships, the manufacturer spends much less on research and development than competing supply chains do.
- A raw material supplier to a food company sent a person to work in the food company's plant for 2 to 3 weeks to help solve a problem. The supplier determined a problem with the raw material they supplied. They fixed the problem and cut the raw material cost for their customer.
- An air carrier working with a company established space allocation each week for the company. Due to the relationship, the two companies worked together

and were able to make packaging enhancements for the company's products, which minimized handling and the air freight costs for both.

- A manufacturer was having a problem with the quality of an expensive part upon its arrival at their plant. A small freight forwarder drove the route the product followed to the plant and found the quality of the roads was damaging the product. They were able to suggest another route to bring the product to the plant, which saved a substantial amount of money in reduced damage for the manufacturer.

Examples of benefits, besides direct cost savings, were also provided by the participants.

- A company built a close relationship with a porter in Hong Kong. During peak season, other companies that dealt with this porter had many days of product sitting idle waiting to be exported. The company with the close relationship was given priority, and their product only sat for 2 to 3 days before export.
- A manufacturer uses a tracking system for delivery of products to their plants. Not only does the manufacturer have constant visibility of the shipments, but the suppliers whose products are being shipped and the carriers that are shipping the products have visibility as well. This allows all parties to have complete information and to act if a shipment problem arises.
- One manufacturer had a problem with a reduction in quality of a product from a longtime supplier. Due to the relationship, rather than abandon the supplier, the manufacturer worked with them. The supplier improved the quality of the product, and the relationship between the two became even stronger.

As this litany illustrates, the benefits that can be achieved are numerous, and participants agreed they all eventually affect the bottom line, whether directly or indirectly. Once companies understand these benefits, they can make the commitment to begin the process of collaborating with key supply chain members. The road is not an easy one, however. Rules, practices, and the "old way of doing things" can all stand in the way. A substantial cost in terms of dollars, time, and managerial risk also impedes progress.

WHAT SHOULD YOU DO?

The enablers and impediments provided by the interview and focus group participants can serve as a guide to implementing supply chain collaboration. The enablers listed in Table 4.1 should be emphasized. The impediments listed in Table 4.2 should be anticipated. Making supply chain collaboration a successful endeavor can reap many benefits for the companies involved (Table 4.3), and should be kept in mind as the reason for overcoming the impediments. The key to supply chain collaboration begins with taking a long-term perspective with your suppliers. Looking beyond immediate costs and benefits to the long term is the first step to supply chain collaboration.

Second, it is important to recognize that supply chain collaboration is not possible with all supply chain members. Identify members of your supply chain who are willing and able to collaborate, and who will create the most benefits, and select key initiatives with which to begin. Key initiatives should be selected based upon their importance to competitive advantage for your supply chain, the degree to which enablers are in place, and the degree to which impediments are not entrenched.

Finally, it is important to recognize that most of the enablers and impediments we discovered in this study were people related. Successful supply chain collaboration is a function of working with your people and the people working for your supply chain partners. Although technology is a considerable enabler, it is not the key to supply chain collaboration; people and an orientation toward long-term partnering are.

The opportunity is great. Mentzer, Foggin, and Golicic (2000) found that the implementation of supply chain collaboration is not widespread, but the benefits are substantial. Thus, the opportunity for considerable competitive advantage can be found in supply chain collaboration.

Company L—The Synergy of Shippers and Carriers

There are tens of thousands of shippers on any developed continent, each looking to move their products domestically and/or globally. In turn, there are many thousands of carriers who concentrate on movement of domestic and/or global freight. Any one of these companies may be following SCM Drivers One and Two, yet still missing supply chain synergistic opportunities. For example, one shipper may outsource the transportation function to a given carrier, who specializes in their core competency of transportation, but neither company is aware that there is a similar shipper moving similar product to similar origins and destinations. Lack of this awareness could cause both shippers to make less-than-truckload (LTL) shipments, which drives up both their transportation costs.

Company L realized the potential synergies in putting many shippers and many carriers together to combine loads and, thus, to reduce total transportation costs for everyone. In fact, Company L often provides illustrations similar to Figures 4.1 and 4.2 to show this synergistic effect. Figure 4.1 illustrates the LTL shipments of a single shipper in the United States. This shipper has numerous small loads going to and from many locations—a situation that generates considerable LTL transportation costs for the shipper. However, when this shipper's transportation needs are overlaid by similar needs for other shippers, Figure 4.2 results! The "thick" transportation lanes provide synergistic opportunities for shippers to combine shipments and obtain truckload (TL) freight rates, rates that are often less than half the per pound LTL rate.

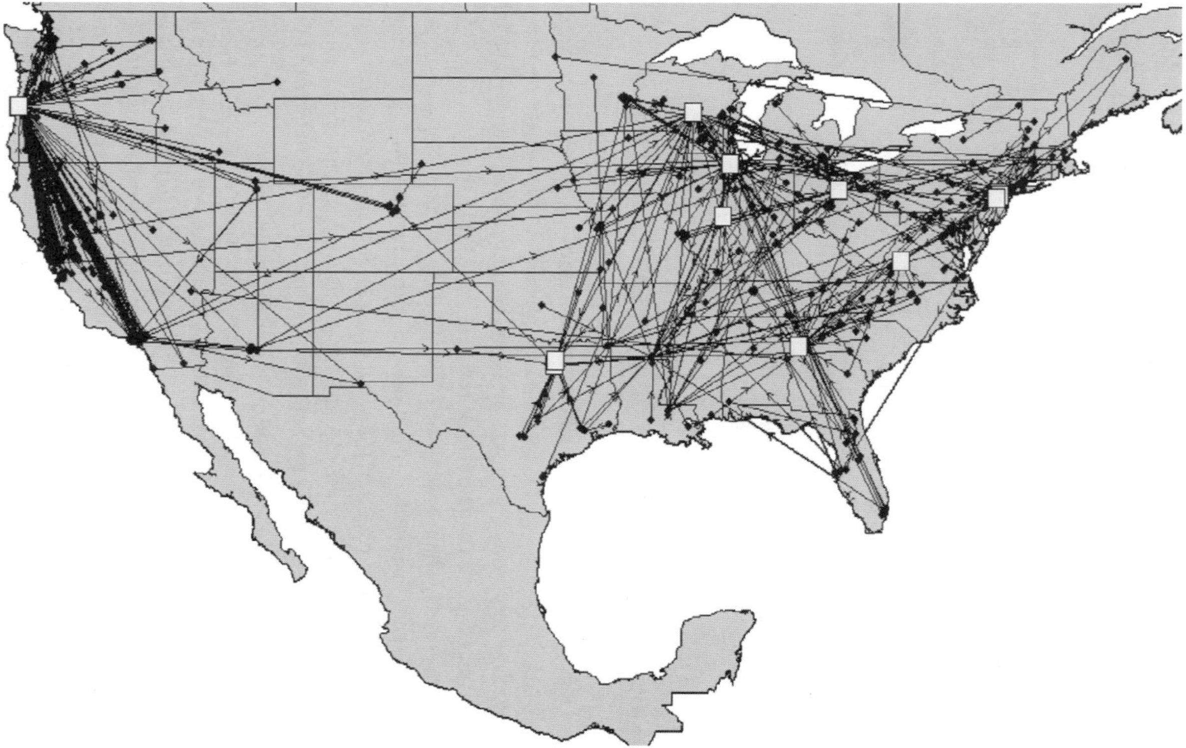

Figure 4.1 A Single Shipper's Freight Network

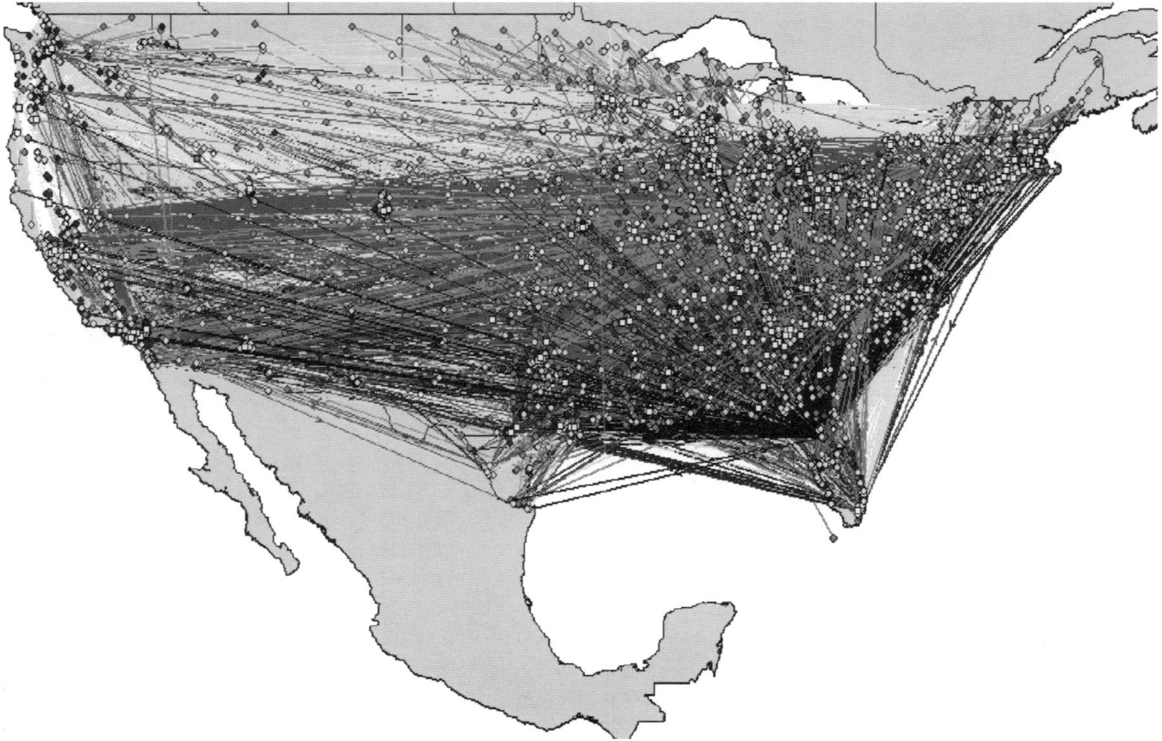

Figure 4.2   A Synergistic Freight Network

But what is the advantage for the transportation carrier? Under Figure 4.1, any individual carrier is guaranteed only the occasional, expensive (but also costly) LTL shipment. However, under Figure 4.2, the carrier is guaranteed (through working with Company L's coordinating database) more of the less costly, more profitable TL combined business.

Let's look at an example of what happens when several companies combine their shipments through Company L. Figure 4.3 shows the shipments of several companies before consolidation through Company L's services, and Figure 4.4 shows the result when the shipments are combined. There are far fewer expensive LTL shipments, and each company substantially reduced their overall transportation expenditures.

In particular, look at the Chicago to San Francisco corridor. This was a daily, high-volume corridor for the shippers involved. When Company L began to investigate this corridor, they found that a railroad sent a unit train from Chicago to San Francisco with empty containers daily. Why empty? Much of the product consumed in the eastern United States is manufactured in Asia, shipped in containers to ports in California where it makes its way (still in the containers) to the east coast. When the containers are emptied, they need to be returned to Asia, thus the collection point in Chicago and the unit train going to San Francisco.

Company L could provide the shippers involved with trucking services from Chicago to San Francisco that took 54 hours, plus or minus 4 hours, and a cost per hundred pounds of $100. When Company L approached the railroad and asked them to bid on the business, their quote was 48 hour delivery, plus or minus 3 hours, at a cost of $35 per hundred pounds! How could the railroad, notorious for being a slow, variable mode of transportation, promise faster, less variable, cheaper performance than the trucking industry? The answer was in the fact that the railroad planned to simply add the shippers' freight each day to the end of the unit train of empty containers. Since it was a unit train, the train never stopped in rail classification yards to pick up and drop off rail cars; it simply ran straight from Chicago to San Francisco, stopping only to change crews. The cheap rate was a result of the railroad realizing they were going to send the train of empty containers anyway, so any additional cars added to the end of the train were of minimal cost to the railroad. Thus, the $35 rate was almost all profit for the railroad. By putting together the synergies of unit trains, coordinated shipments, and the information and coordinating services of Company L, the railroad made money, while all the shippers involved reduced transportation costs on this corridor by more than 65% (remember, the $100 trucking quote was already a TL rate).

This synergistic concept of coordinated shipments can also be extended across multiple shipment corridors and shippers. For example, suppose Shipper 1 has a shipment to move from Houston to Atlanta; Shipper 2 has a

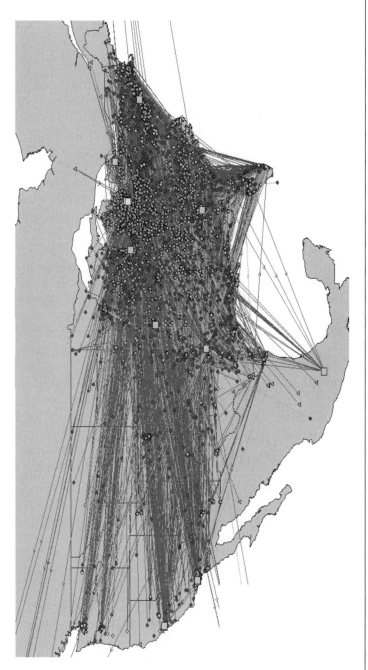

Figure 4.3   Before Consolidation

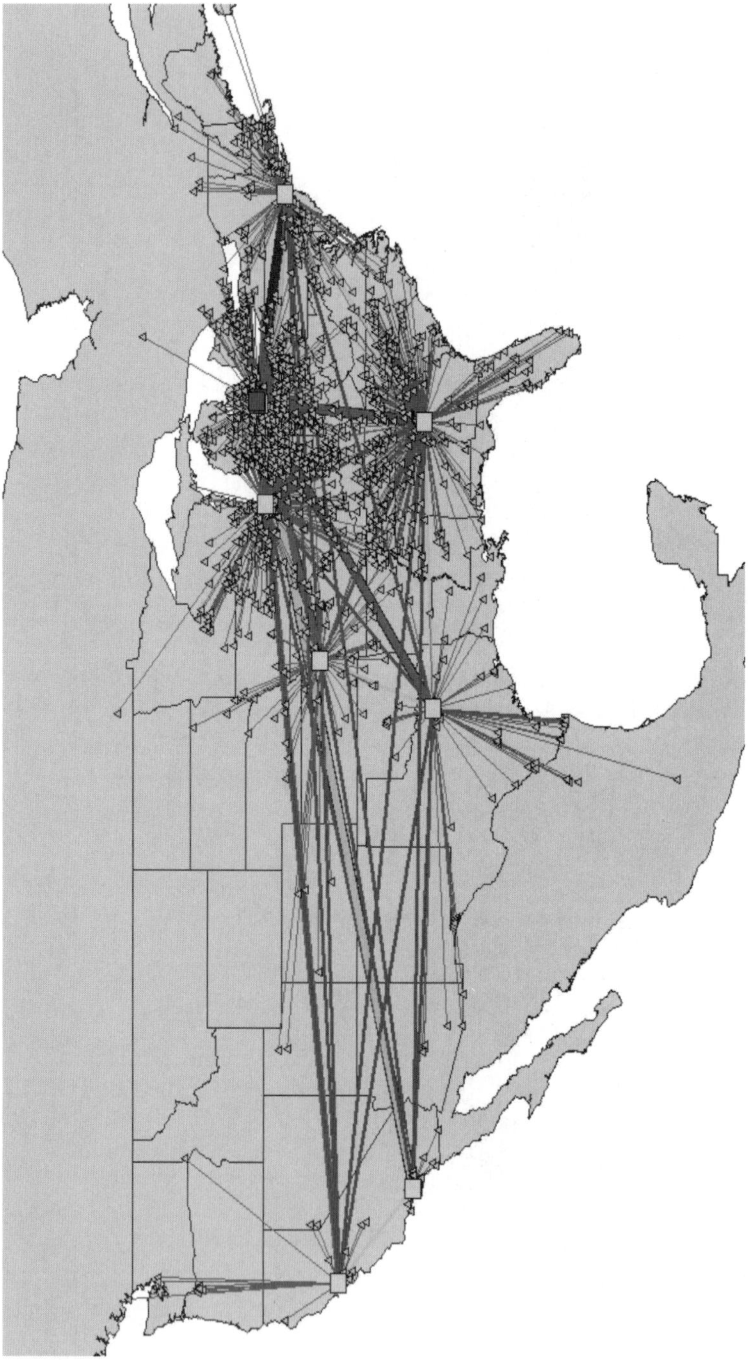

Figure 4.4 After Consolidation

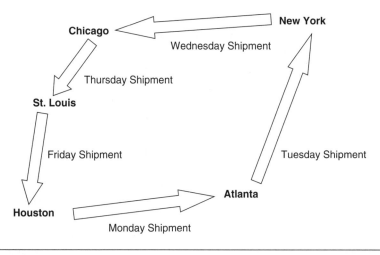

Figure 4.5   A Continuous Shipment Example

shipment to move from Atlanta to New York; Shipper 3 has a shipment to move from New York to Chicago; Shipper 4 has a shipment to move from Chicago to St. Louis; and Shipper 5 has a shipment to move from St. Louis to Houston. Acting independently, each shipper is going to have to contact, negotiate with, and pay a carrier the rate to move their product from the origin to the destination, plus the cost for the carrier to "deadhead" the equipment back to the origin. What Company L provides, by having thousands of shippers and carriers in their database, is the ability to put together the coordinated set of shipments illustrated in Figure 4.5. By approaching one carrier for a bid to handle all five shipments, Company L is offering the carrier the opportunity to obtain five shipments, with little or no deadheading, and have the driver back home for the weekend (which helps with the human resource management function of driver relations). These savings for the carrier are partially passed on to each shipper so they get their individual shipments delivered at a much lower cost. Even with Company L taking a coordination fee, all seven supply chain partners involved (Shippers 1, 2, 3, 4, 5, the carrier, and Company L) make money synergistically.

Company M—The Synergy of Shippers, Carriers, and Vendors

The principles of synergy Company L markets to their shippers and carriers are not limited to such coordination companies alone. Company M is a food service distributor, a company that buys directly from manufacturers the products and supplies restaurants need to operate and sells and delivers these products and supplies directly to individual restaurants. In other words, the core competency of Company M is dealing with all the manufacturers of restaurant products, so an individual restaurant can deal directly only with Company M and not have to purchase directly from hundreds of suppliers.

Company M operates a single large distribution center, into which all their vendors ship products, and out of which every day Company M sends hundreds of trucks to make deliveries to their customer restaurants. Originally, these two functions, inbound shipments from vendors and outbound shipments to customers, were independent operations. Although well managed as separate functions, much synergistic opportunity was missed. On a daily basis, all Company M trucks were dispatched by a routing and scheduling program that optimized customer service requirements, mileage traveled, and truck and driver utilization. Even though this function was well managed, Company M trucks were still running empty (there is that deadheading problem again) 36% of the time. Once the last delivery on a route was made to the last customer, the truck came back to the distribution center empty.

All shipments from vendors inbound to Company M were on a free-on-board (FOB) destination basis, which meant the vendor arranged shipment and then charged Company M for it in their price. Part of the problem of realizing this opportunity was in the fact that inbound transportation cost was not recorded separately by the Purchasing Department. In fact, when management asked, "What part of the purchase price was inbound transportation?" the purchasing manager proudly answered, "None. We negotiated away transportation cost." Now, of course, transportation cost did not simply disappear. It was just included (some would say, hidden) in the vendor price.

Once this was realized, Company M management combined the inbound freight and outbound delivery functions. The routing and scheduling system was changed to take into account any time a truck making deliveries to customers came past a vendor when the truck was empty. If that vendor had a shipment to Company M scheduled, then the Purchasing Department negotiated an FOB Origin price, and the Company M driver stopped at the facility to pick up the order and bring it back on a truck that was coming to the distribution center anyway. The only additional costs to Company M were the incremental miles traveled to pick up the vendor shipment and the costs of loading and unloading. The truck and the driver were coming back anyway.

Taking advantage of this synergistic opportunity (coordinating inbound and outbound shipments) resulted in the percentage of time Company M trucks ran around empty falling to 18%, and a reduction in overall purchasing costs of 11% (the elimination of much hidden transportation cost).

Company N—The Synergy of a Retailer and Their Vendors

Lest we think all examples of SCM Driver Three are transportation examples, let's take a look at Company N, a retailer who took advantage of this opportunity by developing synergies with their top 11 vendors. Company N is a large regional retail chain, with one distribution center in a small town—virtually everyone in town works at the Company N distribution center. Thus, the employees were very loyal and supportive of Company N, but there was no room for human resource expansion.

This created a growth dilemma for Company N. With over 300 stores all served through this distribution center that was operating at physical (storage) and human resource capacity, Company N was constrained from growing any larger without expanding the present distribution center or building another one. Expanding the present center was both unattractive and impractical— unattractive because of the brick and mortar cost of enlarging the facility and impractical because the local labor force was not large enough to support a larger facility.

Almost as unattractive was the idea of a second distribution center in another location. This alternative would cause redundancies (negative synergies) in products carried at each distribution center and stores served by each center. An additional negative synergy would be the increase in inventory caused by not consolidating all store demand in one distribution center. Finally, the human resource dilemma was the ill will that would be caused among workers in the existing distribution center town from the perception that Company N was "deserting us."

The other alternative was to do nothing and simply not grow the company in terms of number of retail stores and geographic area served—very unattractive to Company N management. When Company N management started looking at bottlenecks in the entire supply chain, they realized that 15% of the floor space in the distribution center was taken up by a machine (ironically) called a "space saver." Space saver is the name for a generic category of distribution function machines that move floor space–consuming functions to multiple layers, thus saving space. In Company N's case, the space saver was a machine that went all the way to the ceiling and had 40 employees working full time in it for the sole purpose of putting store labels on the lines of clothing products carried in Company N stores.

The synergy came when Company N realized the labels they were putting on their clothing were not much different than the labels their vendors were putting on the same clothing. This led to a series of meetings between Company N executives and their top vendors to discuss the price vendors would charge to put Company N labels on at the same time the vendor labels were applied. Company N was willing to supply the actual labels but asked each vendor what they would charge for the actual application. The answer, from each of Company N's 11 largest vendors, was they would charge nothing to do this!

Something for free does not sound very likely. In fact, when the incredulous Company N executives asked if they had heard correctly, vendor executives replied, "We have to apply our labels anyway, so (as long as you provide the labels) it costs us nothing extra to apply your labels at the same time we apply ours. After all, it's all done on the same machine." Of course, part of the reason was that Company N is a major customer of each of these vendors and they were more than willing to do something for them that satisfied this major customer and cost the vendor nothing.

A major source of redundancy (negative synergy) in the supply chain was eliminated. As a result, Company N was able to scrap their space saver, freeing up 15% of the floor space and 40 employees—both of which were free increases in capacity in their two critically constrained capacity areas. Company N was now in a position to expand their store base by 15% without either adding bricks and mortar to the present facility or having to locate, design, build, and operate a new distribution center.

This free increase in capacity encouraged Company N to look for other ways to leverage supply chain synergies, and the second came in the form of cross-docking. The Company N distribution center had historically received all inbound product, assigned it a storage location in the building, and moved it to that location, even if the same product was to be pulled the next day from stock and shipped to a store. By coordinating inbound shipment information with storage stocking orders and the receiving and shipping functions in the distribution center (an initiative that took—in keeping with SCM Drivers One and Two—coordination with vendors, transportation providers, the distribution center, and store management), Company N was able to increase their percentage of product that was cross-docked to 22%.

A process was developed that identified what inbound products were going immediately on from the distribution center to stores. The receipt of these products was coordinated with other products already in stock that were also due to be shipped to the same stores. When the truck arrives at the receiving dock, all product is unloaded and sorted into products going into storage and products going on to stores. The product going on is sorted by store and loaded back on the same trucks in the order specified by a routing and scheduling system. Other product pulled from stock going to that store is also loaded.

The result is the stores receive the same level of delivery service as before, but the distribution center serves the same number of stores using approximately one fifth less storage space, thus further adding to the number of stores that can be served through the Company N distribution center. An added benefit is that trucking companies now know that when they deliver a load to the distribution center, they will also be picking up a load. Since their deadheading is reduced, these trucking companies give Company N lower transportation rates. Lower costs and removal of a supply chain bottleneck have given Company N the synergies to further expand their number of stores and the scope of their geographic coverage—all without any additional investment in bricks and mortar.

Summary and an Exercise

These examples illustrate how companies can achieve competitive advantage through coordinating the traditional business functions with their supply chain partners to eliminate functional redundancies and leverage supply chain synergies. Can your company do this? A start is to answer the following questions:

- What does your company do well?
- What does your company not do well?
- What are your core competencies?
- What are your supply chain partner's core competencies?
- Which of your supply chain partner's core competencies are weaknesses of your company? These are functions your company should consider outsourcing to supply chain partners so your company can concentrate on your core competencies.
- Which of your core competencies are weaknesses of your supply chain partners? These are functions your company should consider performing for your supply chain partners to tie them more closely to your company and, thus, give your company a competitive advantage.
- What are the enablers of collaboration with these supply chain partners?
- What are the impediments to collaboration with these supply chain partners?
- What are the benefits of collaboration with these supply chain partners?

By going through the exercise of answering these questions (not always an easy task), you will have taken the first step toward implementing SCM Drivers of Competitive Advantage One, Two, and Three. In particular, if you treat the last three questions as a return on investment analysis (where the enablers and benefits are the "return" part of the analysis, and overcoming the impediments is the "investment" component of the analysis), you get a fairly clear idea of the supply chain partners with which your company should collaborate, and how.

5

Not All Customers Are Created Equal

B usiness strategy has adjusted over the years to challenges from competitive and economic pressures. During the 1960s, marketing strategy primarily focused on developing long-range forecasts and budgets. Since this was a period of economic boom, management had the luxury of long-term planning horizons. During the 1970s, many organizations adopted a product management structure whereby each product was managed by one or more managers. However, market volatility, in the form of high inflation, high unemployment, and a wave of consumer discontent, proved this strategy ineffective in maintaining competitive positioning. The 1980s brought increased global competition that negatively affected consumer loyalty. This decade also brought transportation deregulation, opening the way to strategic logistics options that were once closed to a company. The 1990s were marked by amazing growth in information technology. Such growth paved the way for the development of strategic supply chain relationships and shorter prod-uct-to-market time, and it gave momentum to the growth in consumer power via the Internet. Information technology brought a wave of fast paced strategic challenges to managers who wanted to maintain their competitive advantage (Schewe & Smith, 1983; Williams, 1994).

Porter (1985) defines *competitive advantage* as sustaining superiority of interrelated activities within the firm. Day and Wensley (1988) use the term *positional superiority* or advantage to mean "a relative superiority in the skills and resources a business deploys." Stalk, Evans, and Shulman (1992) refer to "capabilities-based competition" as the ability to sustain competitive position-ing. Although different terms, each describes a similar underlying premise: firms must not only achieve and implement corporate strategies to bring about superiority in their markets, but they must also sustain that superiority. We will call this sustainable superiority in the marketplace *competitive advantage*.

Managers face the daunting task of identifying and developing unique capabilities to achieve a defensible position in the marketplace. The *how* of achieving and maintaining competitive advantage is at the heart of supply chain management. According to resource-based theory, there are two related methods for achieving competitive advantage: (1) assets, which are the resource endowments the business has accumulated (e.g., facilities, brand equity), and (2) capabilities, the glue that brings the assets together (Day, 1994). Capabilities differ from assets because they are so deeply embedded in the organizational routines and practices that they cannot be traded or imitated (Dierkx & Cool, 1989). Supply chain management may involve assets, but it is also the complex set of internally and externally interwoven processes that create a unique advantage that cannot be easily copied.

Porter (1985) argued that companies obtain competitive advantage via one of two strategies: cost or differentiation. Managers following a cost advantage strategy achieve a cost leadership position if they can sustain lower costs. Cost advantage is sustainable if there are entry or mobility barriers that prevent a competitor from imitating its sources. Further, Porter cites "linkages" as a driver of sustainability. *Linkages* are ties "which require coordination across organizational lines or with independent suppliers or channels" (p. 112). It is these linkages that are precisely the essence of supply chain management, and often the "mobility barriers" that prevent competitive imitation.

The second advantage is differentiation. A firm differentiates itself from its competitors if it can be unique at something that is valuable to customers (Day, 1994). The sustainability of differentiation depends on two things: its continued perceived value to customers and the lack of competitor ability to imitate it. Again, Porter defines a driver of sustainability that is related to supply chain management: "The sustainability of a differentiation strategy is usually greatest if differentiation stems from multiple sources, rather than resting on a single factor such as product design" (p. 159). Competitors who want to copy supply chain management strategies find it difficult because it requires unique, experienced, and well-coordinated relationships between multiple parties in the supply chain. Thus, superior supply chain management can lead to competitive advantage, and the infrastructure nature of this superiority makes it difficult to imitate. Therefore, the competitive advantage is sustainable.

According to Day and Wensley (1988), there are two perspectives for achieving competitive advantage in the marketplace: competitor-centered and customer-focused. The competitor-centered approach is based upon direct management comparisons with a small number of competitors. This approach is typically present in industries where the emphasis is on "beating the competition." The key issue is how the company's capabilities and offerings compare with its competitors'. Costs are closely monitored and quickly adjusted to match or thwart competitors' moves. Managers keep a close watch on market share and contracts won or lost to detect changes in competitive positions.

The customer-focused approach (which is the focus of this chapter) begins with a detailed analysis of the customer benefits within the end-use segments and works backward from the customer to the company to identify the actions needed to improve performance. Managers following this approach emphasize the quality of customer relationships.

To achieve competitive advantage, the customer-focused perspective dictates that companies must realize that not all customers are created equal: some are critical to our success, some are less important and should be treated as such, and some are distracting us from serving the first two groups and should not be served at all. To understand these segments of customers, companies first need to answer several questions about their supply chains:

- Who is our customer?
- How do we reach our customer?
- How do we reach competitive advantage with our customer? (Hint: It is not always the product.)

In supply chain management, the answer to the first question is often more complicated than it sounds. Although we can often readily identify the end-use customer, that individual or organization may not be the relevant customer for our company. The relevant customer is the one that provides us with a source of competitive advantage throughout the entire supply chain, an advantage that should lead to greater market share with the final customer. The example of Company A in Chapter 1 was clearly a case of a snack food manufacturer who saw their relevant customer as the retailer. If Company A could deliver greater value to the retailer, that retailer would give better store placement to Company A products resulting in increased market share. This is precisely what happened.

Identifying the customer is the first step in a process illustrated in Figure 5.1. Once we identify who the customer is, we must identify what the customer values, choose the customer values that we will emphasize, provide that value to the customer, communicate to the customer the fact that we are providing that value, and finally (and continuously) assess the customer's satisfaction with the value we are delivering.

To illustrate this process, let us turn to our first example of this SCM Driver.

Company O—Implementing a Supply Chain Value Strategy

Company O is in the auto aftermarket, a supply chain that provides replacement parts to auto repair shops through a network of distributors called warehouse distributors or WDs. Company O held approximately 30% market share

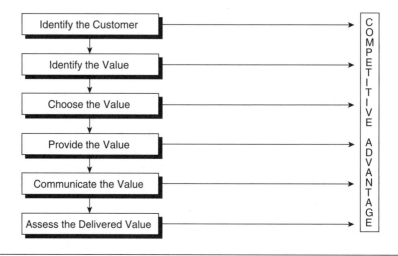

Figure 5.1   Supply Chain Value Strategy

Adapted from Woodruff and Gardial (1996)

in this channel, about the same as their two major competitors, with the remaining 10% divided among minor competitors.

The product in this supply chain eventually is installed by a mechanic as part of an auto repair. As a result, there is virtually no brand recognition in this process. The owner of the car simply wants the car repaired and seldom asks for a specific brand. In fact, market research using a Customer Value Requirements Map (Woodruff & Gardial, 1996) (something we will discuss later in the chapter) to Identify the Value (Step 2 in Figure 5.1) revealed that car owners seldom knew the brand of the product installed on their cars and only valued three things in this process:

1. They wanted their car back the same day they took their car in for repair.

2. They wanted the problem fixed; that is, they did not want the replacement part to fail again as long as they owned the car.

3. They were sensitive to the price of the parts.

This led the auto mechanics (who were also studied with the Customer Value Requirements Map) to value the same three things:

1. They needed the parts within 24 hours of ordering them from the WD so they could be ready for scheduled repair appointments.

2. They were very concerned about product quality.

3. The lower their price on the parts, the higher their margin.

Notice that studying the car owners and the mechanics has now led us to a more in-depth look at Step 1 in Figure 5.1—Just who is the relevant customer in this supply chain?

The results of customer value analysis of these two customers in the supply chain led one Company O executive to describe their company as a "commodity business": there is no difference between the competitors in the market with respect to promotional programs or product quality or features, so the only basis on which to compete was price. However, since the major competitors had near-identical manufacturing processes, identical suppliers, and identical supply chains (the same supplier delivery systems to the plants and the same WDs to distribute the products to the same auto mechanics), their cost structures were very similar and any reduction in price was immediately matched by the competition, a move that simply reduced profit margins for all without increasing overall sales.

In other words, Company O faced the typical profit erosion of a "kinked demand curve" from an oligopoly with identical competitive mixes. If any competitor raised their price, the competition would not follow the higher prices and the competitor lost market share. If any competitor lowered their prices, the competition matched the new price and all competitors had the same market share but with lower profit margins. The industry was a classic example of Porter's (1985) competitor-focused industry.

The road to competitive advantage began when the new CEO of Company O formed a task force to implement his personal vision of the company: to change the corporate vision of the company as a "manufacturer of products in the auto aftermarket" to "a marketer and distributor of products in the auto aftermarket." In other words, to focus the attention of the company not on the product itself but how it got to the customer.

This profound shift in focus of Company O from competitor-focused to customer-centered led to the realization that Company O did, in fact, make a commodity product. The company's customers saw no difference in product quality or features, and the promotional programs were largely ignored by all members of the supply chain. However, this did not mean the company could not come up with marketing and/or logistics services that would differentiate it from the competition. In other words, the CEO realized that having a commodity product does not mean you have a commodity business. There are always services in the supply chain that can be offered with a product that can differentiate it in the minds of the relevant customer.

The important aspect of this point for SCM Driver Four is that logistics services offered with the product often hold the key to differentiating a commodity product from its competition. Company O realized this once their entire supply chain was analyzed. Since all the competitors in the industry used the same suppliers and had the same manufacturing processes, the upstream supply chain was deemed to not hold any sources of competitive advantage.

Similarly, market research focused on the values of car owners and auto mechanics revealed little in how to differentiate Company O from the competition. However, Company O found the WDs were the key to competitive advantage. In other words, the WDs were the relevant Company O customers in the supply chain.

At the time of this example, there were 2,000 warehouse distributors in the United States, which meant that virtually every county with an auto repair shop had at least one WD. Their function in the supply chain is to provide ready access to inventory for the auto mechanic, who carries little or no inventory. When a customer called to schedule an auto repair, the mechanic would assess the likely parts needed to make the repair, call their local WD to ascertain whether the parts were in stock and, if available, would send someone over to pick up the parts. Mechanics expected their WDs to have the parts.

The WD operation usually consisted of a reception area with a counter for waiting on pick-up customers and a huge warehouse out back to hold in inventory all the parts any auto mechanic within the WD's market area would conceivably order. As a result, WDs were small operations with huge inventory levels. In fact, the average inventory turns ratio for a WD was less than 1.0, resulting in huge inventory carrying costs compared with sales levels. Not surprisingly, most WDs were marginally profitable operations. Here lay the source of customer value for the WDs and the source of competitive advantage for Company O.

Company O embarked upon a 3-year plan to develop a wide area network for inventory planning and accompanied this with a plan to stage fast moving inventory at various locations in North America and pull slow movers back to a central distribution center. When these plans were implemented, Company O made the following offer to all WDs: Company O guaranteed that any order placed with them that was not *completely filled* within 24 hours would be *free*. In other words, if an order for 160 different parts was placed and only one of those parts was not delivered in 24 hours, there was no charge for the entire order. Further, each WD was given 1 year to try out the program, and, when they were convinced that Company O never missed a 24-hour delivery, Company O would buy back from the WD their excess inventory. This was an offer hard to resist since the WD would be turning a business liability (the cost of carrying excess inventory) into an asset (cash).

It is important to note that such a dramatic offer was made to the WDs simply to get them to pay attention to the amount of time it took to receive each order. This was due to the fact that WDs were historically accustomed to placing orders and receiving them from Company O or any of its competitors in 10 to 14 days. Thus, WDs simply did not believe Company O could pull off such a dramatic improvement in the delivery time component of customer service. Since each WD was hoping Company O would take longer than 24 hours (after all, doing so meant the WD did not have to pay for the entire order) and after one year Company O had never taken longer than 24 hours for any order (given their self-imposed high cost of non-delivery, no charge, they could not afford to be late), Company O had changed WD perceptions of the value Company O was delivering by Providing the Value (Step 4 in Figure 5.1) and communicating it to the WDs (Step 5 in Figure 5.1).

The competitive advantage for Company O came from the fact that once a WD sold their excess inventory to Company O, the WD no longer had the ability to buy from the competition. WDs were literally faced with the choice of placing an order with Company O and being guaranteed 24-hour delivery or ordering from the competition and having the order arrive in 10 to 14 days, all when the WD was now only carrying, at most, several days of inventory. Over a 2-year period, Company O raised their price 15% above the competition (an act that would have been unthinkable before their new program) and doubled their market share.

What we learn about SCM Driver Four from the Company O example is this: Never confuse a commodity product with a commodity business. Instead, look at all the supply chain participants (Who is the customer?) to determine which values (How do we reach competitive advantage with our customer?) are something the company can use (How do we reach our customer?) to achieve competitive advantage. Again the hint: that "something" is not always the product—it is often a service, such as logistics performance. Company O's new logistics system took several years to develop and implement, but once it was in place, the competition could not match the infrastructure changes. This provided sustainable competitive advantage for Company O that was not based upon a change in their commodity product. It was based upon how that product was distributed and how hard it was for the competition to match that superior logistics infrastructure once it was implemented.

Company O conducted considerable market research to identify what the members of their downstream supply chain—WDs, auto mechanics, and car owners—wanted. They eventually focused on the WDs because therein lay a source for competitive advantage. Auto mechanics and car owners were still important as customers but did not provide the source from which Company O could differentiate itself from the competition. The question we will address next is, Just how did Company O (and others) determine what their customers valued? The answer is the Customer Value Requirements Map we mentioned earlier.

Customer Value Requirements Map

In-depth study of customers' high-end values, the desired consequences derived from these values, and the product attributes that lead to these consequences

Value Requirements	Importance Rating*	Performance Rating**				
		1	2	3	4	5
Requirement 1						
Requirement 2						
.						
.						
.						
Requirement N						

* Importance Rating: From 1 = Essential to 5 = Not Important

**1 = Excellent; 2 = Good; 3 = Fair; 4 = Poor; 5 = Terrible (Map for Company and Competitors)

Figure 5.2   Customer Value Requirements Map

Adapted from Woodruff and Gardial (1996)

(Woodruff & Gardial, 1996) can be involved, complex, and require trained interviewers to conduct the research. However, an effective means to at least determine the value requirements of customers in a supply chain setting can be obtained through use of a Customer Value Requirements Map (Figure 5.2). A Customer Value Requirements Map serves as a guide for company representatives to conduct interviews of customers and provides valuable insights into supply chain strategies to deliver those values.

Now, we do not recommend executives go visit their customers and say, "I need you to fill out this form." Rather, we have trained thousands of executives, managers, and salespeople to visit with customers and say, "We cannot serve your needs unless we understand what you want from us. So tell me what it is about our product/service that is important to you." Good follow-up questions to ask customers in this interview are, "What is it about our product/service that keeps you awake at night worrying?" and "If you had a wish list for our product/service, what three things would be on it?"

Executives are always surprised at how easy it is to get customers to talk about their use-experience with their products and services. When the customer is finished, review the list with them and ask, "Is there anything we did not cover?" What results is a list of things the customer values much like the list in Figure 5.3 that was generated by a customer of a personal computer company.

The next step is to determine the importance of each value requirement. Rather than ask the customer to rank each value requirement on a scale of

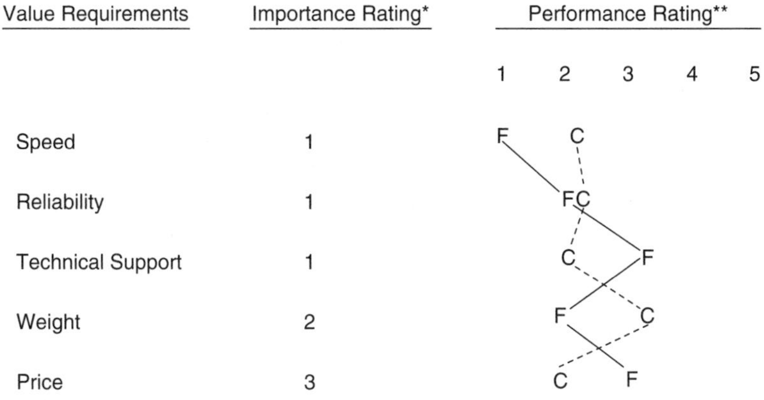

Value Requirements	Importance Rating*	Performance Rating**				
		1	2	3	4	5
Speed	1	F	C			
Reliability	1		FC			
Technical Support	1		C	F		
Weight	2		F		C	
Price	3		C	F		

* Importance Rating: From 1 = Essential to 5 = Not Important

**1 = Excellent; 2 = Good; 3 = Fair; 4 = Poor; 5 = Terrible (Map for
Focal Company (F) and Competitor (C))

Figure 5.3   Customer Value Requirements Map—Computers

1 to 5, as shown in Figure 5.3, simply review the list and ask the customer, "Which of these is most important to you?" This requirement gets a ranking of 1. When they have answered this question, ask them, "Are there any other items on the list that are equally important to you?" These, also, receive a ranking of 1. This is followed by the question, "What is the next most important item?" (which receives a ranking of 2) and so on until all items have been rank ordered.

The result up to this point in the interview is the first two columns in Figure 5.3. Now comes the difficult part. Ask the customer, "On a scale of 1 (meaning we are excellent) to 5 (meaning we are terrible), tell us how well we are doing for you on each value requirement." Then ask them the same question about your number one competitor. It is important at this point to remember that the interviewer's job is not to argue with the customer but rather to simply capture what the customer thinks. The reason for this is that what the customer *thinks* is reality *is* the reality of how they will buy your (or your competitors') products.

The result of this interview is a "map" like the one in Figure 5.3 that shows a company from the customer's perspective: what is important to them and how the company is performing with respect to the company's competitor. Two strategic insights result from this map: operational insights and communication insights. Clearly from Figure 5.3, the focal company has a competitive advantage in the eyes of the customer with respect to speed and weight of their personal computer. However, the customer thinks the focal company's technical support is lacking and the personal computer is overpriced. If the customer is right about the price, then the company faces an operational insight: whether or not to lower the price (sacrificing unit profit margins) and gain value perception in the eyes of the customer (and, thus, possibly gain market share). On the other hand, suppose the customer's perception of technical support is actually wrong. The focal company has much faster and more responsive technical support than the competition. Then the focal company has a communication insight: it needs to more effectively promote and communicate its technical support capabilities to its customers.

The only question now left for the personal computer manufacturer in Figure 5.3 is to interview and/or survey enough customers to make certain these operational and communications insights are widely held among customers. It is important to note at this point that every example provided in this chapter started with the use of this Customer Value Requirements Map to determine exactly what customers valued, how the focal company was performing on each dimension, and how the competition was performing. The results led to the strategic moves discussed throughout these examples.

The use of this map is not limited strictly to consumer products. Figure 5.4, for example, provides similar insights for a company in the forest products industry of their customer's (a printer) perceptions of their and their competitors' products. The only revision to the questions above is to ask the customer, "What is it about your job that keeps you awake at night worrying?" and "If you had a wish list for your job, what three things would be on it?" The discussion should then be led to which of these value requirements are affected by the products and/or services our company sells to them.

Notice that a very similar type of map results for this industrial customer, but the value dimensions are very different. On two of the three most important requirements for this customer, product quality and trust of the supplier, the focal company scores very well. However, in the other number one value requirement, product availability, we again see an example of an operational strategic insight. The customer ranks the focal customer out of line (compared with the competition) on product availability, and this was actually true. If the company wants to improve its competitive positioning with this customer, it needs to improve its performance on this key customer value, having product available when the customer wants it.

A communications insight relates to product variety. Although the customer in this example felt the focal company had a limited variety, this was not actually the case. Thus, the insight for the focal company was to develop a promotional campaign, including trade publication advertising, direct mail, trade

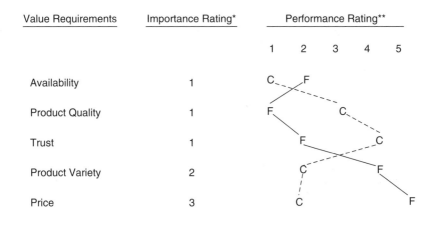

Value Requirements	Importance Rating*	Performance Rating**				
		1	2	3	4	5
Availability	1					
Product Quality	1					
Trust	1					
Product Variety	2					
Price	3					

* Importance Rating: From 1 = Essential to 5 = Not Important

**1 = Excellent; 2 = Good; 3 = Fair; 4 = Poor; 5 = Terrible (Map for Focal Company (F) and Competitor (C))

Figure 5.4   Customer Value Requirements Map—Forest Products

show presentations, and sales force training, to emphasize to such customers the broad product variety the focal company was capable of providing.

An example of an operational and communications insight that the focal company must decide how to address was price. Two options—an operational approach of lowering prices, or a communications approach of training salespeople to emphasize the value to the customer of better product quality and trust, or a combination of both—are open to the focal company. However, the important point to note here is that neither of these insights would have resulted if the focal company had not asked the customer what they valued.

In fact, we have asked thousands of executives and salespeople over the years to go through the exercise of interviewing at least one of their key customers, and, in every case, they have come back and said the same thing: "Our customers told us something they value that we had never thought about before."

The other comment we have heard from over 60% of the executives and salespeople we have put through this exercise is illustrated in both Figures 5.3 and 5.4: "We thought price was the only thing our customers cared about, and they told us it was not even the most important thing."

It is precisely these insights from our customers about what is important to them, and how they think we are doing compared with the competition, that leads to strategies that achieve competitive advantage.

Company P—Do Not
Serve Customers You Cannot Satisfy

One company that effectively used the Customer Value Requirements Map to interview numerous customers was Company P. Company P provides surgical supplies to hundreds of hospitals in North America. They have patents on several sterilization processes, but (after interviewing a number of relevant customers in their supply chain) they found their key to competitive advantage was in how they delivered these supplies to the customers.

However, the first step on this road to competitive advantage was the realization that they could not effectively serve all surgeons. Given the sterilization times needed, and the supply chain planning necessary to deliver supplies (gauze, forceps, sutures, scalpels, etc.) to the surgical theatre, they realized that their key customers were surgeons who planned their operating schedule *several weeks in advance.* Since they had no competitive advantage in delivering supplies to surgeons who schedule their operations *only several days in advance*—and particularly with surgeons who operate in emergency rooms and do not know their operating schedules from one minute to the next—Company P does not even *try* to sell to these potential customers. In the words of SCM Driver Four, the surgeons who planned operations in advance were "more equal" than the others.

Surgeons who planned their operating schedule several weeks in advance perform a variety of types of operations, but all have in common the characteristic of knowing well in advance what operations they will perform in their resident hospitals on a given day, and they know the order in which these operations will be performed. Since these surgeons have brand preferences for many of the suppliers they use, Company P maintains a database for over 16,000 such surgeons in North America, containing the types of operations they perform, the supplies required for each operation, the surgeon's brand preferences for each supply item, and the name and contact information for that surgeon's head surgical nurse and hospital administrator.

The reason for the contact information for the head surgical nurse came from a series of Customer Value Requirements Map interviews, in which it was revealed that what the surgeon most valued was to walk into the surgical theatre, perform the surgery, and never have to stand around waiting for supplies (or anything else, for that matter). The key to making this all happen is the head surgical nurse.

What the head surgical nurse valued most was not having to run all over the hospital to retrieve the supplies required for each operation and then wait around (while the surgeon is becoming frustrated) while these supplies were sterilized. When the operation was over, many of these supplies were now biohazards, the proper disposal of which was the primary value of the hospital administrator.

So Company P devised a supply chain whereby each night, at each customer hospital, for each customer surgeon, something that looks very much like a trash can shows up at the receiving dock. When this patented "trash can" is wheeled into the surgical theatre in the morning, the head surgical nurse (who is already prepped for surgery) opens the can and sees a series of shelves. On the first shelf are all the supplies the surgeon needs (properly sterilized and sealed, of course) for the first planned surgery of the day. The head surgical nurse opens the sealed container, places everything on the surgical tray, and the surgeon has all the supplies necessary for the first surgery.

As the surgery progresses, the head surgical nurse places all discarded surgery supplies in a hole at the back of the trash can, which is the opening to a biohazard container. When the first surgery is completed, the head surgical nurse simply moves to the next tray for the next set of supplies, and the order progresses until all operations for the day are completed. At that point, the trash can (which now only contains the biohazard materials in the back) is wheeled to the receiving dock to be picked up by Company P when the trash can for the next day is delivered. Company P takes the biohazard supplies, recycles what can be resterilized and reused, resharpens any scalpels for reuse if appropriate, and properly disposes of any true biohazard materials. Thus, hospital administrators no longer have to worry about what Customer Value Requirements Map interviews revealed was the item that keeps them awake worrying the most—proper biohazard disposal procedures.

What about health insurance companies? Since Company P delivers all these supplies in a cost-effective manner, lowers the inventory in surgical supplies the hospital needs to keep, and lowers the hospital's biohazard disposal costs, health insurance companies are also receiving something they value: quality healthcare at a lower cost.

At this point, you might ask, "Where is the patient in all this supply chain?" Although the ultimate customer, as one hospital administrator put it, "You have to remember, the patient places a great deal of trust in the surgeon and, through the surgeon, in the surgery team. The patient is not even conscious during this process, so the key to forming the patient's opinion of satisfaction is how satisfied the surgeon is."

Company P is very successful in their supply chain because they realize who their key customers are: (in order) the surgeon, the head surgical nurse, the hospital administrator, the health insurance provider, and only remotely the patient. However, who is not their customer? Surgeons who do not operate in the planned manner that allows Company P's supply chain (suppliers—to Company P—to hospital—to head surgical nurse—to surgeon—to patient—to head surgical nurse—to hospital—to Company P—to biohazard disposal experts) to provide a competitive advantage.

Company Q—Final Customers Versus Trade Partners

What the previous examples teach us is that, for competitive advantage, companies must identify the customer with the value demands that actually present the potential for a competitive advantage for the company in the marketplace. As we said at the beginning of this chapter, it is often not the final customer.

This is not just true in the business-to-business (B2B) supply chains of the previous examples. Many companies in consumer products industries, when asked, "Who is your *consumer?*" will say, "The individuals who buy our products." When asked, "Who is your *customer?*" they will say, "Wal-Mart, Target, CVS Drugstore, Best Buy, Circuit City," or various other retailers that often represent a significant percentage of their overall sales.

One company in the consumer product goods industry has a dramatic example of the 80/20 rule gone crazy. The 80/20 rule says that 80% of your business typically comes from 20% of your customers. However, for this manufacturer of consumer products goods, 90% of their overall North American sales went through only 10 customers, those 10 customers being 10 big retailers. In Europe, 60% of their sales went through only 4 customers, again big retailers. Clearly, this company had millions and millions of final consumers, but only a very small number of customers they had to worry about to create competitive advantage in their supply chains.

Some customers are, quite simply, more important to us than others. Some customers represent such a large percentage of our sales that we should think about ways to create competitive advantage, not for our products, but for our products sold through those customers. The questions have not changed from the earlier examples:

- How do you reach your customers?
- How do you achieve competitive advantage with your customers?

In business-to-consumer (B2C) supply chains, that question often involves more than just the product. We may make a product that is priced no differently than the competition's, has no different brand equity than the competition's, and is promoted no differently. And, in fact, the product looks, for the large part, like a commodity. There would seem to be no basis on which to compete other than price.

However, if we create a cluster of services around a product through the supply chain and through trade partners that gives our company a distinct advantage in the marketplace—not product-based, but supply chain service-based—then we are achieving SCM Driver Four. This cluster of services is often called *logistics leverage* (Mentzer & Williams, 2001).

Many companies competing in global markets have decreased prices (Craig, 1997), improved products (Woodruff & Gardial, 1996), and reduced design-to-shelf cycle times (Camp, 1989), only to find these strategies quickly copied by competitors (Porter, 1985). Yet companies are still actively searching for ways to build a sustainable advantage in the marketplace (Day, 1994; Innis & LaLonde, 1994). Many companies have turned to quality improvements in product design and internal processes to achieve competitive advantage (Stahl, 1994, 1999), only to have them imitated by their competition. Organizations overcome this competitive matching by focusing on delivering customer value to obtain competitive advantage (Woodruff & Gardial, 1996).

In the current environment, it is difficult to maintain competitive advantages that accrue from changes in product, promotion, or price. Many of today's products, albeit manufactured in different global locations, have become homogenized and indistinguishable to the customer (Daugherty, Stank, & Ellinger, 1998). Given the ever shortening technology cycle, companies trying to create or maintain differentiation in the marketplace often find product changes quickly greeted by a countermove from competitors. Likewise, changes in promotion and price may be quickly duplicated. A particular challenge for supply chain strategy today is determining how to promote products whose features are perceived as homogeneous by customers. Because, for many companies, any change in product, promotion, or price has only a temporary impact in their markets, the way to sustainable differential advantage may not lie in changes in the product, promotion, or pricing strategies of the company but rather in improving ancillary supply chain services, such as logistics (Bowersox, Mentzer, & Speh, 1995). For this reason, logistics has been suggested as the strategic "battleground . . . displacing manufacturing, marketing, and quality as the focus of top management" (Woods, 1991). Many firms now stress logistics capabilities as a means of creating differentiation (Anderson & Narus, 1995).

Such service improvements are most likely to yield a sustainable competitive advantage (Day & Wensley, 1988) in the market when implemented through changes in the corporate infrastructure: people, technology, facilities, and/or strategic corporate relationships. Logistics leverage is defined by Mentzer and Williams (2001) as *the achievement of excellent and superior, infrastructure-based logistics performance, which—when implemented through a successful marketing strategy—creates recognizable value for customers.* As such, logistics leverage represents a sustainable competitive advantage for the company: value added services that the customer recognizes as important and (as it requires changes in the corporate infrastructure) that the competition cannot readily match.

The question managers face is how to maintain such an advantage given factors such as the homogenization of products and shortening product-to-shelf cycles. A careful review of the work by Porter (1985), Bowersox, Mentzer, and Speh (1995), and Innis and LaLonde (1994) reveals some insights. Each refers to logistics as instrumental and central to providing competitive advantage. Unlike a product change or enhancement, achieving logistics superiority (because it involves changes in the people, technology, facilities, and/or strategic corporate relationships infrastructures of the company) is a capability difficult to imitate. In addition, regardless of whether managers define their market as competitor-focused or customer-driven, achieving competitive advantage through leveraging logistics is likely to achieve and maintain competitive superiority.

Perhaps the most popular indicators of marketing effectiveness and competitive advantage are market share and profitability (Dess & Robinson, 1984; Jaworski & Kohli, 1993; Kohli & Jaworski, 1990; Narver & Slater, 1990, 1991; Slater & Narver, 1994). Firms that are able to create value for their customers by satisfying their needs and wants generally increase their market share. Logistics, the last point of contact between the firm and its customers (Coyle, Bardi, & Langley, 1996), has a direct impact on customer satisfaction and, thus, impacts market share.

Day (1994) supports this position by stating, "What really matters is achieving a defensible cost position" when faced with the challenge of achieving superior performance. Logistics has historically been concerned with cost reduction (Coyle, Bardi, & Langley, 1996). The primary basis for transportation deregulation in the United States was to decrease transportation-related logistics costs (Krapfel & Mentzer, 1982; Mentzer & Krapfel, 1981a, 1981b). Thus, achieving logistics success will, at a minimum, involve cost reductions.

Leveraging logistics success can reduce costs and increase customer satisfaction and, therefore, positively influence the firm's profitability. Profitability is a desirable outcome because it creates shareholder value. When consistently and substantially maintained, it ensures the firm's longevity (Groves & Valsamakis, 1998).

But how can this logistics leverage be applied to achieve market share and profitability in the supply chain? Company Q, a major global manufacturer of consumer appliances, provides us some insight. Company Q long based its competitive positioning on the development of excellent quality products with recognizable features that customers wanted. This strategy established Company Q as a respected brand in consumer appliances, but most of its product innovations were quickly copied by competitors, and the level of quality maintained by Company Q was no different, in the eyes of the consumer, than any other manufacturer. To make matters worse, other competitors spent considerably greater amounts of money on advertising, thus creating greater brand equity than Company Q. This brand equity led to a perception by retailers that Company Q competitors were better at creating retail store traffic than Company Q (remember from the Company A example in Chapter 1 that traffic is one of the key value concerns of retailers).

Company Q decided to focus its attention not just on the final consumer of their products but upon the retailers (Company Q refers to them as trade partners) that sell their products. Company Q implemented logistics leverage in the form of a series of changes to their supply chains that allows Company Q to guarantee (given certain information provided by the retailers on point-of-sale [POS] demand and inventory levels) availability of product and on-time delivery to the stores a much higher percentage of the time than any of their competitors. In fact, Company Q became so proficient at this that they managed to reduce their days sales outstanding (DSO), or the amount of finished product in inventory, while simultaneously raising their in-stock percentage by five points. Since a lower DSO means less inventory carrying costs, this positively affects Company Q profitability. Since better availability meant retailers could depend upon Company Q and, thus, were more willing to carry their product, Company Q market share dramatically increased. (Company Q combined this strategy with increased advertising to create great final consumer brand equity and, thus, overcome the retail store traffic concerns of the retail customers.) In fact, one retail customer simply stopped carrying competitive brands and only stocked Company Q products.

Following SCM Driver Four, Company Q even stopped selling product to some retailers (these retailers were not created as equal as other key retailers) because they would not provide Company Q with the POS data Company Q needed to make their version of logistics leverage work. Even though these retailers wanted to stock Company Q products, the answer from Company Q executives was, "We cannot make money for us and for you the way you want to do business, so we would rather you did not carry our products." Of course, since the Company Q logistics leverage strategy was making money and gaining market share for both Company Q and its trade partner retailers, these nonparticipating retailers suffered an ever decreasing share of this appliance business—and became even less important to Company Q's success.

Company R—Managing Trade Partner Assets

Company R is in a sector of the consumer appliance business that is similar, but noncompetitive, with Company Q. They have also applied the logistics leverage concept by training their salespeople (who sell exclusively to retail customers) to see themselves, "not as account managers, but as asset managers." This change in orientation is very similar to the Company Q case, where salespeople see their job as not selling product to retailers but rather as selling product through the retailer to the final consumer (Company R brand equity is such that it does help create considerable retail store traffic) to achieve profitability for both the retailer and the vendor. Company R trains their salespeople to help the retailers manage their own inventory levels.

Given the fact that retailers can depend upon Company R to have the product desired in stock and deliver it quickly, salespeople help retailers change their inventory management decision rules to carry less inventory (a source of profitability for the retailers). In addition, salespeople work with retailers to determine the fast selling items, which items affect sales of other items, and which items create the most store traffic, and to share successful merchandising strategies across noncompetitive retailers. The result is greater profitability for the retailers (one retailer credits Company R's advice with saving it from bankruptcy) and greater sales for Company R. Further, since from the retailer's perspective Company R provides not only retail store traffic-creating products but also expertise, retailers are very loyal to this company and work with Company R to sell more of their product, often to the exclusion of competitors.

From Company Q and Company R we see two manufacturers who are achieving greater profitability (greater sales with lower inventory levels) and increasing market share, not just from making a quality product but from realizing who their key customers are, what they value (retail store traffic and sales, with lower inventory levels), and treating them well. In the case of one retailer, Company Q even takes this SCM Driver to the individual store basis. Realizing that one of their retail chain customers has a dozen "flagship stores." Company Q makes certain they never miss a delivery to these stores—that is, they provide a 100% customer-service level. This inordinately high service level is a recognition that when upper management wants to know how a vendor is performing, they invariably ask the managers of these 12 stores, managers who think Company Q can do no wrong. Thus, Company Q realizes that, for this particular chain, the managers of these 12 flagship stores are more important than any other customers in this particular supply chain and treat them accordingly.

Company S—Shifting Resources to Satisfy Customers

Company S is in the machine tool business, a supply chain where the principal product may cost as much as $15 million. In fact, the capital cost of these machines is so large that customers of Company S (manufacturers who use the machine tools in making their products) estimate the costs of machine tool downtime in thousands of dollars per hour. These machines are marketed and distributed by Company S worldwide, so Company S must maintain a downstream supply chain that can deliver the machines, and replacement parts, anywhere in the world.

Although the machines are expensive capital items, Company S found (through market research, again, involving Customer Value Requirements Maps) that the major source of customer dissatisfaction with Company S and its competitors was the delivery of replacement parts (parts that often cost less than $50). For example, when a customer in Singapore has a broken part on the machine, their satisfaction with the machine and the manufacturer of that machine is largely dependent on how fast they can obtain a replacement part and get the machine back in operation. This satisfaction, in turn, has a significant effect upon repeat sales and word-of-mouth reputation. To keep customer dissatisfaction from becoming a problem, Company S staged inventory all over the world (an expensive decision in its own right) and routinely shipped replacement parts to customers by overnight delivery—an international transportation service that often cost more than the actual value of the part. The result was that Company S spent tens of millions of dollars staging inventory and expediting shipments to make overnight commitments, and the customers were still dissatisfied! That is, Company S would often proudly deliver a $3.50 part overnight to a customer (at a cost of over $50!), and the customer would complain that their $15 million machine had been down for 24 hours!

As a result of this Customer Value Requirements Map insight (and in an effort to turn a customer dissatisfaction problem into a customer satisfaction advantage), Company S embarked upon a 4-year plan to implement a dramatic new logistics leverage strategy that was embodied in this phrase: "We guarantee we will deliver replacement parts to any customer worldwide *before* they order it." Notice that this zero-delivery-time strategy embodies two key elements of logistics leverage: (1) excellent logistics performance (in this case, the ability to meet this guarantee), and (2) the ability to market this performance to customers (in this case, the dramatic promotional statement that easily conveys the superiority of their performance over the competition).

To accomplish this strategy, Company S began installing cellular phones in every machine they sold (a minor cost compared with the overall purchase price). No matter where the machines are in the world, every day each machine conducts a diagnostic analysis of its performance, calls the Company S home office, and transmits the results of these diagnostics. Company S computers analyze these diagnostics every night, determine whether any parts are beginning to fail, and if they are, the computers issue shipment orders to the distribution center. Within several days (usually at least a week before the part actually fails), the plant manager of the customer company receives a package from Company S containing the part and with instructions that the part is about to fail and should be replaced in the next regular maintenance session. Thus, the customer receives the replacement part before they ordered it!

Notice that this system eliminates the need for Company S to stage inventory all over the world (they now have only one global distribution center) and employ high-cost expedited modes of transportation. Because the order is no longer a rush order and can be sent far enough in advance by slower, less expensive modes of transportation, Company S has been able to substantially lower its inventory and transportation costs while simultaneously dramatically raising customer satisfaction levels. The higher customer service levels eventually resulted in dramatically increased market share. Customers could buy their machine tools from one of several equally competent manufacturers, but only one of these (Company S) had the logistics system to eliminate their customers' unproductive downtime while waiting for replacement parts. As a result, customer perceptions actually changed to a belief that Company S made a higher quality machine than the competition. Typical comments from customers were, "Company S makes a great machine. It never breaks down." Of course, the real answer is that Company S simply has developed the logistics infrastructure to replace parts before they fail, but the customer perception is that the machines are of superior quality.

This is a slightly different example of the communication insights illustrated in Figures 5.3 and 5.4. In both of those figures, the customer perceived that the company was worse at something—relative to the competition—than they really were. This resulted in a communications challenge for the company: how to convince the customer they were actually performing well when the customer did not perceive it as so. In the Company S example, the customer actually perceives the machine tool as higher quality when in fact the initial quality is no better or worse than the competition. Company S is simply better at keeping their machines running by using logistics leverage to prevent breakdowns. However, the improved customer perceptions of Company S products are a competitive advantage that Company S enjoys regardless.

What we learn about logistics leverage and SCM Driver Four in this case is that excellent logistics performance means nothing if the customer is not aware that it exists. Company S lowered its logistics costs dramatically by implementing the logistics aspect of this strategy. However, the dramatic increases in customer satisfaction, product quality perceptions, and market share only came as a result of properly marketing this performance, a marketing strategy that was built around the dramatic and catchy promotional phrase, "We guarantee we will deliver replacement parts to any customer worldwide *before* they order it."

It is important to also realize that an effective logistics leverage strategy derived from SCM Driver Four comes from insightful market research (which is back to SCM Driver One, coordinating business functions). Rather than just asking customers about the product, Company S asked customers questions *the customers* thought should be asked. As a result, Company S discovered a

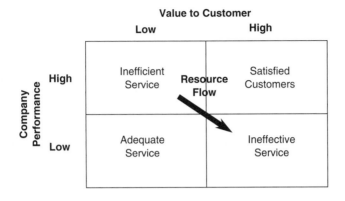

Figure 5.5   Managing Customer Value Resources

source of competitive advantage. Companies can only ask questions customers care about if they first conduct qualitative interviews with customers to determine what customers value, and then, what satisfies and dissatisfies them about these requirements they value. Only then can the company design customer satisfaction questionnaires. It is precisely this qualitative/quantitative market research approach that Company S followed, an approach that led them to develop a logistics leverage strategy based upon what the customers told them was important.

Notice again that the competitive advantage of logistics leverage came from the fact that Company S only announced this strategy after several years of installing cellular phones in their machines (something the competition was not doing) and several years of reconfiguring their logistics inventory, transportation, and information systems to accommodate this strategy (something the competition was also not doing). The result was that once Company S announced its new replacement parts guarantee, the competition was in no position to match it and was faced with several years of expensive changes in how they manufacture and distribute their product (their infrastructure) before they could match it.

Company S helps us illustrate one additional point about strategically implementing SCM Driver Four: shifting resources from areas customers do not care about to areas customers do care about. As Figure 5.5 illustrates, a simple matrix can demonstrate for companies whether their expenditures of resources match what customers really care about. The quadrant labeled "Satisfied Customers" is what we typically hear about in customer satisfaction examples, the instances where the company performs exceptionally well at something the customer also cares about. We hear such phrases as, "the customer is number one," "exceeding expectations," and "delighting the customer," surrounding examples of companies that have loyal customers because they seldom fail on the dimensions the customers value.

What we hear much less about, but what is nevertheless an equally valid example of SCM Driver Four, are companies that do not perform well on things customers do not care about. Although this *seems* to run athwart the concept of Total Quality Management (TQM), there are some things we just do not try to do well. This, in fact, is completely consistent with TQM, which is a management philosophy that says we should concentrate on the total quality of only two things:

1. anything the customer cares about;

2. anything that lowers our costs and the customer does not care about.

Notice that Company S did both of these. Company S became much less effective at rapid parts delivery—pulling inventory back to a central location (not giving customers inventory that was close to them) and using slower modes of transportation (not promising rapid transportation) because the customer did not care about either of these. What the customer did care about was never having the machine out of service, so Company S is superb at managing the quality of this aspect of their supply chain.

The key to effective and efficient management of customer value is moving resources from the Inefficient Service quadrant of Figure 5.5 (spending resources managing the total quality of something the customer not only may not care about, but may not even notice) to activities that fall in the Ineffective Service Quadrant of Figure 5.5 (things the customer does care about that the company is not good at accomplishing). Notice that this is precisely what Company S (and the other companies in the examples in this chapter) did. They took resources away from things their customers did not care about and redistributed those resources to what the customers did care about, usually with resultant dramatic increases in market share and/or profitability.

Company T—Understanding the Customer Gaps

There are multiple opportunities for supply chain partners to misunderstand each other. These "gaps" in understanding are illustrated in Figure 5.6. A beverage bottler, Company T, realized that numerous opportunities existed in their supply chain for misunderstandings between what their customers (retailers) wanted and what Company T delivered. Although customer expectations of quality are formed by various factors—past experience in the supply

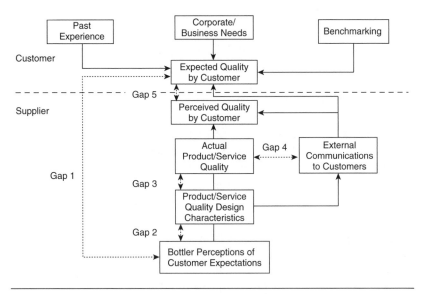

Figure 5.6   Expected Versus Perceived Performance

Adapted from Parasuraman, Zeithaml, and Berry (1988)

chain, the needs of the retailer and their customers, and benchmarking information from other companies—the bottler did not always fully understand what those expectations were (Gap 1). This could happen for various reasons: the retailer did not tell the bottler salesperson what they wanted, the salesperson did not tell the bottler, or the salesperson and/or the bottler misunderstood what was expected. In any of these cases, the bottler loses the ability to give the retailer what they expect because they do not know, accurately, what it is.

Even in cases where Gap 1 did not exist, the bottler found that, internally, there was often a gap between what the retailer wanted and what the bottler's own internal staff designed to fill that expectation (Gap 2). Further, a difference often existed between what was designed and what was actually produced (Gap 3, caused by not following SCM Driver One—that is, not coordinating the business functions). Following on this lack of internal coordination of business functions, what was communicated to customers was often different than what was actually produced by the bottler. Not surprisingly, the resultant perception of the retailer of what was delivered by the bottler was often far different than the original customer expectation (Gap 5). The result was a largely dissatisfied retailer base, who believed, "Company T just does not listen to us or care about what we want." This, of course, was far from the truth, but Company T's supply chain gaps created an image that they gave the retailer what Company T wanted and not what the retailer wanted. It took considerable effort to identify key customers, identify their expectations (SCM Driver Four), and coordinate Company T internal operations (SCM Driver One) to accurately deliver what the customer wanted and communicate that accuracy to the customers.

Dell Computer

And, finally, as an illustration of SCM Driver Four, we will discuss an undisguised company. In 1984, a University of Texas student who had been selling rebuilt PCs out of his dorm room thought about entering the emerging PC market. Ordinarily, entering a relatively established market would have been a ridiculous idea. It was conventional wisdom that Intel and Microsoft Corporations had taken all the margins out of the PC business, and all the products were viewed as commodities (there is that mistake again: assuming the only basis on which to compete is the product itself, without considering the services that accompany it). In addition, all the key players in the industry were building massive structures to produce everything a computer needed from disk drives to memory chips and applications software. Certainly, a new entrant could not compete.

The young college student, Michael Dell, decided to enter the market and, by doing so, totally revamped the industry. Dell Computers is now the undisputed industry leader. Dell applied a customer focus, supplier partnerships, mass customization, and Just-In-Time delivery to implement the strategy of virtual integration to create and sustain customer value.

By selling directly to customers via the Web, Dell Computers uses e-commerce to communicate with customers, maintain low costs, and customize products according to customer specifications. Dell Computers is driven by the desire to create value for the customer. Michael Dell himself said, "Looking for the [customer] value . . . is most important" (Magretta, 1998a).

Through the use of the Internet, Dell's customers gain access to the same product, service, and catalog information as Dell's employees. Tailor-made Internet cites called Premier Pages give customers direct access to purchasing and technical information about the specific configurations they buy from Dell. Thus, customers can order, configure, and even gather technical advice online, thereby turning a commodity product into a customized product offering.

For those customers who want or need more personalized assistance, Dell will send out one of more than 10,000 service technicians to their site. However, only a small number are Dell employees. Most are "virtual employees" that dress like Dell employees, talk like Dell employees, even cater to the customer like Dell employees, but are actually contract employees (supply chain partners). According to Michael Dell, this allows Dell's employees to focus on activities that create the most value for customers.

Activities such as coordination with its virtual manufacturing facilities and inventory velocity and reduction are of primary concern for Dell because they result in lower costs to customers. Dell has a virtual manufacturing arrangement with key suppliers such as Sony. Sony employees work in the Dell facility on joint planning and product development. Because of this close relationship, and its reputation for building reliable computer monitors, Dell decided not to perform quality checks on Sony monitors. Thus, they determined there was no reason to maintain inventory. So, Sony manufactures monitors Just-In-Time for Dell. When needed, Dell instructs UPS or Airborne Express to pick up 10,000 monitors from Sony's plant in Mexico and a corresponding 10,000 computers from Dell's facility in Texas. UPS or Airborne Express match computers with monitors in the delivery process, eliminating the need for Dell to have an expensive distribution center to perform these functions (SCM Driver Three).

Dell strives to implement virtual integration because it allows them to meet customer needs faster and more efficiently than any other PC maker. If customers want, Dell will install company-specific software before delivery. They will also put an asset tag with the company's logo on the machine and keep an electronic register of the customer's assets. This saves the customer the time and expense of having their employees place asset tags on the equipment. Dell also places technicians at major customers' sites. Thus, Dell becomes the customer's virtual IT Department (applying SCM Driver Two), instead of just a traditional supplier.

Logistics leverage is at the core of Dell's virtual integration strategy. Customer value is created and sustained in this highly competitive industry because no one can duplicate the customization, the logistics infrastructure, the employee infrastructure, and the unique supply chain partner relationships, all of which have resulted in decreased costs and increased customer service. Even when retailers aligned with Dell's competitors began charging higher rates for servicing and supporting Dell products, customers remained loyal (Dell had placed their customers in the Satisfied Customers quadrant of Figure 5.5).

Leveraging logistics allows Dell to have long-term special relationships with both key suppliers and key customers (remember: not all customers are created equal). Unique product offerings and cost reductions have resulted in loyal customers and sustainable position. Thus, Dell has used logistics leverage to reduce cost and focus on creating value for customers.

Summary and an Exercise

These examples illustrate how companies can achieve competitive advantage through understanding what their customers value and developing the operational and communications strategies to deliver that value.

An exercise to start your company down a path to the successes similar to those in this chapter is to regularly interview customers and fill in the Customer Value Requirements Map in Figure 5.2. The goal should be to answer the following questions:

- Who is our customer?
- What do these customers value?
- What are we doing to provide these values?
- What are we doing to communicate our delivery of these values?
- How satisfied are our customers with our delivery and communication of these values?
- Are we spending resources on things the customers do not value?

By going through this exercise again and again with many customers, you will have taken the first step toward implementing SCM Driver of Competitive Advantage Four.

6

Identify and Manage the Supply Chain Flow Cycles

There are numerous flows in supply chains (Figure 6.1). Product flows from suppliers through manufacturers, through distributors, through retailers, to final customers. The product arrow in Figure 6.1 flows both ways because many supply chains (soft drink bottlers, for example) must manage the flow of the remains of the consumption (empty bottles) back up the supply chain. In the 1970s, when Michigan passed a "bottle ban" law, which required all plastic, metal, and glass containers to have a deposit, the supply chain was not ready for the volume of product flow back up the supply chain that resulted. The supply chains for these products were primarily focused on getting the product to the retailer, not taking the empties back to the manufacturers. The results for several months were huge piles of empties in the parking lots outside the retailers (often piles larger than the actual store), until the supply chains were reconfigured to not only deliver product to the retailer but to also take the empties away from the retailer.

Other supply chains (e-commerce and catalog supply chains, for example) must contend with a large percentage of returned products. One large clothing retailer has conducted research that indicates 60% of all its sales are unplanned purchases (the customer came into the store for something else but saw and bought other items on impulse). Thus, when this retailer developed a Web site for their products, one of the marketing messages emphasized on the Web site was the ease of returning purchased product that did not fit, was not quite the right color, or for any other reason (a large problem for most clothing e-commerce supply chains). Instead of having to repackage the product, take it to UPS or Federal Express and incur the cost of shipping it back, this retailer encouraged customers to simply bring it to the returns desk at any of their stores.

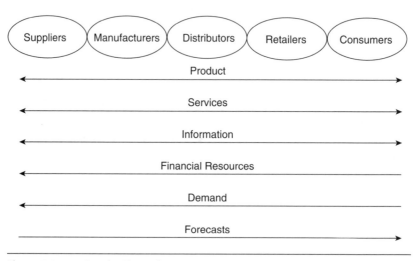

Figure 6.1　　Supply Chain Flows

This was more convenient for the customer, and the retailer did not incur higher logistics costs as the returned product could be placed in stock at that store or returned to the distribution center on trucks making deliveries to the store. More important, the returns desk was all the way at the back of each store, so customers returning e-commerce purchased products had to walk all the way through the store (impulse buying as they went). Thus, their e-commerce supply chain product flow management increased in-store sales.

Still other supply chains (automotive parts, for example) must deal with used parts that are remanufactured and redistributed for reuse by the final customer. In the automotive industry, for instance, entire industries exist around these remanufactured products. The supply chain must encourage customers to turn in their used parts and encourage supply chain partners to move the used parts from the point of consumption back to the remanufacturers.

Services need supply chain support equally as much as product supply chains do—a dentist, for example, cannot perform the service of replacing your old tooth filling unless the machinery (drill, etc.), the tools, and the supplies (filling materials) have all been moved to the dentist office in anticipation of the procedure. In addition, we have talked throughout this book about various services that accompany product flows in supply chains—inventory, transportation, order processing, financial, and information management; market research; and advertising, to name just a few. These services flow both up and down the supply chain.

Information about product/service availability, inventory location, transportation options, customer values, finances, the location of shipments, the quality of goods that are being produced, when goods are being produced, in what quantity, demand by location—in fact, information about any aspect of supply chain management—also flows up and down the supply chain. As we discussed in our first example (Company A), these flows are critical aspects of supply chain management and largely affect the profitability of not only individual companies but the supply chain as a whole. Although financial flows are ultimately up the supply chain from the final customer to all supply chain participants, the timing of those flows (again, as Company A illustrated) is a critical aspect of supply chain management.

Finally, demand for products and services flows up the supply chain, and the ability to forecast, anticipate, and plan for those demand flows has a huge impact on the viability of the supply chain. Demand starts with the final customer, flows through the initial point of contact for the customer to the supply chain, and up through the various supply chain partners. In return, the forecasts about potential future demand flows down through various supply chain partners. The horizon for those forecasts depends on how far in the future that demand occurs. Without such flows, inventory builds up at the wrong locations, transportation and production costs go up as we expedite shipments to meet unplanned demand, and customer service at all locations suffers.

Coca-Cola Bottling Company Consolidated (CCBCC) is Coca-Cola's second largest U.S. bottling company (Murphy, 2002a). CCBCC retailers engaged in aggressive advertising and promotion of Coca-Cola products, often without sharing any of this information with CCBCC. The result of the lack of managing these information and demand flows was that CCBCC suffered stockouts in some products while carrying excess inventory in other products. In a project to manage these flows, CCBCC set three goals: cut inventory in half (from 12 to 14 days to 6); reduce stockouts and improve customer service by having the right product available; and reduce large-scale capital investments in warehouses. By increasing visibility of production and operations plans (information flows) and regularly updating forecasts based upon new demand information (forecast and demand flows), CCBCC cut inventory in half, improved customer service, eliminated 12 warehouses, and prevented the expenditure of $50 million on new warehouses. As Brian Wieland, director of Demand Planning at CCBCC, put it, "What is so important about this is that we can change the forecast as things happen, and within an hour or less we can rerun the entire plan and know what our new needs are: what we now need to replenish, what we need to schedule from a production standpoint, and even the raw materials we now need to order. In a matter of minutes we can have a whole new look."

It is not just large companies that can manage these supply chain flows (Murphy, 2002b). Fox Electronics designs and manufacturers quartz crystals and oscillators to provide accurate timing to a variety of devices. One reason for its success is the ability to provide customers with customized products in 10 days or less, rather than the industry standard of 12 weeks!

It is the understanding of the timing of all these flows—how long each takes, and where bottlenecks to efficient supply chain flows exist—that SCM Driver Five addresses. By coordinating the various flows, and their timing across supply chain partners, individual companies and whole supply chains can significantly reduce costs and obtain competitive advantage.

Company U—Managing the Supply Chain Flows

SCM Driver Five requires us to identify and manage the supply chain flow cycles. The supply chain flow cycles are different than what we typically talk about in the business of managing order cycles—the amount of time it takes between placing an order and receiving the order.

To illustrate the impact on the supply chain of managing these flows, let's examine a particular supply chain's flow cycles. How long does it take for information about a customer buying the product to move from the point of consumption to any partner in the supply chain? The answer will probably surprise you. When we talk about demand information flows, the answer is typically, "Well, we have EDI (electronic data interchange) in our supply chain, so the information flows instantaneously."

However, let's take an example of a piece of women's clothing, a skirt (Figure 6.2). A skirt could be bought in various locations. One is a retail store in a local mall—the retail store being part of a larger retail chain. The customer walks into the store, buys the skirt, pays for the skirt, either in cash or with a credit card at the cash register, and leaves. How long does it take the manufacturer of that skirt to find out that a sale has actually occurred in that style, in that color, in that size, in that particular store? Again, the typical answer is, "Well, they know instantly. We have EDI." But EDI is the amount of time it takes for the retailer to place an order to their supplier—not the amount of time between the customer buying the product and the retailer placing that order with their supplier. In point of fact, when the customer came in and bought the skirt, the answer to the question of what immediately happens is "nothing!" What happens when the customer buys a product and leaves the store in a typical, traditional supply chain? Absolutely nothing!

What happens is inventory is decreased by one skirt and nothing happens in the typical supply chain until inventory levels in that retail store hit a magic number called a reorder point. Typical inventory management procedures establish reorder points and order quantities for each product (in all its style, color, and size variations) in each store. When inventory gets down to the reorder point, the store system places an order for a predetermined order quantity to replenish that store.

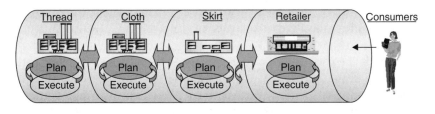

Figure 6.2   Supply Chain Flow Cycles

Where does the order go? Well, in the particular example of retailers served by Company U, the order goes from the store where the skirt was sold (and, by the way, it may take several days or even weeks before inventory levels get down low enough for the retailer to actually place an order) to the retail chain's regional distribution center. The regional distribution center replenishes supplies for all the stores until they hit their reorder point, at which point they tell corporate that it is time to place an order with the supplier. However, before notifying Company U (the supplier) of an order, the retailer checks inventory levels in all other regional distribution centers. If any of these RDCs have excess inventory, it is "transshipped" to the RDC that needs it and sent on to the retail store to fill the order. When all RDCs have hit a systemwide reorder point, only then does the retailer place an order with Company U.

The supplier (Company U) is a manufacturer of women's clothing and, in this particular case, is located in the United States. The order is processed. Remember that once the order is placed from the retailer headquarters to the manufacturer, the order is transmitted instantaneously. However, consider the time that has elapsed between the customer buying the skirt and the retail chain finally placing an order with Company U.

Even though Company U and its retailers have EDI, let's look at how long it takes, on average, between a customer buying a skirt and the manufacturer finding out that a sale has actually occurred. The answer may surprise you. On average for this particular supply chain, the time between a sale in the store and an order being released to the manufacturer was 23 days. It took 23 days, almost a month, for the manufacturer to find out the demand had occurred— even though they have EDI!

When the order arrives at the manufacturer, they either fill the order from inventory on hand, or they schedule production. For this manufacturer, production happens in several stages. When they have received the cloth from their supplier, they go through a process called "cut, color, and sew." *Cutting* is cutting the cloth to the patterns for the particular style of the particular skirt, in the size that the skirt will eventually be. Once this is done, it goes into inventory to be held while awaiting orders for particular colors. When a color is received, the product is dyed to the particular color and then sewn into the final product.

This is the concept of postponement that we discussed earlier in this book—not committing to the final color and sewing of the product until an actual order exists. However, postponement takes time. The time between cutting the product, coloring the product, and sewing the product in this particular company can take up to 2 weeks.

Now, when this company has shipped enough product to retailers that they have hit their own reorder point for the cloth Company U needs, what do they do? They also have EDI with their suppliers. They instantaneously place an order with their supplier, a cloth manufacturer also in the United States. But from the 23 days it took them to get the order from the retailer, on average it is 2 weeks until they go through their entire cut, color, and sew production cycle and have to schedule orders to their supplier, which has now brought the supply chain flow cycle in this particular supply chain up to 37 days (23 plus 14).

The cloth manufacturer instantaneously receives (remember, it is EDI) the order on average on day 37 and goes through various weaving processes to make the product, which adds another week to the supply chain flow cycle.

The final step in this particular supply chain is a manufacturer of thread, also in the United States, and they also instantaneously receive orders from the cloth manufacturer because of EDI. We now are up to 44 days (23 plus 14 plus 7) from when the customer actually bought the product in the store.

So how does the thread manufacturer, still in the United States (not even a global supply chain involved here), manage this supply chain? Every month, they try to forecast what the demand is going to be for 6 weeks (i.e., the average of 44 days) into the future. They are constantly trying to forecast the demand at the store level so they can back that supply chain flow information up to their production schedule.

Now, let's reconfigure this supply chain (just as Company U did) for these four companies in the United States. Let's replace the supply chain flow cycles of the thread manufacturer trying to forecast demand for thread 6 weeks out, and the cloth manufacturer trying to forecast demand for cloth a month out, and the clothing manufacturer trying to forecast demand for skirts 3 weeks out. Let's replace this with only one company forecasting demand for skirts at the retail level and sharing that information with all four supply chain partners.

What they all need is information, and the information (called "point-of-sale demand") can be provided by the retailer. And that point-of-sale demand is not just a history of skirts as they sell, but is also information on local advertising, merchandising strategies, and so forth by the retailer, so that whoever is doing the forecasting can look at the effects of different marketing strategies on retailer demand. In this particular supply chain, the cloth manufacturer had the most effective forecasting system. So only one company in the supply chain was doing forecasting. Here is an important principle of supply chain management that we will revisit in Chapter Seven—every supply chain only has one point of what is called "independent demand." All other demand in the supply chain is "derived demand." The independent demand in this particular supply chain was at the retail level. It is independent because it is difficult to forecast when different shoppers are going to come into which stores to buy what styles and colors and sizes of skirts. That is the one demand point in the supply chain we have to forecast. All other supply chain partner demand is derived from this independent demand.

We can drastically reduce many of the supply chain flow cycles in this example by instantaneously sharing the one forecast of independent demand with all other supply chain partners. So the thread manufacturer—instead of waiting 44 days to get an order and, as a result, trying to forecast 44 days out—at any given point in time knows both what the demand is at the retail level and what forecast the supply chain as a whole (not the individual companies) is using for operations and planning. Thus, the thread manufacturer can look out 44 days and see what the demand is going to be that will affect their order processing system a month and a half from now. The thread manufacturer is no longer forecasting. They are planning demand that is derived through the supply chain consisting of the retailer, the skirt manufacturer, and the cloth manufacturer.

The impact of the decrease in the supply chain information flow cycle, from 44 days or 37 days or 23 days for various supply chain members, is that information is now instantaneous throughout the supply chain. Companies no longer have to wait till the other supply chain members pass on relevant and critical information (the information flows) to plan their operations (the product flows). The impact of this change on this particular supply chain is that this chain still sells the same number of skirts. Market share has not significantly changed, which means the demand for cloth and demand for thread (product flows) have not changed, but these four companies systemwide are doing the same amount of business with 40% less inventory in the supply chain.

The service flow in this example is Company U providing the service of forecasting independent demand and sharing that information (the demand and forecast flows) with all four companies. All four companies, in turn, share information on inventory levels, production plans, and shipping and receiving schedules (the information flows) with each other, so each company can plan when the independent demand is going to affect their particular operations (the derived demand).

The final flow in this example is finances. The 40% reduction in inventory was not uniform across companies. In fact, far greater financial savings from reduced inventory levels and smoother production schedules were experienced by the cloth manufacturer and the thread manufacturer than by the retailer or Company U. Realizing this, and sharing the savings so that all companies were sufficiently compensated to be willing to participate in managing these supply chain flows, was a crucial success factor in this example (and is an idea we will revisit with SCM Driver Twelve). Unless the financial flows are monitored and managed so all supply chain partners are fairly rewarded, the long-term viability of such an example as Company U is in jeopardy.

Summary and an Exercise

These examples illustrate how companies can achieve competitive advantage through understanding the various supply chain flows and bottlenecks of these flows in their supply chains. It is helpful to estimate the impact of these bottlenecks on supply chain performance by following a product through your supply chain.

As an exercise, take a product and determine the same information discussed in the example for Company U for all levels in your supply chain. Determine how much inventory could be eliminated if all that information was shared real-time by all supply chain partners. The result is the impact, for one of your supply chains, of managing the supply chain flows.

7

Manage Demand (Not Just the Forecast)

L ittle attention has been paid to the role of sales forecasting and demand
management in the supply chain or how that role might change depending
upon the position in the supply chain that a company occupies. As discussed in
Chapter 6, two of the supply chain flows are the information (forecasts) related
to demand (orders) as they flow up and down the supply chain.

From a SCM perspective, however, the question arises, "Do all members of
the supply chain need to forecast demand?" In fact, taking a SCM perspective
reveals that any supply chain has only one point of *independent demand (the
amount of product demanded, by time and location, by the end-use customer of
the supply chain)*. Whether this end-use customer is a consumer shopping
in a retail establishment or online (B2C), or a business buying products for
consumption in the process of conducting their business operations (B2B),
these end-use customers determine the true demand for the product that will
flow through the supply chain.

The company in the supply chain that directly serves this end-use
customer directly experiences this independent demand. All subsequent companies in the supply chain experience a demand that is tempered by the order
fulfillment and purchasing policies of other companies in the supply chain.
This second type of supply chain demand is *derived demand* because it is not
the independent demand of the end-use customer but rather a *demand that
is derived from what other companies in the supply chain do to meet their demand
from their immediate customer (the company that orders from them)*. It is important to note that only one company in any given supply chain is directly
affected by independent demand. The rest are affected by derived demand.
Equally important, the techniques, systems, and processes necessary to deal
with derived demand are quite different from those of independent demand. In

fact, many companies develop elaborate sales forecasting techniques, systems, and processes when, in fact, *they do not even need to forecast!*

Recognizing the differences between independent and derived demand, recognizing which type of demand affects a particular company, and developing techniques, systems, and processes to deal with that company's particular type of demand can have a profound impact on supply chain costs and customer service levels. We first explore the implications of independent and derived demand, followed by a model of the demand management function in SCM.

Derived Versus Independent Demand

Figure 7.1 depicts a traditional supply chain, with a retailer serving the end-use customer, a wholesaler supplying the retailer, a manufacturer supplying the wholesaler, and a supplier providing raw materials to the manufacturer. The source of independent demand for this supply chain is 1,000 units for the planning period. However, the retailer (as is typically the case) does not know this with certainty. In fact, the retailer has a reasonably good forecasting process and forecasts end-use customer demand to be 1,000 for the planning period. Since the forecast has typically experienced +/–10% error in the past, the retailer places an order to their supplier (the wholesaler) for 1,100 units (1,000 units for expected demand and 100 units for safety stock to meet expected forecasting error). It is critical to notice in this simple example of a typical, *unmanaged* supply chain that the demand the wholesaler experiences is *1,100 units, not 1,000.*

The wholesaler, in turn, has a reasonable forecasting system (note that the wholesaler is not forecasting end-use customer independent demand but is inadvertently forecasting retailer derived demand) and forecasts the demand affecting the wholesaler at 1,100 units. Again, the wholesaler believes forecasting error to be approximately +/–10%, so the wholesaler orders 1,100 plus 10% (or 1,210) units from the manufacturer. If the manufacturer and the supplier both assume the same +/–10% forecasting error, then they will each add 10% to their orders to their suppliers.

As Figure 7.1 illustrates, simple failure to recognize the difference between independent demand (which needs to be forecast) and derived demand (which can be derived and planned)—even in a supply chain where forecasting error is only +/–10%—adds greatly to the safety stock carried in the supply chain. In fact, since each member of the supply chain only needed 1,000 units to meet the actual demand, plus 100 units for the potential forecasting error, this particular supply chain is carrying 705 too much inventory: $(210 - 100) + (331 - 100) + (464 - 100) = 705$, or a 16.0% supply chain–wide inventory overstock: $(705/4, 400) = 16.0\%$, for the actual end-use customer demand.

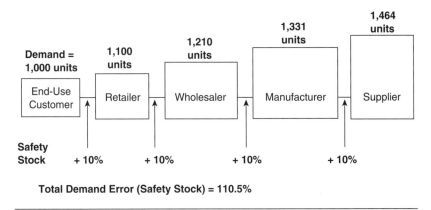

Figure 7.1   Demand Error in a Traditional Supply Chain

Inventory carried for total demand error (safety stock) in this supply chain is 1,105 (100 + 210 + 331 + 464), or 110.5% of actual end-use customer demand! This example allows us to introduce the supply chain concept of *demand planning,* which is *the coordinated flow of derived demand through companies in the supply chain.* Demand planning was partially illustrated in the Company U example in Chapter 6 and is diagrammed in Figure 7.2. In the Figure 7.2 supply chain, end-use customer demand is the same as in Figure 7.1, and the retailer's faith in their forecast (+/−10%) is unchanged. What has changed, however, is that the other companies in the supply chain are no longer even attempting to forecast the demand of their customers. Rather, each member of the supply chain receives point-of-sale (POS) demand information from the retailer and the retailer's planned ordering based upon this demand. Combined with knowledge of the time-related order flows through this supply chain, each company can plan its processes (including orders to their suppliers). The result is that each member of the supply chain carries 1,100 units in inventory, a systemwide reduction in inventory of 13.81% from 5,105 (1,100 for the retailer, 1,210 for the wholesaler, 1,331 for the manufacturer, and 1,464 for the supplier) to 4,400 (1,100 each for the retailer, wholesaler, manufacturer, and supplier). More important, the inventory carried for forecasting error (safety stock) drops from 1,105 to 400 (from total demand error of 110.5% to 40.0%) for a reduction of total demand error inventory (safety stock) of 63.8%: (1,105 − 400)/1,105.

Notice, however, that the inventory reductions are not uniform across the supply chain. Whereas the supplier has a reduction in safety stock of 78.4% (from 464 to 100), the retailer experiences no reduction. In fact, the further up the supply chain, the greater the safety stock reduction. This illustrates a paradox of demand planning in any supply chain: the very companies that are most

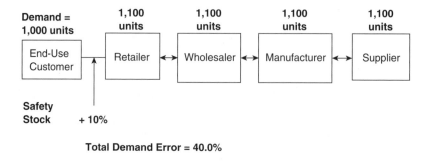

Figure 7.2   Demand Error in a Demand-Planning Supply Chain

needed to implement supply chain demand planning (implementation of systems to share with suppliers real-time POS information held by retailers) have the least economic motivation (inventory reduction) to cooperate. This leads us to the concept of demand management.

Demand management is *the creation across the supply chain and its markets of a coordinated flow of demand.* Much is implied in this seemingly simple definition. First, the traditional function of marketing creates demand for various products, but often does not share these demand-creating plans (such as promotional programs) with other functions within the company, much less with other companies in the supply chain.

The marketing function in one consumer durables company, for example, was planning and implementing promotional plans but not sharing this information with the logistics managers responsible for planning production schedules and deliveries of products to stores. Thus, marketing often created increased demand for products for which no increased inventory levels were available—resulting in dissatisfied customers (and the perception by marketing managers that the promotion had not worked—after all, demand did not go up). This creation of demand that the company cannot fill is often called "advertising for the competition," in other words, spending advertising/promotional money to create demand among customers for which company inventory will not be available, so the customer buys the competitors' products (often simultaneous with being dissatisfied with the advertising company for being out of stock). It was only when the manufacturer started managing the overall demand flows that promotional, production, and logistics plans were coordinated with ordering schedules for the manufacturer's suppliers.

Second, the role of demand management is often to decrease demand. This may sound counterintuitive, but demand often exists for company products at a level management cannot realistically (or profitably) fulfill. A clothing manufacturer (the Company C example earlier in this book) was capacity constrained and, as a result, was having trouble filling orders for certain lines of clothing to their existing customers. However, the sales force was given a bonus for each new customer account they opened! The result was that not only could the company not fill the orders of its established customers, but they were also paying salespeople to open accounts with new customers they could not hope to satisfy. Demand management implies an assessment of the profit contribution of various products and customers (all with capacity constraints in mind), emphasizing demand for the profitable ones and decreasing demand (by lessening marketing efforts) for the unprofitable ones.

Finally, as we mentioned earlier, considerable supply chain savings can result from demand planning, but the rewards are not always consistent with the need to obtain collaboration from all companies in the supply chain. Thus, an aspect of demand management is *supply chain relationship management,* which is *the management of relationships with supply chain partners to match performance with measurements and rewards so that all companies in the supply chain are fairly rewarded for overall supply chain success (measured as cost reduction and increased customer satisfaction).*

A Model of Supply Chain Demand Management

These examples and concepts lead us to an overall model of the role of demand management, demand planning, and sales forecasting in the supply chain. Figure 7.3 illustrates these roles. Supply chain management has many aspects (many of which we discuss in this book), only one of which is demand management. As previously illustrated, demand management encompasses the traditional marketing functions, along with the coordination of marketing activities with other functions in the company and the supply chain.

However, the traditional demand creation role of marketing is tempered in supply chain management by a desire to coordinate the flow of demand across the supply chain (demand planning) and the creation of incentives for supply chain partners (more on this in Chapter 13) to help manage those flows (supply chain relationship management). First, this role of marketing and supply chain relationship management in demand management will be explored more fully by looking at the role of the salesperson in demand management and sales forecasting. The nature of demand planning for derived demand will then be examined. This will be followed by discussion of the sales forecasting function as it tries to anticipate independent demand and how world-class companies assess their performance in the supply chain. Examples, as usual, will follow this discussion.

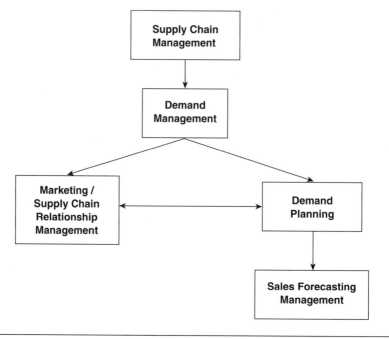

Figure 7.3   Demand Management in Supply Chain Management

The Sales Force Role in Demand Management and Planning

Supply chain partners have to share tactical and strategic information on a timely basis to accomplish demand management. They also must engage in cooperative, problem-solving, integrative behaviors. Of all the functional areas within the organization, the sales force is particularly well positioned to implement, coordinate, and facilitate many of the required supply chain relationship management behaviors and activities.

In most companies, however, the sales force's potential in effective supply chain relationship management is not fully leveraged. There are a number of reasons for this. For one, the traditional view of sales runs counter to the broader, more strategic perspective required in supply chain management. For another, built-in reward and compensation programs inhibit the development of the behaviors and activities required. That needs to change if the sales force is to reinvent itself as a value-added contributor to the supply chain.

THE TRADITIONAL VIEW OF SALES

Traditionally, personal selling has focused mainly on transactional prepurchase activities. An examination of the many popular books on selling bears this out. A great deal of attention is paid to making sales presentations, handling customer objections, closing sales, signing the contract—all transactional, prepurchase activities. The primary objective has been to increase sales, profits, and new business.

Personal selling also has been primarily tactical in nature and not strategic. While there are exceptions in every industry, salespeople, for the most part, have been concerned with selling their products rather than leveraging their company as a strategic resource or a partner to the customer. Most salespeople spend the majority of their time detailing product features, benefits, and advantages instead of exploring how they can help customers reach *their* strategic goals and objectives.

In many ways, traditional sales practices are counterproductive to supply chain management objectives. For example, appropriate inventory management throughout the supply chain is key to overall supply chain performance. Yet traditional selling practices often encourage salespeople to stock customers with high inventory levels (having the opposite effect of the inventory reductions in Figure 7.2). Typically, they do this to meet or exceed their monthly sales volume quotas (more on this in Chapter 13). These traditional practices, which still linger in many sales organizations, hinder the attainment of supply chain goals. While many salespeople continue to concentrate on the prepurchase activities, their supply chain partners now are more concerned with postpurchase activities like managing the relationship and streamlining intercompany demand management and demand planning processes.

In many situations, salespeople are simply displaying behaviors that have been ingrained through a culture of traditional selling beliefs, training programs, and sales management practices. This culture has reinforced a traditional view of selling that is *not* aligned with supply chain management. Many sales training programs are focused primarily on product knowledge and selling techniques. Yet these topics do little to prepare the salesperson to add value in the supply chain. In fact, traditional sales programs pay hardly any attention to managing relationships, leveraging logistics expertise, and explaining supply chain management roles. If salespeople develop any supply chain management skills at all, it is likely *ad hoc* or by chance.

Performance evaluations and reward structures, which strongly influence sales force behavior, also inhibit the broader supply chain perspective. Many companies still evaluate and reward their salespeople based on increasing sales volume, profits, and new business. These measures encourage and reward short-term financial results. And this often causes salespeople to take a short-term perspective (increasing this month's sales volume) over a more advantageous long-term perspective (improving supply chain relationships). Under a traditional selling model, salespeople focus more on ringing up short-term sales to reach their monthly quota than on whether the transaction is in the supply chain partner's best interest.

In short, the traditional sales force role is not aligned with supply chain management. To maintain long-term financial performance, companies need to engage in key supply chain activities, like demand management and demand planning, and become value-adding supply chain partners. To attain this goal, the sales force needs to take on new supply chain management roles.

NEW ROLES FOR THE SALES FORCE

Salespeople are centrally positioned to add real value to the supply chain. But if they are to fulfill this potential, they need to

- Develop a new selling orientation
- Interface more effectively with logistics
- Take on new activities and adopt new behaviors
- Gain expertise in supply chain management

DEVELOP A NEW SELLING ORIENTATION

Changing the cultural belief of personal selling is extremely difficult. Salespeople must replace their prepurchase orientation with a postpurchase focus on delivering solutions that create value for supply chain partners. They need to move from a selling to a service orientation, with the purpose of meeting the needs of various supply chain partners and continuously improving performance of the supply chain. In short, they need to become relationship managers.

Salespeople also need to work with and develop relationships with various supply chain partners, both upstream and downstream. The traditional mindset of focusing on a "once removed" downstream customer is too limited. World-class companies today recognize the value of extending that focus to the customer's customer to add value to that downstream partner. Looking upstream, sales may be involved in relationships with vendors as part of the demand management and demand planning processes of delivering superior value to downstream customers. Partnering and negotiating skills that are traditionally associated with managing major customer accounts can be used effectively in working with suppliers, distributors, and other partners in the supply chain.

INTERFACE MORE EFFECTIVELY WITH LOGISTICS

In many business environments, sales and logistics are becoming closely intertwined. In leading organizations, salespeople are even leveraging logistics as a competitive weapon in acquiring new business and retaining existing customers. This is a positive development, and companies that are not already moving in this direction are at a competitive disadvantage.

Salespeople often are required to solve customer problems that center on logistics needs and operations (Garver & Mentzer, 2000). Although salespeople may not design or implement logistics processes or systems, they need to be familiar with them to add value to supply chain partners. This underscores the point that salespeople and logistics managers need to work together to solve supply chain partners' demand management problems. Although the logistics manager may be the primary person designing logistics solutions, the salesperson must take a leadership role in ensuring that the solutions satisfy the supply chain partners' demand management needs and requirements. Teamwork and knowledge are the keys. Both logistics and sales professionals must be able to communicate effectively and speak the same language, that is, the supply chain partner's language.

The sales force, of course, interacts with many departments within the organization. But with supply chain management, the integration with logistics is particularly important. To be effective supply chain team members, as well as effective service providers, problem solvers, and relationship managers, salespeople must broaden their experience base and gain logistics and supply chain management expertise. Training programs that focus on logistics and supply chain management expertise are one way that companies can develop this competency. Furthermore, allowing salespeople the opportunity to gain cross-functional experience in logistics, or vice versa, is another way to develop supply chain experts in the sales force.

TAKE ON NEW ACTIVITIES AND ADOPT NEW BEHAVIORS

The supply chain sales force should be involved with any demand management activity that goes beyond organizational boundaries. More specifically, it should be an integral part of implementing cooperative behaviors such as joint planning, evaluating, and forecasting; mutual sharing of information; and nurturing supply chain relationships.

COOPERATIVE BEHAVIORS: PLANNING, EVALUATING, AND FORECASTING

To achieve the goals of the supply chain, partners need to work toward developing common strategic and tactical demand plans. These plans must be synchronized to realize synergies throughout the supply chain. To gain these synergies, the sales force must be actively involved in joint demand planning sessions throughout the supply chain. Although these joint demand planning sessions should also include representatives from other functional areas (marketing in particular), sales needs to play a prominent and active role. Sales can bring their expertise about supply chain partners, the market, and competitive supply chains. This input is invaluable in coordinating demand activities among supply chain partners.

Cooperative planning also should include joint evaluation of overall supply chain performance. Because the sales force is a facilitator of many boundary-spanning activities, it knows where performance is meeting, or failing to meet, expectations. By living in the supply chain partner's world, the salesperson is in close contact with the partner, often the first to identify new emerging needs and problems in performance. With this knowledge, salespeople may be better able than others to understand their own company's strengths and weaknesses from the supply chain partner's perspective. With this knowledge, the salesperson can represent the "voice of the supply chain" to drive continuous improvement internally, while at the same time building external relationships.

The sales force also can readily identify roadblocks and barriers to effective interfirm demand management. Once these barriers are identified and overcome, supply chain performance is enhanced. Morgan (1995) gives an example of how a sales manager provided a materials manager with critical demand information so that the company could dramatically reduce its inventory.

To further enhance joint demand planning and evaluation, many companies now place sales representatives directly at the supply chain partner's location. Through this arrangement, the on-site salesperson is constantly available to share his or her expertise about company products and supply chain processes. The salesperson can offer real-time solutions to various problems that arise. This arrangement allows supply chain partners to share accurate demand information on a real-time basis, information not contained in a Web site or shared database. For example, SC Johnson has sales and supply chain support people working in Wal-Mart's Bentonville corporate headquarters. Similarly, medical supply distributors and their hospital partners have implemented comparable programs with great success (Garver & Mentzer, 2000).

Beyond demand management and demand planning, accurate sales forecasting is essential to effective supply chain management. If forecasts are accurate, then the supply chain partners can maintain the appropriate inventory levels that allow them to meet customer expectations on product availability while eliminating redundant inventory investment. When this occurs, supply chain partners are satisfied at the lowest total supply chain cost. Conversely, when forecasts are inaccurate, supply chain partners either experience stockouts or are forced to carry excess inventory.

Through joint demand planning and evaluation, reinforced by frequent personal contact, salespeople can play a pivotal role in determining the partner's demand requirements, both short and long term. Best-practice companies statistically derive forecasts that are then qualitatively adjusted by salespeople. The emergence of CPFR (Collaborative Planning, Forecasting, and Replenishment) in consumer products supply chains is also an attempt to bring real-time POS forecasts to all supply chain participants (Garver & Mentzer, 2000). However, regardless of the supply chain, the salesperson's knowledge of supply chain partners offers invaluable insight into the forecasting process and supply chain partner's demand requirements.

MUTUAL SHARING OF DEMAND INFORMATION

Sharing accurate demand information on a timely basis, at both tactical and strategic levels, is important to supply chain performance. Much of this information involves not just independent demand but also logistics, operations, integrated processes, and systems issues.

Because salespeople are boundary-spanning agents, they can play a key role in the mutual sharing of this strategic and tactical demand information, up and down the supply chain. Li & Fung offers an excellent example. This Hong Kong–based multinational trading company locks up capacity of weaving and dying suppliers with the promise that they will get an order of a specific size even though product specifications and orders are not currently known (Magretta, 1998b). This is made possible by Li & Fung salespeople working closely with customers to capture market demand and then sharing this demand information with suppliers on a real-time basis. As an added benefit, the open communication has led to high levels of trust between the trading company and its supply chain partners, an essential ingredient in strong supply chain relationships.

One highly effective way of sharing supply chain demand information, of course, is through Web sites and databases. Yet not all information can be shared in this manner. Valuable and complex demand information often is qualitative and cannot be downloaded from the Internet or shared through a database. When supply chain partners need insight or complex demand information, the salesperson may be the one they turn to.

RELATIONSHIP MANAGER

The number one priority for salespeople across all industries is to improve supply chain relationships (Garver & Mentzer, 2000). However, salespeople still remain responsible for sales volume and profit. As relationship managers, salespeople are responsible for ensuring that their companies focus on meeting the needs and requirements of the supply chain partners. This includes partners upstream and downstream, including the customers' customers and the suppliers' suppliers. Once needs and requirements are understood, salespeople can take the lead role in communicating, sharing, and disseminating the demand information to all functional areas within the organization. This helps ensure that internal processes are configured to meet demand requirements. As relationship managers, salespeople are integrators—both internally (synthesizing technological capability to meet market needs) and externally (bringing the customer into the organization to drive the design, development, and adaptation of products, services, and internal processes to meet demand).

Is the Traditional Sales Force Equipped for the Challenge?

Does the traditional sales force possess the expertise to effectively implement and enhance supply chain management performance? Earlier, we discussed supply chain roles for the sales force, such as cooperative behaviors, information sharing, and relationship management. The new roles demand a new set of beliefs, skills, and expertise that differs dramatically from the traditional selling model.

In adapting to this new model, organizations have to address the following issues: How much experience and expertise do our salespeople possess in supply chain management? How much training have salespeople received in this area? How much training have they received in cooperative behavior, demand information sharing, and relationship management? How strategically oriented are they? How much operations expertise do they possess? How do salespeople get to the point where they fit the description of a "great salesperson"? The starting point is a fundamental knowledge of supply chain management.

GAIN SUPPLY CHAIN MANAGEMENT EXPERTISE

Salesperson expertise traditionally has been associated with competencies, skills, knowledge, or experience related to the seller's offering. In today's business environment, however, sales expertise must go well beyond product knowledge to include supply chain management, including the supply chain partner's processes and operations. This expertise needs to go beyond a working knowledge of supply chain management and includes a deep understanding of the activities and issues. Without a clear understanding of these activities, it is difficult for a salesperson to provide unique solutions that create value for the supply chain partner. Importantly, these solutions need to be both tactical and strategic in nature. In the past, salespeople have been far more oriented toward the former than the latter.

	External Expertise	Internal Expertise
Tactical Expertise	Needs and Requirements for • on-time delivery • inventory levels • order processing • order cycle lead times	Short-Term Capabilities: • on-time service rates • fill rates • packaging designs • order processing systems • information systems
Strategic Expertise	Strategic Goals and Objectives • Customer capabilities? • What capabilities does the customer want to develop? • What do they need from a supplier to reach their supply chain goals and objectives? • What type of logistical service does this customer want to deliver to its customers?	Strategic Capabilities: • on-time service rates • fill rates • packaging designs • order processing systems • information systems

Figure 7.4   Salesperson Supply Chain Expertise

Adapted from Garver and Mentzer (2000)

The salesperson's knowledge and expertise must extend across the entire supply chain. This "big-picture" perspective incorporates the following dimensions:

- Internal (company) logistics expertise
- External (supply chain partner) expertise
- Tactical logistics and supply chain expertise
- Strategic logistics and supply chain expertise
- Knowledge of the overall supply chain

Supply chain management expertise allows salespeople to better conduct new supply chain activities and behaviors (Figure 7.4). To conduct supply chain behaviors effectively, salespeople need to have the supply chain expertise to guide these activities and behaviors. Without this expertise, how can the sales force be effective in the supply chain?

Internal Expertise

Salespeople need to fully understand their own company's supply chain processes and systems to add value in the supply chain. Can the salesperson implement, facilitate, and coordinate supply chain tasks efficiently and effectively? In the case of a back order, do they understand their own processes sufficiently to recommend the most effective plan of action for delivering product in a timely manner? Can the salesperson expedite orders in case of an emergency? Can he or she discuss how the company's supply chain capabilities can be leveraged into a tactical or strategic weapon for the customer? Can the salesperson suggest ways to reduce the buyer's supply chain flow cycles (see Chapter 6)? Does he or she understand how the various components of the internal processes work together to deliver value to the customer?

External Expertise

A salesperson that understands the supply chain partners' demand management and service needs can better coordinate company resources to meet and exceed those needs. This requires expertise in acquiring knowledge about supply chain partners, as well as in-depth knowledge of the partner's demand management requirements.

Real expertise means being able to answer the following questions: How do the supply chain partner's operational processes work (a key to the demand planning function of translating independent demand into derived demand)? What is the current state of their supply chain systems? What is the best way to bridge this gap between existing supply chain systems and desired systems? How much inventory does the supply chain partner hold in stock for demand planning reasons? What are their inventory goals and objectives? What is the current state of supply chain operations, and how could they be improved? Where does the partner want to go with their supply chain processes in the future? One large chemical manufacturer stated that its future competitive advantage hinged on how well its salespeople understood the business operations of the supply chain partners (Garver & Mentzer, 2000).

Strategic Supply Chain Management Expertise

Strategic knowledge means the salesperson knows the partner's strategic plans and objectives and the shared goals of the supply chain as a whole. It also means the individual knows how to help supply chain partners reach those strategic objectives by coordinating supplier resources and capabilities. Today's salesperson needs to become a boundary-spanning agent that assists in planning, designing, and implementing strategy as well as tactics. Salespeople need to possess skills and knowledge in strategic thinking, which requires the salesperson to understand the strategic direction of the supply chain and that of supply chain partners.

Tactical Supply Chain Management Expertise

The salesperson needs to understand the short-term, tactical demand planning requirements of supply chain partners. He or she often is called upon to supply information that puts out fires that arise on a daily basis. Many of these are related to demand management: arranging emergency deliveries, expediting orders, substituting available product, or tracking certain invoices.

To develop this tactical capability, salespeople need to fully understand the day-to-day intricacies of the partners' operations. More specifically, they need to know the intricacies of the customer's demand patterns, order cycle, order processing, packaging, inventory policies, and delivery requirements for the various product lines. In case of a stock-out, what does the supply chain partner expect? In case of an emergency, can the salesperson intervene in a timely fashion and recommend specific corrective actions?

Knowledge of the Entire Supply Chain

A holistic view of the supply chain is necessary to fully understand how different pieces of the supply chain work together. Salespeople need to have a big-picture perspective to effectively manage interactions on demand management issues with supply chain partners. Where is the supply chain heading in the future? What are the goals and objectives of the supply chain? What are the strategic plans to reach this destination? How does the supply chain plan to differentiate itself from competing supply chains, now and in the future? How is technology transforming demand information sharing throughout the supply chain? These are the kinds of questions salespeople must address to develop a supply chain–wide perspective.

THE ROLE IS STILL EVOLVING

To effectively perform their new role in this era of supply chain management, salespeople must adopt a whole new approach that incorporates cooperative behaviors, information sharing, and relationship management in supply chain management. Before this can happen, certain inhibitors need to be removed. Among these are the traditional sales force performance evaluations and compensation. Evaluating and rewarding short-term financial performance has told salespeople that these activities, which may be detrimental to long-term goals, are the most important aspect of their jobs. Evaluation and reward practices have shaped traditional selling beliefs and activities, and they must be modified to reward and motivate supply chain behaviors. Companies like Xerox and IBM are taking steps in the right direction by evaluating and compensating their sales forces for how well they meet the needs of their customers (Garver & Mentzer, 2000). While these measures need to include more supply chain relationship behaviors, they are a start in the right direction.

Sales managers also need to enhance and support the supply chain perspective. Sales training programs should be used to educate the sales force on supply chain management practices and reinforce the salesperson's new role in the supply chain. Sales force activities discussed in this chapter could be used as relevant topics. Developing supply chain expertise should be the end goal of such training programs. As they develop this expertise, salespeople should be better equipped to deliver value-added services to the supply chain partners. As the art and science of supply chain management evolves, so will the role of the sales professional. It is crucial that sales management practices keep pace with this evolution of the role of the sales force in demand management and demand planning.

The Sales Force Role in Sales Forecasting

We have extensively discussed the role of the sales force in the derived demand functions of demand management and demand planning, but what is the role of the sales force in forecasting independent demand in the supply chain?

Any sales forecast should be thought of as a best guess about expected levels of customer demand for a company's goods or services, during a particular time horizon, given a set of assumptions about the environment (Mentzer & Bienstock, 1998a). Frequently, historical demand follows patterns, and statistical approaches to forecasting are designed to identify those patterns and then project those patterns into the future. Time series techniques are designed to identify historical demand patterns that repeat with time, whereas regression techniques are designed to identify historical patterns that exist between demand and some other variables. These techniques are extremely helpful and should almost always be an element of a company's sales forecasting process.

But consider the example of a European company that sells very high value weapons systems to governments around the world. While it is certainly possible to track historical sales patterns, both based on time series and other regression variables, such statistical analysis is not particularly useful for this company. The reason for this is that the future seldom looks like the past. For one thing, this company has very few, but very large, customers, who order weapon systems very sporadically. One year, a large customer might order 200 tanks but then not order another tank for 10 years, then order 200 tanks 3 years in a row. Each individual customer has a very large impact on the overall sales forecast for the entire company, but no individual customer follows any time-based patterns. In addition, those variables that might cause changes in demand patterns are themselves nearly impossible to predict. These variables include changes in governments, including events like coups d'état and changing political climates, as occurred in the late 1980s in Eastern Europe. For this company, then, statistical forecasting tools are not very useful. Instead, this company relies heavily on the judgment of its salespeople.

The above example demonstrates the two primary conditions under which it makes sense for a company to ask its salespeople to provide forecasting information. First, salespeople should forecast when they have insights into changing demand patterns at their customers. As mentioned above, quantitative forecasts are based on the assumption that future demand will follow the same patterns as historical demand. When salespeople become aware through their interactions with customers that these historical demand patterns are likely to change in some significant way, they should participate in the forecasting process so that this intelligence can be incorporated into forecasts.

An example is a manufacturer of consumer packaged goods. While such products often do follow predictable historical demand patterns, the sales team responsible for a large retail account became aware that new store openings would be cut dramatically for this particular customer. Because of their close relationship with this large customer, this sales team gained important intelligence that could be shared in their consensus forecasting process, and the resultant forecasts were significantly improved.

The second circumstance that necessitates forecasting participation from the sales force is when salespeople have insights into the probabilities of securing large orders. Many companies have "lumpy" demand patterns that are the result of large orders placed by large customers. Another company is a major supplier to the electronics industry, and their 15 largest global customers make up 70–80% of their global sales volume. In this case, it is critically important that the salespeople share their honest insights concerning the probability of large orders coming from these large customers. Huge forecasting errors could result if one of these large customers were to unexpectedly place a large equipment order, or conversely, if one of these large customers who had been expected to place a large order, suddenly decided to cancel that order. In such a circumstance, the *honest* insights from the sales organization are critical to a company's ability to accurately forecast, and then effectively plan for, these lumpy demand patterns.

It is a common circumstance that salespeople either have insights about changing demand patterns at their accounts, or insights about the probabilities of securing large orders. It is because these circumstances are so common that sales force participation in the forecast process is a key element of achieving SCM Driver Six.

Improving Salespeople's Forecasts

Moon and Mentzer (1999) provide four keys that a company should focus on if it wants to improve the forecasting performance of its sales force: make it part of their jobs; minimize game playing; keep it simple; and keep it focused.

MAKE IT PART OF THEIR JOBS

Salespeople resist forecasting responsibilities. Many salespeople feel it is simply not their job to forecast. A common sentiment is that time spent doing forecasting is time taken away from their "real job," which is calling on customers and selling products and services.

It is critical that sales managers communicate to their frontline salespeople that, in many cases, it is in fact their job to forecast. The job of a salesperson is, as one executive from a chemical company explained, like a three-legged stool. The first leg is building and maintaining relationships with customers. This part of the job is clearly an investment: success at building and maintaining relationships with customers ultimately results in those customers buying more of the company's goods and services. The second leg of the three-legged stool is providing intelligence back to the company about customers, competitors, and the environment. Forecasting is a part of this leg of the stool. The final leg is selling—by knowing the customers—generating revenue and profits by selling the company's goods and services to its customers. Unfortunately, many organizations have not been successful at communicating to their salespeople that providing intelligence back to their company—including forecasting intelligence—*is* part of their job.

There are several steps that a company can take to communicate to salespeople that forecasting is part of their jobs. First, it can make sure that salesperson job descriptions clearly state that monthly sales forecasts are a requirement of the job. This documentation is important, but those words are not particularly meaningful without incentives for high performance in forecasting and consequences for poor performance. It was very typical for salespeople to report that although their managers tell them to spend time and energy forecasting, in fact there are no incentives for good performance. In other words, managers' words are not supported by their actions. Because salespeople are often paid on a variable compensation plan like a commission, they are sometimes reluctant to spend time working on tasks that do not directly lead to outcomes that may be beneficial to the company but for which they are not directly rewarded. Therefore, perhaps more so than others in a company, it is important to place "carrots" in front of salespeople to encourage them to spend the time and energy required to make their forecasts as accurate as they can be. These carrots can consist of monetary rewards, but they can also consist of special recognition. One company awards a special brightly colored ribbon to all salespeople who achieve a predetermined target for forecast accuracy. At the annual sales meeting, being the owner of one of those ribbons is an important source of pride, and this reward clearly drives behavior.

Another way that managers can make forecasting important to salespeople is to provide them with feedback on their own performance, as well as the training that is needed to help them improve that performance. Many salespeople report that although they are asked to forecast monthly, they seldom if ever receive any feedback as to the accuracy of those forecasts. Forecasting management systems have been developed that allow tracking of forecast accuracy down to the level of the individual salesperson, and unless salespeople receive regular reports of those accuracy numbers, they have little incentive to strive for improved accuracy.

A final tool that managers can use to communicate the importance of forecasting to salespeople is training. Training for salespeople should have two different focuses. First, it should help salespeople understand the importance of accurate forecasts throughout the company. Many salespeople report that they do not know what happens to their forecasts after they are completed. In other words, these salespeople do not understand the impact that inaccurate forecasts have on the company's supply chain. Salespeople need to appreciate the effect that poor forecasting has on inventory control, production planning, logistics planning, purchasing, finance, and capacity planning. Second, once salespeople understand why forecasting is so important, they need to be provided with skills training to help them improve their own forecasting efforts. They need to be taught how to approach customers with questions concerning expected future demand patterns, and they need to be taught how to interact with the forecasting systems that are in place to maximize their own performance. Quite simply, when there is no training made available to salespeople on forecasting, the company is inadvertently sending a message that forecasting is not important. And the key here is to communicate in as many ways as possible that for a salesperson, forecasting is *critically important.*

MINIMIZE GAME-PLAYING

At one company, none of the forecasts delivered by the sales organization are believed, but the reason for the lack of credibility varied depending on the time of year. In the first half of the year, all product planners believed that the salespeople would pad their forecasts with "phantom" orders. This was because many of the products sold by this company were capacity constrained, and the salespeople felt that if they overforecast, then when *real* orders came in, there would be enough to go around. In the latter half of the year, the product planners believed that the salespeople would "sandbag" their forecasts, because the salespeople felt that the sales quotas that would be assigned to them for the following year would be based, at least in part, on their sales forecasts. In both instances, creating accurate forecasts was not the prime consideration for the salespeople. They had other objectives, and to achieve those other objectives, salespeople in this company were guilty of "game-playing."

The most common form of game-playing results from salespeople's perceptions that forecasts and quotas are intermingled. This perception can have two opposite effects on salespeople's forecasting behavior. On one hand, salespeople have a tendency to "lowball" forecasts so that future quotas will be attainable. Even if the quota-setting process is not, in fact, influenced by forecasts, salespeople have an incentive to underforecast if it is their *perception* that the two are intertwined. On the other hand, salespeople may have a tendency to be overly optimistic with their forecasts to avoid the reprisals that come from not reaching their targets. At one company, a sales manager made the statement that "It would be suicide for a salesperson to forecast anything less than his or her quota." At this company, salespeople prefer to get in trouble once, at the end of the year when they fail to make their numbers, rather than each month from forecasting that the quota will not be met. In both of these cases, salespeople's game-playing behavior relative to their forecasts results in forecasts that have little credibility throughout the rest of the organization.

There are three actions that management can take to minimize salespeople's game-playing. First, they can make forecasting accuracy an important outcome for salespeople. As discussed in the previous section, if sales volumes are the only measured outcome for salespeople, then their behaviors will focus exclusively on that single outcome. Game-playing is much more likely if there are no repercussions associated with inaccurate forecasts. Therefore, managers can minimize the tendency to game-play by measuring each individual salesperson's forecast accuracy and making valued rewards available for excellence in forecasting, as well as for excellence in generating sales volumes.

The second action that managers can take to disengage forecasting from quotas, and thus minimize game-playing, is to have forecasts and quotas expressed in different units. For example, forecasts are most useful for planning purposes when they are expressed in physical units. Therefore, salespeople should be asked for unit forecasts. Quotas, on the other hand, can be expressed in other units, such as dollars or points. By dealing with different numbers that are expressed in different units, salespeople have less tendency to intermingle forecasts and quotas, and this helps minimize game-playing.

Finally, managers can help salespeople disentangle forecasts from quotas by separating the time horizons. Quotas are most typically assigned either quarterly or annually. Forecasts, on the other hand, should be prepared on some sort of a rolling monthly schedule, such as rolling 24-month, or current-year plus 12 months. These distinct time horizons, similar to distinct units of analysis, help salespeople keep these two processes separate, and minimize game-playing.

KEEP IT SIMPLE

When salespeople are asked to forecast, they tend to do a relatively poor job. Even when salespeople are provided with a history of their customers' demand patterns, they frequently either see patterns that do not exist or fail to see patterns that do exist. However, salespeople's insights and knowledge about their customers can contribute to more accurate forecasts if they are asked to *adjust* statistically generated baseline forecasts. Salespeople truly can contribute value to the forecasting and demand planning processes when they have insights as to how the future will not follow the same patterns as the past. By asking salespeople only to adjust statistically generated forecasts, they are doing what they do well—providing insights about the customer—while avoiding tasks that they do poorly—finding patterns in historical data.

Another way that companies can keep it simple for salespeople is to provide them with adequate tools to allow them to complete their forecasting work as efficiently as possible. One company has implemented a system that takes advantage of the corporate intranet to distribute statistically generated forecasts to each of their more than 300 salespeople worldwide. It is then the responsibility of the salespeople to examine projections that the system has made, make any adjustments that are necessary, and quickly enter their reasons for adjusting the forecast. Although the developers of this system initially met with resistance from sales management, who felt that asking salespeople to provide this type of information would take them away from their "real job," the implementation has proven relatively painless for the salespeople, and the overall forecasting accuracy for this company has improved significantly.

KEEP IT FOCUSED

The final key to improving the effectiveness of salespeople's forecasts is to keep them focused only on those forecasts on which they can make a significant contribution to the company's overall forecasting effectiveness. This focus comes by asking the salespeople to concern themselves only with those combinations of customers and products that are truly important to forecast accurately. In many organizations, the 80/20 rule holds firm, in which 80% of sales is generated by 20% of the customers, as well as 20% of the products. When this concentration of either customers or products exists, salespeople provide the most benefit when they focus their forecasting attention on those customer/product combinations where they can provide real insight and where that insight can significantly affect the company's supply chain.

One company has set as one of its objectives having their sales organization "touch" only 10% of the forecasts that are generated each month. This company has established revenue and inventory cost guidelines that are used to classify products as A, B, or C level products and revenue or "strategic" guidelines which are used similarly to classify customers. Then, each month, the salespeople are only asked to think about and possibly adjust statistically based forecasts of the A level products demanded by their A level customers. For this company, any time spent by salespeople adjusting forecasted demand for less important products by less important customers is not cost-effective. Continual monitoring of both products and customers keeps these "ABC" classifications up to date and ensures that salespeople are using their forecasting time effectively. In addition, by minimizing the number of product/customer combinations the salespeople are asked to work with monthly, the task becomes far less onerous and the salespeople are far less likely to resist.

Salespeople in the Forecasting Process

The first step any company needs to take to implement the keys discussed above is to convince senior sales managers that excellence in sales forecasting is critical to the health and well-being of their company. Without effective sales forecasting, not only will sales managers be unable to develop realistic sales plans for their territories, but the rest of the company will be unable to develop effective demand plans for the supply chain. This will affect customer satisfaction levels and jeopardize supply chain relationships.

Once senior sales managers accept the importance of excellence in sales forecasting, the next step is to convince those same senior managers that this excellence can only be realized when their salespeople become active participants in the process. Forecasting and demand planning are more effective when salespeople are involved. Of course, salespeople should not be the only source of forecasting intelligence, but they are in a unique position to identify changes in customer demand patterns and to assess the probability of securing large orders. Yet companies frequently fail to take advantage of this valuable source of intelligence. By following these guidelines—make it part of their jobs, minimize game-playing, keep it simple, and keep it focused—companies can realize the significant enhancement to their overall demand management effectiveness that can come from tapping into the unique intelligence available from their salespeople.

Company V—Sales Forecasting and Demand Planning: From a top-line perspective, companies cannot take advantage of demand for their products and services if, first, they fail to accurately forecast that demand and, second, they fail to develop and implement appropriate plans to build the required supply chain capacity to fulfill that demand. From a bottom-line perspective, effective customer demand planning allows a company to minimize its supply chain costs by minimizing inventory, purchasing, logistics, and production costs (Kahn & Mentzer, 1996; Moon, Mentzer, & Thomas, 2000).

One large industrial company recognized the leverage available from effective customer demand planning (Company V) and made improvements over several years but still faces challenges in this area. Company V established an organization, as well as a core business process, called "Customer Demand Planning," or CDP. The CDP process is a business planning process enabling sales teams, marketing, and customers to develop product/application demand forecasts as inputs to inventory and production planning, revenue planning, services planning, and supplier planning processes.

Many companies use *forecasting* and *planning* almost interchangeably, but Company V recognizes that they are separate, and sequential, processes. Forecasting is seen at Company V as the process of developing the most probable view of what the level of future independent demand will be, given a set of assumptions about the economy, competitors, pricing, marketing expenditures, and sales efforts. Planning, on the other hand, is seen at Company V as the process of making management commitments that allow the company to efficiently and effectively respond to the demand forecast. Forecasts at Company V precede plans—it is not possible to make a management commitment, for example, to production scheduling or to purchasing and inventory levels (supply chain/business plans), until a forecast is developed that gives a reasonably accurate, most probable view of independent demand over the forecasting horizon.

Company V regards CDP as critically important to its business because of the large number of internal and external stakeholders that must be satisfied by providing accurate, credible forecasts. Following is a list of the various supply chain processes that cannot function effectively without the forecasts that are provided via the CDP process:

- Finished goods inventory planning
- Production requirements planning
- Commitments to external customers and to internal Company V sales teams
- Production reservation scheduling
- Allocation of limited supply products
- Supplier coordination
- Strategic planning gap analysis
- Engineering/installation/distribution planning
- Global product demand forecast data repository
- Allocation of inventory
- Revenue forecasting and planning

The CDP organization at Company V sees itself as an interfunctional process planning and management organization that oversees the collection of data from different organizational functions, such as sales, marketing, operations, and supply chain partners, and then provides information that facilitates effective forecasting and decision making back to other organizational functions, such as logistics, finance, and manufacturing.

The CDP process involves over 2,000 different users from 33 countries. Input is provided by 79 sales teams worldwide, as well as direct sales input by

29 key external customers and 15 marketing organizations. The CDP process supports production planning and scheduling at 20 factories or joint ventures around the world. There are over 16,000 monthly forecasts generated for over 2,000 forecast lines, using a single global schedule, data repository, and set of procedures. Significant CDP system training has been implemented to support this forecasting organization, consisting of 14 tele-training classes as well as traditional classroom and video techniques. In addition, there is significant user support available, including extensive documentation, and a Web site and hotline designed to answer questions and resolve problems.

The CDP forecasting system focuses on forecasts in units, which can then be converted to revenue forecasts using historical average price data. The CDP system directly provides information to the production scheduling systems at Company V's manufacturing sites and to key suppliers' production-scheduling systems.

The CDP system is designed to be user-friendly for those people in the sales organization at Company V who are inputting information into the forecast. There is an emphasis on graphical tools, and the user interface is designed to provide a point and click environment. To provide salespeople with the most recent information to help them forecast, there are year-to-date and the past 3 years' global customer demand history included in the system, and this history is updated weekly. In addition, known future demand, which takes the form of long-term contract business for which there are not yet specific orders, is detailed for 12 months into the future. Also, order-level information is available for the previous 3 months and for all future committed orders. The system also provides the capability for sales teams to enter subjective information, such as forecast risk and significant upside or downside variables.

While the CDP system is very well engineered, it did not just happen. Accuracy measures were not originally at a level that the company felt was acceptable, and this led Company V to undertake a sales forecasting audit in a continuous improvement effort to evolve the CDP process.

The Sales Forecasting Audit

Company V management came to the realization that forecast accuracy was at unacceptably low levels. Management had established overall targets of 75–85% accuracy across all major product lines and businesses, yet accuracy numbers were consistently in the 60% range. In addition to this, there was a major internal operations reengineering program under way, which created an environment that was conducive to changing a number of key business processes. Finally, management changes took place that resulted in new executive ownership of the forecasting process. In combination, these factors created an atmosphere in which a comprehensive audit of the entire forecasting process could be supported across different levels of the organization.

To help identify opportunities for improvement, a team of academic experts who had performed similar audits for over forty companies (Mentzer & Moon, 2003; Moon, Mentzer, & Smith, 2003) was commissioned to perform this audit. This choice was critical for two reasons. First, because the audit team was not a part of Company V, those involved in forecasting could honestly report their problems and concerns without fear of retribution. Second, because the audit team brought with them more than 3 decades of experience in sales forecasting and the perspective of the other companies they had audited, new ideas and approaches that might have been outside the normal thought processes at Company V could be considered.

The process for conducting the forecast audit at Company V began with a 2-day meeting between the audit team and representatives from the Company V CDP organization. At this orientation meeting, the audit team was given a detailed description of how the current forecasting systems and processes were intended to work. Detailed documentation of the CDP process was provided to the team for analysis and evaluation. Over the next month, 21 teleconference interview sessions took place with 64 different process stakeholders. Effort was made to include a wide range of individuals from different organizations in this data collection process. The audit team interviewed personnel who were forecast process owners; who contributed input to the forecasts, such as sales and marketing personnel; and who were users, or customers, of the forecasts, such as manufacturing and logistics personnel. It was truly a global data collection effort with personnel from China, Europe, India, Japan, and the United States included in the interviews. For each interview, two members from the audit team were present to facilitate inter-rater reliability. All interviews were audio taped to allow for clarification and to resolve disagreements at the time of data analysis. Following collection of the data, the audit team met to reach agreement on how Company V compared with other companies in their database and to develop a set of recommendations that would help Company V improve.

The findings from the audit could be summarized into four major themes. First, the audit team found significant "islands of analysis" at Company V. These islands of analysis can be thought of as separate information systems and processes that are not interconnected, either physically, electronically, or conceptually. Second, it was found that performance was not adequately measured and, as a result, there was a lack of performance evaluation. In other words, there were no rewards for anyone at Company V for doing a good job of forecasting, nor were there any negative consequences for poor performance. Third, the forecasting process, which on the surface appeared to be quite rigorous, was, in fact, based almost entirely on qualitative, or judgment-based, techniques. There was minimal use of statistical tools to uncover patterns of historical demand and project those patterns into the future. Finally, the audit team determined that there was a limited commitment to sales forecasting as a business function. This limited commitment was manifested in a number of ways, including lack of training for those who provided inputs to forecasts, limited financial commitment to system resources, inadequate policy directives that could provide uniform guidance to forecasters worldwide, and limited use of performance metrics along with insufficient opportunities for reward and recognition for forecasting excellence.

In terms of specific recommendations, the audit team presented Company V with four major categories of recommendations:

1. *Training.* While members of the forecasting group at Company V were adequately trained in how to manage Company V's CDP system, there was inadequate training in the role of forecasting in the organization as well as the opportunities to employ statistical analyses to improve forecasting accuracy. In addition, the sales teams at Company V provided the bulk of forecast input, and although those individuals had received training on how to interact with the system, they had received no training in how to forecast. The audit team recommended enhanced training programs to address both these deficiencies.

2. *Reward and Recognition.* The audit team recommended that Company V institute a program of rewards and recognition that would be directly linked to forecast performance. It was recommended that this program go beyond the forecasting group and include members of the sales organization, whose input was so critical to the process. The audit team pointed out that this reward and recognition program needed to be significant—there needed to be enough at stake that forecasting would "get on people's radar screens." Compensation is an ideal way to reward forecasting excellence, but there were also opportunities to employ recognition events and programs as a way to get people to pay attention to this critical process.

3. *Metrics.* It was pointed out in the audit that Company V did not have adequate performance metrics in place, which is clearly a critical requirement of a reward and recognition program. Unless performance can be measured, it cannot be adequately recognized and rewarded. The audit team emphasized in their report that the contribution of every individual who interacts with the forecast must be measured and that feedback mechanisms must be put into place so that all those individuals know whether their contributions to the forecast have been positive or negative.

4. *Process.* The audit team recommended that Company V put into place a knowledgeable core group that would use statistical tools such as time series and regression models to develop an initial forecast view. These initial statistical forecasts could then be distributed to those knowledgeable individuals, such as marketing directors and sales teams, for their adjustment. It was recommended

that this core group have enough clout and visibility to be able to truly influence the forecasting behaviors of others in the organization.

IMPLEMENTATION OF THE AUDIT RECOMMENDATIONS

Within each of the four broad areas of recommendations outlined above, Company V had some successes and some challenges. Following is a progress report on how Company V dealt with each of the recommended changes, approximately 14 months after the audit recommendations were delivered.

TRAINING

Following the recommendation given by the audit team, Company V significantly enhanced the training opportunities available to its employees. Of most interest was a series of training videos that were aimed specifically at the sales teams located around the world. These videos were designed to give salespeople an appreciation of the importance of forecasting in the effective operation of the business, as well as skills in how to adjust statistical forecasts, given their knowledge of current market and customer conditions. Several hundred copies of these tapes were distributed, and the videos were also made available for viewing over Company V's intranet.

REWARD AND RECOGNITION

This proved to be the area of most challenge to Company V. The management of the forecasting group has not been fully successful in convincing upper management that salary or other compensation should be linked to forecasting performance. The message that has been delivered to forecasting management is that such linkages are inconsistent with corporate compensation directions. In spite of this, some progress has been made to develop broad recognition programs, which have had some success at getting the attention of members of the sales organization.

METRICS

The audit team's report and recommendations were successful at giving impetus to more widespread use of accuracy metrics. Soon after the completion of the audit, an extensive software enhancement was completed that allowed calculation of these metrics in a multitude of ways, including by individual forecaster. Thus, because these metrics are now available, the forecasting group has the tools in place to be able to implement the reward and recognition programs discussed above.

PROCESS

As for organizational changes, it is often the case in large, global organizations that changes in executive leadership and corporate reorganizations come frequently, and these can have an impact on the speed with which process change takes place. This occurred at Company V, and as a result of such leadership changes and reorganizations, some of the organizational process recommendations were implemented and some have yet to be addressed. For example, Company V implemented an extension of the CDP process that supports capacity planning by the engineering, provisioning, and installation resource units within the company. This was the first time that resources across the company were planned from a common baseline. This process also established the capability to monitor the monthly most-probable-forecast view against the budget as the year progressed. However, Company V is still struggling to properly engage its various marketing organizations, and some supply chain partners, in the forecasting and demand planning process. This has proven difficult in part because of frequent internal restructuring, as well as the independence given to each of its business groups.

RESULTS

Even with the challenges to implement the recommended changes, Company V achieved some significant improvement following the sales forecast audit. Specifically, forecast accuracy in the upper 50% to lower 60% range prior to the audit increased to consistently in the 80–85% range. In addition, there has been broad-based improvement across the various sales teams. Before the audit, a forecasting package had been implemented that allowed the final forecast to be a combination of quantitative and qualitative techniques, but there was wide variance from one sales team to another in terms of the quality of their qualitative forecasts. After the audit, that variance was reduced, and accuracy improved across the board. Significantly, Company V met its on-time customer delivery objectives, met its sales growth objectives, and brought inventory levels under control. Each of these corporate accomplishments points directly to improved forecasting and demand planning performance as an important contributor.

What We Should Learn From Company V

The experience of going through a sales forecasting audit was extremely beneficial for Company V. Considerable effort went into development of the CDP processes and procedures prior to the audit, but the CDP team was receptive to learning from the audit that forecasting practices at Company V had room for improvement. There was tremendous value in obtaining the insights from experts who had not "grown up" in the Company V environment and who were not influenced by previous experience with the CDP process. These insights provided the company the opportunity to rethink fundamental process design and deployment. The audit also provided a platform for affecting organizational change, and a framework for continuous improvement.

One of the most important insights from Company V is that companies must be prepared to confront clashes with corporate culture and entrenched ways of doing business to improve the demand planning process. Because of these inevitable conflicts, change agents must above all else be patient and tenacious. It will not always be possible, for various cultural or political reasons, to immediately accomplish everything that should be accomplished in order to become world-class in forecasting and demand planning. Instead, it is important to win small victories and demonstrate success—thereby building the momentum that may be needed to make more substantive changes. This is the road of continuous process improvement.

Discussion of other things learned from Company V can be organized around the four focus areas that emerged from the audit: training, reward/recognition, metrics, and process. First, in terms of training, the experience at Company V reinforced the importance of extending forecasting training beyond the forecasting department. Because they rely heavily on the input from their sales organization, Company V felt that it was necessary to deliver forecasting training to its sales teams, operations and marketing personnel, and key supply chain partners. Every company should identify those individuals whose input is critical to sales forecast accuracy, and then develop and deliver training programs that help those individuals understand both *how* to forecast and *why* it is so important to the demand planning process of the organization and the supply chain that forecasts be accurate.

Second, on the subject of rewards and recognition, Company V discovered that this area was the most difficult to address. Although there was no disagreement at Company V with the axiom "What gets measured gets rewarded and what gets rewarded gets done" (Mentzer & Bienstock, 1998a), changing the way that people are compensated may have been the most politically charged issue they faced. While it may be politically charged, there is no better way to influence people's behavior relative to the forecasting and demand planning processes than through a well-designed reward and recognition program for forecasting and demand planning excellence.

Third, in terms of metrics, an important learning that emerged from the audit process at Company V was that individual behavior cannot be influenced unless a process is in place to measure individual contribution to forecast accuracy and demand planning. These metrics should capture how accurate the forecast would have been *without* an individual's contribution, and how accurate the forecast was *with* that individual's contribution. Such measures are not only important to enable the reward/recognition efforts discussed above; they are also important in deciding whether or not an individual *should* provide input to a particular forecast.

In terms of process, Company V learned that obtaining perspectives from multiple sources makes forecasts better. For example, they learned that asking salespeople to forecast at the customer level, over a relatively short time horizon, made forecasts more accurate. They also learned that asking marketing people to forecast at the product line level over longer time horizons made the forecast better. In other words, people who have insights about future demand patterns should be asked to provide input to forecasts, but only at the level and time horizon at which they normally operate.

Finally, we learn from Company V that all companies can enhance forecast accuracy if they use a combination of quantitative (statistical) techniques to find patterns in historical demand, along with qualitative (judgment) techniques to adjust those statistical forecasts.

In summary, the forecast audit process at Company V was successful in two critical ways. First, after implementing a number of the recommendations that emerged from the audit, Company V improved their forecast accuracy dramatically. This improvement led to reductions in operations and marketing costs and improved levels of customer service. Second, the audit provided Company V with a framework for continuous improvement of their demand planning processes. Although this continuous improvement process is always challenging and occasionally painful, the rewards have been clearly worth the cost.

A final question, after studying Company V, should be, "Are there broader conclusions we can learn from the audits of numerous companies, beyond what we learn from Company V?"

What We Should Learn From the Audit Database: The audit process involves three stages: the "as-is" state, the "should-be" state, and the "way forward."

1. The As-Is State

Assessment of the company's sales forecasting and demand planning processes as they are at the time of the audit involves the dimensions of sales forecasting management and strategic themes. The four dimensions of sales forecasting management articulated in Mentzer, Bienstock, and Kahn (1999) are a useful diagnostic and prescriptive framework to define both the as-is and the should-be states:

1. *Functional integration* is concerned with the role of collaboration, communication, and coordination of the sales forecasting function with the other business functional areas of marketing, sales, finance, production, and logistics.

2. *Approach* is concerned with which products and services are forecast, the forecasting techniques used, and the relationship between forecasting and planning.

3. *Systems* addresses the evaluation and selection of hardware and software combinations to support the sales forecasting and demand planning functions, as well as the integration of forecasting systems with other planning and management systems in the organization.

4. *Performance measurement* considers the metrics used to measure sales forecasting and demand management effectiveness and its impact on business operations.

Moon et al. (2003) reported several strategic themes that emerged from auditing the demand planning processes of a number of companies. These strategic themes are issues that cut across multiple dimensions of demand management and which are so pervasive or which cause such wide-ranging problems that they demand special attention and discussion.

Blurred Distinction Between Forecasts, Plans, and Goals

Forecasts are a projection into the future of expected demand, given a stated set of environmental conditions, whereas plans are managerial actions proposed by the organization to capture and supply as much of the forecasted demand as possible (Mentzer & Bienstock, 1998a). Evidence of this theme can be found in these actual statements from audits: "We forecast up to plan," or "It would be suicide for me to forecast anything different than the plan." Such statements indicate these organizations are creating forecasts based upon plans or sales targets, rather than their best judgments about future customer independent demand and supply chain derived demand.

Limited Commitment to Sales Forecasting and Demand Planning

This theme manifests itself in a number of different situations, including insufficient commitment of resources to training, documentation, systems support, or reward and recognition programs; relegating the sales forecasting and demand-planning functions to relatively low levels in the organizational hierarchy; unwillingness to designate a forecasting champion; and lack of accountability throughout the organization for forecast accuracy. At one company, this theme was manifested by the failure to fill an open director-level forecasting position for over a year. Because of this lack of leadership, the company's forecasting and demand-planning improvement efforts were unfocused and unsupported by other constituent organizations in the company (a violation of SCM Driver One).

Islands of Analysis

This is the situation in which a company has nonstandard, noninterfacing systems or procedures for performing similar tasks, or forecasting and demand-planning systems that fail to connect with other enterprise systems like production planning or finance. These "islands" can range from each forecasting analyst having his or her own homemade spreadsheet with unique characteristics and assumptions, to separate forecasting systems installed and operating in different departments of the company, to the manual transfer of data either into or out of a forecasting system. An extreme example of this phenomenon occurred at one audited company where three separate forecasting systems had been installed over time: a mainframe-based legacy system, which was the "official" forecasting system, an AS/400-based system installed by production planning, and a PC-based system installed by logistics. These latter two were described as "black market" forecasting systems, and were installed because the forecast user organizations did not trust the "official" forecast and so created their own forecasting systems.

From these two sources (dimensions and strategic themes), the portrayal of the audited company's "as-is" state of forecasting management practices is complete. The second stage of the audit process is the description of the "should-be" state of sales forecasting management practices for the company.

2. The "Should-Be" State

Although understanding the current status of sales forecasting management (the "as-is" state) is important, managers cannot take steps toward excellence without guidance on the directions to take. For this reason, it is important to provide a clear picture of the "should-be" state of forecasting management in the company. The "should-be" state is a return on investment decision that analyzes the cost (investment) to improve sales forecasting and demand management processes, and the bottom line impacts (returns) of these improvements (for more on this analysis process, see the shareholder value section later in this chapter).

3. The "Way Forward"

Any audit process should provide the audited company with a "way-forward" roadmap through a series of concrete recommendations. Although the recommendations are unique for each company, based on the current status of their forecasting and demand management practices, these recommendations usually fall into four categories.

Process recommendations refer to the way forecasts are created and used. For one company, process recommendations included instituting a consensus forecasting process, where different people from different parts of the company work together in a forum characterized by open information sharing to create a consensus forecast. On the other hand, for another company's forecasting practices, statistical tools were not used effectively to uncover patterns in historical demand data. Thus, the process recommendations included implementation of a process where baseline forecasts are generated statistically and then distributed to knowledgeable experts, such as sales or marketing people, for adjustment.

Training recommendations refer to specific situations where company personnel who are involved in forecasting have inadequate skills or knowledge to perform their forecasting tasks effectively. For example, salespeople are usually in a position to provide forecasting intelligence, but in few companies do salespeople have any training on why forecasting is important (functional integration), or how to make qualitative adjustments to baseline forecasts (approach). Similarly and surprisingly, in many companies the people in the forecasting group receive no training on how time series and regression analysis can be used to create baseline forecasts (approach).

System recommendations refer to the way computer and communication systems can be enhanced to develop and communicate forecasting information more effectively. In one company, sales forecasting and demand planning systems were not integrated with other corporate systems, in this case finance and materials requirements planning (MRP) systems, resulting in manual transfers of data. Therefore, the system recommendations included creating electronic linkages that allow data transfers between systems. Also, in several companies where islands of analysis exist, characterized by multiple processes or systems performing similar tasks, system recommendations include specific procedures designed to eliminate such islands and standardize on a single set of sales forecasting and demand planning processes.

Finally, *performance measurement recommendations* refer to specific metrics that should be put in place to measure forecasting performance adequately. For example, in many companies the salespeople are asked to make adjustments to baseline forecasts, but the accuracy of those adjustments are not measured and communicated back to the salespeople. Similarly, in many companies, accuracy is the only sales forecasting metric used. Thus, other metrics designed to assess the impact of forecasting accuracy on overall supply chain costs and customer service are needed.

Moon et al. (2003) note considerable variance in management responses to audit recommendations. Management reaction typically falls into one of three categories: "address the problems," "assign the blame," or "why should I care?" Companies that fall under the address-the-problems category tend to have an organizational culture oriented toward solutions, regardless of which department is "to blame." Companies in this category also tend to recognize that responsibility for complex organizational problems is usually shared across functions and thus look for cross-functional solutions.

Companies in the assign-the-blame category tend to have an organizational culture oriented toward identifying the source of organizational problems, and when that source is identified, that department becomes responsible for solutions. Since forecasting problems tend to be cross-functional, it is usually impossible to identify a single source of forecasting problems. Thus, companies in this category tend to bog down in assigning blame rather than in pursuing solutions.

Companies in the why-should-I-care? category tend to view forecasting as an unimportant activity. In these companies, there is no understanding at the senior management level of how sales forecasting and demand planning improvements can dramatically enhance the company's key performance indicators.

One company in particular provides an excellent example of the address-the-problems response. This organization, which was in stage one on all four dimensions of sales forecasting management audit dimensions (Mentzer et al., 1999), responded by assigning a cross-functional project team first to perform a detailed review of the recommendations, and then to propose a prioritization scheme, followed by an action plan. Three months after the conclusion of the audit, this project team met with the audit team to review their proposed priorities and action plan, and this was followed by a 2-year-long effort to reengineer their approach to sales forecasting. As a result of that reengineering effort, this company now approaches stage four on all four dimensions of sales forecasting and demand management, and their supply chain costs have been reduced dramatically. In fact, the company estimates their entire implementation effort cost less than $1 million, but the savings in raw material purchasing costs alone (buying more on long-term contracts based on accurate forecasts and less at the last minute on the spot market) during 1998 were in excess of $7 million. Thus, the return on investment from implementation has been considerable. It is important to note that this $7 million saving was seen by upper management as an accomplishment by all departments involved in the forecasting effort, not just purchasing.

Another company provides an example of the assign-the-blame response. At this organization, which was primarily at stages two and three on two of the dimensions and stage one on the other two dimensions, the auditors' final presentation to senior management degenerated into a heated discussion between executives over which department was at fault for the problems identified by the audit team. Although these executives agreed that problems existed, none were willing to acknowledge that performance improvements were needed in their individual departments. As a result, no consensus could be reached on how to effect change, and no reengineering effort was carried out. Over the next 18 months, this company experienced considerable supply chain disruption and customer service problems due to an inability to forecast demand hitting their supply chain.

Finally, at an audited company that exhibited the why-should-I-care? response, during the question and answer portion of the final presentation to senior management, the executive vice president of marketing rose from his chair and stated that all the company really needed was a new "killer product," and with such a new product, all this attention to forecasting improvement would not be necessary. At another company, the CEO spent the time during the final presentation to management doing other work and gazing absently around the conference room. At a third company, the audit team was told that because they had moved to a "just-in-time" (JIT) environment, forecasting was no longer important (an unrealistic answer, since JIT systems depend upon either stable or accurately forecast demand). None of these companies, to date, has made any changes in sales forecasting and demand management and, thus, none has realized any of the supply chain cost savings and customer service benefits achieved at the other companies.

Schultz (1984) cites the presence of top management support as the top-ranked predictor of implementation success and lack of top management support as the top-ranked predictor of implementation failure. In the examples cited above, top management support was clearly present in the address-the-problems response profile, and top management support was clearly lacking in the assign-the-blame and why-should-I-care? responses. Obtaining such top management support is one of the key contributions from a forecasting champion (Mentzer, Moon, Kent, & Smith, 1997). Consistent with Schultz, one conclusion from the auditing research is that the existence of a sales forecasting champion, along with the top management support for forecasting improvement such an individual can obtain, is critical to long-term organizational success in sales forecasting management.

The Impact of Sales Forecasting and Demand Planning on Shareholder Value

No company was ever successful simply from more accurate sales forecasting (Mentzer, 1999). Unless these more accurate forecasts can be translated into higher levels of customer service and lower supply chain costs, the impact of improved forecasting accuracy is lost on corporate profitability. By the same token, "C-level" executives (CEO, COO, CFO, etc.) are not interested in investing corporate dollars to improve forecasting performance unless it can be translated into higher returns for the shareholders. After all, return on shareholder value is the primary concern of upper management. Although improved forecasting accuracy often has a profound impact upon corporate profit and shareholder value, it is seldom presented as such to upper management.

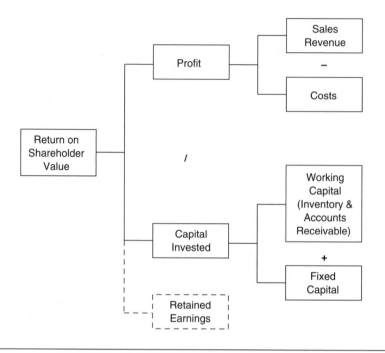

Figure 7.5   Impact of Forecasting Improvements on Shareholder Value

Adapted from Mentzer (1999)

Given this reality of business management, what is the most effective way to demonstrate the impact of improved demand forecasting performance? The answer lies in the translation of forecasting accuracy into improved operational plans and execution and improved service to customers. The former results in lower costs per dollar of sales, and the latter results in increased sales.

A MODEL OF RETURN ON SHAREHOLDER VALUE

The improvement in shareholder value resulting from improvement in forecasting accuracy can be visualized with the help of the "du Pont model" of financial performance. The du Pont model is a framework for viewing the impact of changes in sales, capital, and operating expenses on return on net assets. A slight revision in this model gives us a return on shareholder value model (see Figure 7.5). In this model, we start with sales revenue and subtract from it all the costs of doing business. Notice this is not a gross margin calculation, where only the costs of goods sold are subtracted from sales revenue, but rather all costs (fixed and variable) are subtracted to give us the profitability of the business unit.

In the lower right part of the model, we examine the total investment by shareholders in capital, both working (primarily accounts receivable and inventory) and fixed. Ordinarily, to this is added retained earnings of the company to arrive at shareholder value. However, retained earnings are a financial decision made by the board of directors and the shareholders to leave money not invested in capital in the company or take it out. Further, since we are solely concerned here with the impact of operations decisions on shareholder value, retained earnings is irrelevant and, thus, left out of the decision model in Figure 7.5.

Dividing profit by shareholder value (capital investment) gives us a return on shareholder value, or the percentage of capital invested that is returned in the form of profits each year. This is a primary factor for any decision made by chief executive officers, chief operating officers, chief financial officers, and, in fact, any executive in the business unit.

AN ACTUAL EXAMPLE

Figure 7.6 illustrates an actual example of how improved forecasting performance affects shareholder value. Although the numbers have been slightly altered to protect the identity of the example company, this company originally had sales revenue of $2 billion and total costs of $1.9 billion (annual profit of $100 million), on a working capital base of $200 million. The fixed capital base (consisting primarily of plant and equipment and three distribution centers) was $500 million. This resulted in a return on shareholder value (RSV) each year of 14.29%.

Based on a sales forecasting audit, a number of areas for potential improvement were discovered. As a result, management authorized a series of actions to implement recommended improvements to these processes, actions that included a new sales forecasting package to provide a more accurate base forecast; a revised process that included greater input from marketing, sales, and operations to the base forecast to arrive at a final revised forecast; a computer and communications system to augment this process; and a new performance evaluation system to measure and reward everyone involved in the forecasting process who improved forecasting accuracy or who used those improved forecasts to lower supply chain costs and/or improve customer service.

From the start of this effort, upper management insisted upon dollar measures of the impact of these more accurate forecasts upon lower operations costs and increased sales from improved customer service. It was quickly realized that the latter of these two could not be fully and accurately measured, so the company settled for documenting only when the more accurate forecasts led to improvements in inventory available to meet customer demand—in other words, when sales were made because the inventory was available, as opposed to a lost sale due to stockouts.

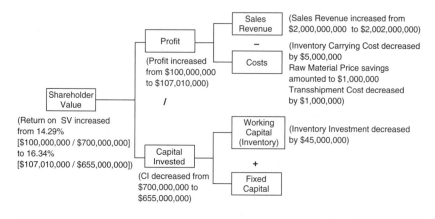

Figure 7.6   An Example of Impact of Forecasting Improvements on Shareholder Value

Adapted from Mentzer (1999)

The results of this documentation are illustrated in Figure 7.6. Increased sales as a result of improved in-stock situations were $2 million, while the operating costs of meeting total demand decreased by $7 million, resulting in increased profit of $7.01 million.

The operating cost savings fell into three main categories. First, more accurate forecasts led to a reduction in the amount of inventory held by the company to meet uncertain demand variations (safety stock) in the amount of $45 million (also note that the reduction in inventory resulted in lower working capital). This resulted in savings in the cost of money on those invested funds, lower risk costs on the inventory (obsolescence, shrinkage, and insurance), and lower facility costs. The total of these three cost components is typically referred to as "inventory carrying cost," which was reduced $5 million per year.

Second, more accurate forecasts led the company to buy more of their required raw materials on long-term contract from supply chain partners rather than on the spot market. The reduction in price between these two methods of procurement led to a $1 million annual savings.

Finally, the company often faced the situation of producing a certain product and shipping it to their East Coast distribution center to meet anticipated demand, only to find the demand was lower than forecast on the east coast and higher than forecast on the West Coast. As a result, some of the inventory of that product that had already been shipped from the production facility (located in the Midwest) to the East Coast distribution center would have to be moved (transshipped) to the West Coast distribution center.

Improved forecasting accuracy by product and by distribution center lowered the incidence of this scenario and its accompanying costs in the amount of $1 million a year.

Although fixed capital was negligibly affected by these changes, working capital (money invested in inventory) decreased by $45 million. This resulted in a decrease in capital invested in the company by the shareholders of $45 million. As we mentioned, whether this $45 million is paid out to the shareholders as a dividend or kept in retained earnings for future investments is irrelevant to the financial impact being evaluated here.

The result of all these changes in forecasting performance was improvement in profit by $7.01 million each year, the capital investment base went down by $45 million, and return on shareholder value increased from 14.29% to 16.34%. The total cost of all the improvements in sales forecasting management was approximately $1.65 million—for a return on investment result of 7.01 million/1.65 million, or 425%! All this clearly shows that improvement in forecasting accuracy can have a dramatic effect on corporate profitability and shareholder value.

LESSONS LEARNED

The most important lesson learned from this example is that we should estimate the potential impact on RSV *prior to* making investments in sales forecasting and demand planning improvements. We make a serious mistake in sales forecasting and demand management when we go to upper management with a proposal to spend money to improve forecasting accuracy without indicating what *impact* it will have on revenues, on supply chain costs, and, subsequently, on shareholders.

To properly document the impact of improved sales forecasting performance, forecasting managers must answer the following questions:

1. What will be the total investment in all improvements to the sales forecasting and demand planning processes (packages, systems, staffing, training, performance rewards)?

2. What will be the estimated improvement in forecasting accuracy?

3. To what degree will this improved accuracy reduce the incidence of stockouts? In which products? By how much?

4. To what degree will this improved accuracy reduce inventory levels? What is the total dollar investment in this inventory that will be reduced? What is the cost of money for this investment? How much are the risk costs pertaining to obsolescence, shrinkage, and insurance reduced because of reductions in inventory? How much are facility costs related to receiving, handling, and shipping reduced because of reductions in inventory?

5. How much savings in production (overtime, expedited operations, etc.—see the upcoming example of Company W) will result from more accurate forecasts?

6. How much procurement savings will result from more accurate forecasts?

7. How much saving in transshipments will result from more accurate forecasts?

Answering these questions provides the information needed to prepare a proposal similar to Figure 7.6, a proposal that touches the heart of C-level decision makers.

In conclusion, it is important to remember that there is nothing wrong with projecting improvements in accuracy, but without carrying this to the final step—the ultimate impact on shareholder value—we are not providing upper management with the information necessary to make informed business decisions about improvements in sales forecasting and demand management.

Company W—Separating Sales Forecasting From Demand Planning

Company W thought they had a forecasting problem. Many of their products were "slow movers, with spikes." This is that daunting forecasting problem where 4 units sell one week, 3 the next, 5 the next, 10,000 the next, 3 the next, 6 the next, 20,000 the next, 1 the next, and so on. The spikes are seemingly unforecastable (come in different size spikes, at irregular times, not related to promotional events) and cause huge supply chain disruptions (expedited production and overtime or excessive inventory to meet the order, disruption to supplier operations resulting in higher procurement costs, or outsourcing the large orders resulting in lost margins).

Company W is a manufacturer of numerous lighting products, but one of their slow movers with spikes is called a ballast. Ballasts are little transformers that take electrical energy and convert it into an energy beam that passes through a fluorescent bulb. When this energy beam passes through the fluorescent bulb, the paint on the inside of the bulb begins to glow and gives off light. This is how fluorescent bulbs work, and without the ballast, they do not work.

So let's look at how the supply chain for ballasts works. An individual comes home from work after an arduous day (probably trying to manage a supply chain), turns on the kitchen light, and the fluorescent bulb does not come on. This individual changes the bulb and finds it still does not work. Being a do-it-yourselfer, this individual knows there can only be one of two reasons for this—either there is a short circuit, or the ballast is out. Checking the circuit breaker, our do-it-yourselfer determines there is nothing wrong with the circuit, gets a screwdriver, removes the ballast, goes to the local home supply store, and says to the person at the counter, "Give me one of these." We now have our slow mover that sells one at a time as a replacement for ballasts already in use as they wear out (part of the independent demand in this supply chain). As this independent demand affects the ordering policies of the various home supply stores in the Company W supply chain, we get the fairly smooth, slow-moving component of derived demand that Company W experiences.

However, there is another source of independent demand for ballasts. The owners of a large office building decide to retrofit all the ballasts in their building. This is a return-on-investment (ROI) decision because old ballasts use more electricity to light the fluorescent bulb than a new ballast would (at some point, the cost of replacing the ballasts can be justified on the basis of the savings in electric bills). The office building in question has—you guessed it—10,000 ballasts that need replacing. When the building owner decides to retrofit the ballasts in the building (generally in connection with some other renovations), bids are solicited from several electrical contractors, and one is chosen to do the job. The winner of the contract then works with the other contractors involved in the renovation to decide when to start the ballast retrofitting part of the overall project, usually weeks if not months in the future.

Unfortunately, traditionally in this supply chain the electrical contractor does not tell Company W about the independent demand for ballasts until the week before they are needed. Since it typically takes Company W 3 weeks to fill an order of this size, all the supply chain costs mentioned above (expedited production costs, costs of higher inventory levels, spot market procurement costs, outsourcing production to higher-cost alternatives) associated with expediting a large order occur, and Company W makes far less (if any) money on this large order.

By recognizing that the demand affecting Company W was derived demand (derived from the contractor's ordering policies), not independent demand, Company W shifted its emphasis from forecasting the spikes in independent demand to demand planning for the derived demand. The result was a new demand planning policy in this supply chain—Company W now offers contractors a 3% price discount on any orders in excess of 10,000 that are placed with Company W 5 or more weeks before they are needed. This is a considerable savings for the contractors (3% off an order of 10,000 units, each of which typically costs in excess of $20!), and resulted in increased sales for Company W.

More important, however, Company W turned the unplanned large spikes hitting their operations systems into demand that could be planned weeks before needed. Under the new demand planning system, Company W knows about spikes (that take 3 weeks to fill) 5 weeks in advance. This means instead of expedited production, overtime, higher procurement costs, and unwanted, expensive outsourcing of production, Company W can actually produce the products to fill the order anytime during the 5-week window, usually in slack production times. This smoothing out of their production scheduling system saves Company W millions of dollars every year, all with increased market share among the contractors. This would not have been possible without the realization that the demand Company W was trying to forecast was actually derived demand that could be planned.

Summary and an Exercise

Many companies have recognized how the various supply chain aspects discussed here can have a profound impact on their sales forecasting and demand planning practices. As these companies have improved their sales forecasting and demand planning practices, they have experienced reductions in supply chain costs and increases in customer and employee satisfaction. The reductions in supply chain costs accrue from reduced inventory levels; lower raw material costs; and lower production, logistics, and transportation costs. Increases in customer satisfaction accrue from more accurately anticipating and planning demand and, subsequently, more often fulfilling that demand. Increased employee satisfaction comes from a more understandable process, easier information access and transfer, and clear rewards tied to performance. But the first step that any company must take before realizing these benefits is to recognize the importance of sales forecasting and demand planning as management functions. With this recognition comes a willingness to commit the necessary resources to improve this critical process.

As a first step to accomplish this, we encourage readers to answer the questions in Figure 7.7. The first question is an assessment of the independent and derived demand in your supply chains. Remember that the goal of supply chain management is to develop sales forecasts of the independent demand and share those forecasts with supply chain partners (along with inventory levels and ordering policies, the second question in Figure 7.7) to derive demand

> What is the source of your company's independent demand?
>
> What demand planning information does your company
>
> receive from supply chain partners?
>
> What does your company forecast?

Figure 7.7   Demand Management Exercise

plans. The answer to the third question is often a revelation for supply chain managers—they often discover they are forecasting the demand that is derived from their supply chain partners when this demand can be planned (with the information from the second question) and does not require forecasting. Recognizing this and separating forecasting of independent demand from planning for derived demand (SCM Driver Six) can profoundly affect the competitive advantage of the supply chain.

8

Substitute Information for Assets

Think back 15 years. How many of you had a cell phone? A fax machine in your home? An e-mail account? EDI in your company? A wireless personal computer? Information technology is changing at an incredible rate of speed. The cost of obtaining that information is also getting cheaper and cheaper. At the same time, the costs of the assets to run a supply chain are not decreasing rapidly. The cost of inventory, plants, equipment, people, and storage facilities, to name a few, is not getting cheaper. Thus, the key to SCM Driver Seven is how to use increasingly available and inexpensive information and information technology to reduce investment in other, more expensive supply chain assets.

A key aspect of supply chain management is the ability to make strategic decisions quickly, based on accurate information. Every supply chain has an information chain that parallels the flow of product (Andel, 1997). Information is vital for a supply chain to function. Without information relayed at the right time to the right place, there are no purchase orders, no shipment messages, no payments, no coordinated marketing and sales efforts, and the supply chain shuts down (Zuckerman, 1998). SCM is based on the exchange of substantial quantities of information among buyers, suppliers, and carriers to increase the efficiency and effectiveness of the supply chain (Carter, Ferrin, & Carter, 1995). At the ultimate level of information integration, all member links in the supply chain are continuously supplied with information in real time (Balsmeier & Voisin, 1996).

Information is at the center of virtually every aspect of business, especially in today's dynamic, uncertain, and highly competitive environment. The competitive environment is undergoing major change: markets are becoming more international, dynamic, and customer driven; customers are demanding more variety, better quality, and greater service in terms of reliability and response time; product life cycles are shortening; and product proliferation is expanding (Fliedner & Vokurka, 1997). E-commerce applications and e-enabled capabilities that rely on efficient information transfer have the potential to completely revolutionize existing supply chain environments. We will explore information systems that are internal to the company, between companies, and across entire supply chains, all with the usual appropriate examples. In fact, let's start with an earlier example but examine this company from the perspective of substituting information for assets.

Company S—Information for Assets to Satisfy Customers

Company S (first introduced in Chapter 5) is in the machine tool business, a supply chain in which the principal product may cost as much as $15 million. In fact, the capital cost of these machines is so large that customers of Company S (manufacturers who use the machine tools in making their products) estimate the costs of machine tool downtime in thousands of dollars per hour. These machines are marketed and distributed by Company S worldwide, so Company S must maintain a downstream supply chain that can deliver the machines, and replacement parts, anywhere in the world. This required considerable investment in replacement parts inventory assets.

Although the machines are expensive, capital items, Company S found (through market research involving Customer Value Requirements Maps) that the major source of customer dissatisfaction with Company S and its competitors was the delivery of replacement parts (parts that often cost less than $50). For example, when a customer in Singapore has a broken part on the machine, their satisfaction with the machine and the manufacturer of that machine is largely dependent on how fast they can obtain a replacement part and get the machine back in operation. This satisfaction, in turn, has a significant effect upon repeat sales and word-of-mouth reputation. To keep customer dissatisfaction from becoming a problem, Company S invested in replacement parts inventory all over the world (an expensive decision in its own right) and routinely shipped replacement parts to customers by overnight delivery—an international transportation service that often cost more than the actual value of the part. The result was that Company S spent tens of millions of dollars staging inventory and expediting shipments to make overnight commitments, and the customers were still dissatisfied! That is, Company S would often proudly deliver a $3.50 part overnight to a customer (at a cost of over $50!), and the customer would complain that their $15 million machine had been down for 24 hours!

In an effort to turn a customer dissatisfaction problem into a customer satisfaction advantage, Company S embarked upon a 4-year plan to implement a dramatic new logistics leverage strategy that substituted information for replacement parts inventory investment, and was embodied in this phrase: "We guarantee we will deliver replacement parts to any customer worldwide *before* they order it." To accomplish this strategy, Company S began installing cellular phones in every machine they sold (a minor cost compared with the overall purchase price). No matter where the machines are in the world, every day each machine conducts a diagnostic analysis of its performance, calls the Company S home office, and transmits the results (information) of these diagnostics. Company S computers analyze these diagnostics every night, determine whether any parts are beginning to fail, and if they are, Company S computers issue shipment orders to the distribution center. Within several days (usually at least a week before the part actually fails), the plant manager of the customer company receives a package from Company S containing the part and with instructions that the part is about to fail and should be replaced in the next regular maintenance session. Thus, the customer receives the replacement part before they ordered it!

Notice that this information-driven system eliminates the need for Company S to stage inventory assets all over the world (they now have only one global distribution center) and employ high-cost expedited modes of transportation. Since the order is no longer a rush order and can be sent far enough in advance by slower, less expensive modes of transportation, Company S has been able to substantially lower its inventory and transportation assets, while simultaneously dramatically raising customer satisfaction levels. The higher customer service levels eventually resulted in dramatically increased market share. Customers could buy their machine tools from one of several equally competent manufacturers, but only one of these (Company S) had the information system to eliminate their customers' unproductive downtime while waiting for replacement parts. As a result, customer perceptions actually changed to a belief that Company S made a higher quality machine than the competition. Typical comments from customers were, "Company S makes a great machine. It never breaks down." Of course, the real answer is that Company S simply has developed the logistics and information infrastructures to replace parts before they fail (with considerably lower investment in replacement parts inventory—i.e., information has been substituted for assets), but the customer perception is that the machines are of superior quality.

This example of achieving SCM Driver Seven through information obtained across many companies (Company S, its customers, and its transportation providers) leads us to a discussion of intracompany, intercompany, and supply chain information systems.

Intracompany Information Systems

Managers have identified information substitution—the intensive use of information to achieve better control and visibility, resulting in lower costs and higher customer service (in other words, SCM Driver Seven: substituting information for assets)—as a major trend (Perry, 1991). Information systems now provide better visibility of physical goods as they move within the company (Lewis & Talalayevsky, 1997). Accurate, timely information facilitates better decision making. Substituting information for inventory assets influences strategic decisions and enables significant cost reductions (Rogers, Dawe, & Guerra, 1992). High levels of information enable companies to develop unique capabilities to achieve competitive advantages (Gustin, Daugherty, & Stank, 1995). According to Dröge and Germain (1991), information on customer service levels (such as fill rate and on-time delivery) and service quality levels (such as a number of credit claims and number of damaged shipments) are most valuable for logistics.

A survey conducted by Gustin et al. (1995) found that the successful implementation of the integrated logistics concept was related to high levels of information availability. More information provides greater decision-making capabilities at the strategic, tactical, and operational level. Gustin et al. (1995) also found that companies with integrated logistics functions exhibited enhanced information systems performance compared with nonintegrated companies. The difference between mediocre and excellent logistics is often the company's information technology capabilities (Rogers et al., 1992).

Market orientation—a fundamental concept in supply chain management (Min & Mentzer, 2000)—is dependent on three organizationwide, coordinated behaviors: generating, disseminating, and responding to market information (Kohli & Jaworski, 1990; Slater & Narver, 1994). Information systems are also valuable in promoting learning within the company, which consists of information acquisition, dissemination, and shared interpretation of information across the functions within a firm (Sinkula, 1994). Information systems that permit free flowing information are of great benefit to all functions of the firm and the supply chain, such as marketing, sales, R&D, logistics, production, purchasing, and finance. Not having an effective information system, which allows free information flows within the firm and across the supply chain, can be very detrimental as it can lead to distrust and antagonism, resulting in ineffective supply chain processes.

Information systems have been developed within specific functions that are ideally suited to meet the needs of the function. To manage the logistics component of their supply chains, most companies have purchased single-point solutions, that is, applications designed to oversee specific tasks such as warehousing, transportation, order management, or inventory control (Cooke, 1999).

Enterprise Resource Planning (ERP) systems allow companies to replace their existing information systems, which are often incompatible with one another, with a single, integrated system, thereby streamlining data flows throughout an organization and promising dramatic gains in a company's efficiency and bottom line (Davenport, 1998). ERP systems have helped companies reduce inventories, shorten cycle times, and lower costs, which in turn have helped improve overall supply chain management practices and investment (Minahan, 1998).

Intercompany Information Systems

Intercompany information systems and technologies are those systems that facilitate information flow between the focal firm and a supplier or customer associated with the flow of the physical goods, services, and finances. These systems typically deal with a single supplier or single customer, instead of a supply chain focus.

However, simply linking information systems between the company and its customers and suppliers in the areas of product, service, and financial flows has benefits. Andel (1997) suggests that interconnecting information systems leads to improvements in the manufacturing scheduling processes, reduces finished product inventories, improves efficiency of loading and distribution operations, reduces requirements for paper and rework, lowers prices, and provides better value to the consumer. Partnerships with cooperative efforts to develop shared information systems have the potential benefits of eliminating redundant pools of inventory and duplicate service operations and, therefore, reducing costs (Narus & Anderson, 1996). The promise of intercompany integration over the Internet suggests unlimited potential to gain productivity through information technology (Parker, 2000). Three specific examples of intercompany information systems, EDI, JIT, and cross-docking, are discussed here.

EDI

Electronic data interchange (EDI) is a significant change in intercompany information systems (Kahn & Mentzer, 1996). In many supply chains, long-term strategic relationships are replacing the short-term transactional relationships of the past, and EDI is often the glue that ties long-term relationships together (Bowersox, 1988; Williams, 1994). EDI plays an important coordinating role in managing the interfaces between companies as business processes go beyond the boundaries of the company.

EDI is intrinsically different from other types of message exchange such as postal, fax, and telex because of the speed of message exchange and the ease of data capture with high reliability (Sheombar, 1992). The purpose of EDI is to act as an external information accuracy enabler (Zacharia, 2000c). EDI takes externally produced and transmitted information and allows it to be electronically received into the host system while also allowing the host system to electronically send information to another external computer system (Peters, 1996). EDI and information technology systems are assuming an increasingly significant role in purchasing by eliminating many of the time-consuming steps involved in traditional information flows (Pagell, Das, Curkovic, & Easton, 1996).

EDI allows the incorporation of more timely and accurate information into internal planning and scheduling systems such as JIT and inventory systems (Emmelhainz, 1988). EDI is also used to communicate and track sales and increase sales as buyers can make more frequent and smaller orders, keep less inventory, and react quickly to changes in demand (Emmelhainz, 1988). As computer and telecommunication technologies become more powerful and cost-efficient, EDI continues to directly influence business practices (Walton & Marucheck, 1997). EDI is viewed not only as a tool for improving transaction efficiency but also as a tool for improving customer service (Emmelhainz, 1988). EDI linkages speed up information flow and, thus, decision making (Rogers, Daugherty, & Stank, 1992). As a result, flexibility is enhanced. Examples of integrated EDI transactions can be found with many of the large retailers where inventory is set up on bar code scanners. Every time an item is sold, it is scanned, and the information goes to the supplier, who will replenish the item as needed. The major benefits that users of EDI technology receive are (Balsmeier & Voisin, 1996) quick access to information, better customer service, reduced paperwork, better communications, increased productivity, improved tracing and expediting, cost efficiency, competitive advantage, accuracy, and improved billing.

JUST-IN-TIME

Just-in-time (JIT) manufacturing was first developed at Toyota in the early 1960s by Taiichi Ohno as part of their lean production process (Womack, Jones, & Roos, 1990). JIT is the concept that parts are only produced at each step in the supply chain to supply the immediate demand of the next step. This concept was extremely difficult to implement because inventories between the different production steps were practically eliminated, so if one small part was not available, the entire production system failed (Womack et al., 1990). The logistics function became directly involved when JIT was further expanded outside the factory to include suppliers in the Toyota production system. The success of JIT manufacturing within the company led to the development of JIT beyond the company through information systems technology.

To achieve the gains in productivity that are possible from JIT, real-time information sharing is needed between suppliers and buyers (Lewis & Talalayevsky, 1997). Among the many impediments to implementing JIT is the need for direct access to suppliers through information technology to enhance communication and coordination. Richeson, Lackey, and Starner (1995) found that information flow between manufacturers and suppliers is important to the synchronization of production operations of both partners. For JIT to work effectively, good supplier relationships are needed, but for an effective supply chain with JIT, this is even more important (Bowman, 1996).

CROSS-DOCKING

Cross-docking is a system where the incoming shipments are turned into outgoing shipments without entering warehouse storage. The goal of cross-docking is to reduce materials handling and storage by moving goods directly to the end user, eliminating the need for storage (Witt, 1998), thus reducing warehousing investment. Since it requires considerable supply and demand synchronization, effective information and planning systems must be in place for cross-docking to work. According to Witt (1998), the key to getting the most out of cross-docking is to identify the needs of the information system, as well as the needs of the physical system. Information technology allows managers to have faith in inventory accuracy and delivery time accuracy, both key components of a successful cross-docking system. Cross-docking literally allows a company to receive and ship at the same time through an effective information system.

Supply Chain Information Systems

A valuable, initial element to managing a supply chain is developing supply chain information systems. It is especially critical that supply chain partners have access to information on activities they do not control (Gustin et al., 1995). Supply chain management is built on the functional integration of SCM Driver One, which is supported and often catalyzed by information (Larson, 1994). As businesses embrace supply chain management, they must maintain instant communication between computers in different corporate departments as well as with partners outside the company walls. Companies can use SCM to develop close partnerships in which each partner collaborates using shared information streams to forecast, produce, ship, and assemble in a true just-in-time scheme (Donlon & Galli, 1998). Such supply chain information systems allow companies to coordinate production with demand, slash inventory and cycle times, better manage logistics, improve customer satisfaction, and reduce overall costs and investments.

Information systems are shrinking the logistics and marketing channels that separate suppliers from end consumers. Through information technology, suppliers are able to drastically cut response times (SCM Driver Five), the number and type of intermediaries are reduced, and distribution is recognized as an interorganizational process requiring the cooperation of all parties. Information technology allows suppliers real-time access to the point-of-sale information necessary for SCM Driver Six. Where exactly a company's products are and how long it takes to get them from Point A to Point B is essential information to retailers and manufacturers as they strive to find profit by cutting inefficiencies and investments out of the supply chain. For example, Dell Computer's direct relationships with its customers create valuable information that, in turn, allows the company to coordinate its entire supply chain back through manufacturing to product design (with other companies) (Magretta, 1998a). This coordination eliminates considerable supply chain investment in inventory and storage facilities.

Several systems have become popular recently through advances in information systems technology that uses accurate point-of-sale (POS) information and eliminates substantial variability in the performance cycle (Bowersox & Closs, 1996), which, again, reduces inventory investment. Quick response (QR), efficient consumer response (ECR), vendor managed inventory (VMI), and automatic replenishment (AR) all focus on rapidly replenishing inventory based on real-time sales data.

QR is implemented by monitoring retail sales using POS data and sharing that information across the supply chain. Continuous information exchange reduces uncertainty in the total supply chain and creates the opportunity for reduced inventory investment and improved availability.

ECR originated in the grocery industry where the focus is on a consumer-driven system in which members of a supply chain work together and is dependent on timely, accurate, paperless information flow. One ECR study, sponsored by the Food Marketing Institute, estimated 42 days could be removed from the typical grocery supply chain (SCM Driver Five), freeing up $30 billion in current costs, and reducing inventory investment by 41% (Sengupta & Turnbull, 1996).

VMI is a modification of QR in that the vendor does not have to wait for the replenishment order but assumes responsibility for directly replenishing the retail inventory. The goal of VMI again focuses on having a flexible supply chain that is updated continuously with real-time sales information.

Automatic replenishment (AR) extends QR and VMI by giving suppliers the right to anticipate future requirements and replenish accordingly (Bowersox & Closs, 1996). Suppliers accept responsibility for inventory in return for access to retail stores, and retailers reduce the cost of holding and managing inventory.

QR, ECR, VMI, and AR only work with effective information flow throughout the supply chain. Better information systems improve coordination between all members of the supply chain and increase the opportunity to improve the operational efficiency and investment of the entire supply chain. However, an important point often ignored in discussions of these systems is the supply chain implications of this information for marketing. The ability to see real-time, POS reactions of customers to various product, promotion, and pricing strategies can have profound impacts upon marketing strategy and implementation, thus improving the ability of the entire supply chain to react to customer demands with optimal supply chain investment.

Increasing sophistication of Internet technologies has led to the development of electronic marketplaces. Supply chain information systems are increasingly reliant on information that resides in networks rather than on the premises of a particular company (Andel, 1997). Major ERP vendors are adding supply chain capabilities and functionality. SCM ERP systems are designed to utilize the information in these electronic marketplaces to streamline production schedules, slash inventories, find bottlenecks, respond quickly to orders, and provide final market information. Used properly, these supply chain information systems remove supply chain barriers by creating a seamless flow of supplies and finished products (Willis, Klimek, & Hardcastle, 1998). SCM ERP applications take data from ERP orders or past sales history and create forecasts to aid in planning (Minahan, 1998). SCM ERP systems help large companies reduce inventories, shorten cycle times, lower costs, and improve global supply chain management investment and practices (Minahan, 1998; Tyndall, 2000).

Company M—Information for Assets to Create Availability

Company M, which we first introduced in Chapter 4, is a major distributor in the food service industry in the United States. The food service industry is the supply chain that provides food, supplies, and equipment to restaurants, both freestanding and in hotels, and also to restaurants that are parts of chains. Company M looked at their competitive position several years ago and found themselves wanting. They delivered the same brand name products to restaurants as their major competitors did. They delivered in largely the same way. They charged the same prices. Restaurant managers would switch from one supplier to another strictly based on several pennies per case of a product. How do we achieve competitive advantage in this marketplace when the customer sees no difference between us and our competitors?

To answer that question, let's examine how a restaurant manager decides what products to order for the next day. The salesperson from a food service distributor comes into the manager's office and asks, "What products do you need?" The manager looks at their menu for the next day and their typical demand and says, "I need a case of ketchup, two cases of canned beans, and 200 chicken cordon bleu for tomorrow." The salesperson writes the order down, tells the manager the price, shakes hands with the manager, and says, "I'll fax this into the office tonight and, if we have it in stock, it will be here tomorrow." When the salesperson leaves the manager's office, what is the restaurant manager lacking? They are lacking any idea of whether they will actually have food to sell the next day.

So Company M reconfigured the way it performed this function for restaurant managers in their market area. Today, Company M sales representatives walk into the restaurant manager's office, set up their laptop computer (which has wireless capability), and dial directly into the Company M inventory management system. When the manager says, "I need 200 frozen chicken cordon bleu," the salesperson types that order directly into the computer and says to the manager, "We have that item in stock. The price is $10 per item. What's your next item?"

The salesperson is directly accessing the inventory system of the food service distributor. When the restaurant manager has told the salesperson every item he wants, the salesperson says, "Of the 12 things you asked me for, 9 of them are in stock. I can guarantee you 100% of the time we will have those items here for you within 24 hours. The other 3 items are not in stock so we can tell you right now we can't get those items for you. You should call one of our competitors and order from them."

What is the basic value this food service distributor has provided to the restaurant manager? What they've provided is information. They haven't provided a better product. They haven't provided a lower cost. What they have done is told the manager not to worry about the nine items just ordered from Company M. They will be here. As a matter of fact, 99.99% of the time, when the salesperson tells a restaurant manager the product will be there the next day, it arrives. That one small fraction of a percent when it is not delivered is the very rare occasion when the truck is involved in an accident and the product is damaged.

Equally important for Company M, they can provide this level of value to their customers with less inventory. Because the salesperson enters orders directly into the inventory management system, Company M can better manage their inventory. In other words, Company M is substituting information (the salesperson's direct input to the inventory management system) for assets (inventory carried in stock).

Company M is continuing to stay ahead of the competition through services offered (and the related information) around the food service function. As other companies are starting to add inventory control and inventory status systems similar to the one Company M has, Company M is moving into other forms of substituting information for assets. They are providing cell phones to all their delivery drivers, and they are providing access to a computer system to all their major restaurant customers. So at 10:00 in the morning, a customer expecting a delivery at 3:00 in the afternoon can go on the system, find out where the truck is, call the driver on their cell phone, and inform them that they are having a slow morning and that it would be more convenient for them if the order was delivered in the morning instead of the afternoon. The driver is given the authority to make that change in the routed schedule for their more important customers (remember SCM Driver Four). Through greater supply chain information, Company M is better utilizing their delivery assets (the trucks and the drivers), while also providing better service to key customers.

Company M is also enhancing their inventory management system so that now a salesperson can sit in the restaurant manager's office and tell the restaurant manager whether the salesperson thinks the manager's projections of demand are reasonable. For instance, the restaurant manager in the earlier example asked for 200 chicken cordon bleu. The salespeople can call up order history and tell the restaurant manager, "In the past when you have run this particular menu item, the demand for chicken cordon bleu was only 170 . . . you've typically had 30 left over." So the salesperson can suggest to the restaurant manager that they actually lower the order. As a matter of fact, the system today allows the salesperson to make suggestions on menu planning and even download for the restaurant manager full-color inserts to go in the menu that have been market tested and shown to help promote the particular items the restaurant manager is featuring that week in the restaurant. Thus, the salesperson no longer is seen by the restaurant manager as someone selling to them but rather as consultants to the supply chain. This idea of consultative selling is an important aspect of building collaboration between supply chain partners. In this case, it is based upon the ability of Company M salespeople to substitute their information for the restaurant manager's assets (inventory). The result is competitive advantage for Company M.

Company X—Shipping Information for Customer Assets

Company X, a global shipping company, offers their customers (shippers) a Web site where they can look up the status of any of their shipments. This is possible because all Company X containers have GPS (global positioning system) transponders. The customers look up precisely (to within 50 feet) worldwide where their container is. Through the Company X tracking system, the customer can also find out if the container is on a ship, when the ship will be in port, when the container is going to be unloaded, when it will be placed on a railcar, when the train will leave port, and an estimate (based upon this information) of when it will be delivered to its final destination. They also have the ability through the Web site to monitor and control the temperature and relative humidity on refrigerated containers. Thus, the competitive advantage Company X is offering their customers is not just transportation services but the location information, shipping status, and product condition anytime around the world. Company X has achieved competitive advantage by allowing customers to substitute Company X information for assets (excess inventory carried at destinations due to lack of information on delivery time for the next order, smoother production operations due to information on raw material delivery times, lower incidence of damage in transit due to temperature and humidity problems).

Company Q—Retailer
Information for Inventory Assets

Company Q, first introduced in Chapter 5, is a major global manufacturer of consumer appliances. Company Q long based its competitive positioning on the development of excellent quality products with recognizable features that customers wanted. This strategy established Company Q as a respected brand in consumer appliances, but most of its product innovations were quickly copied by competitors, and the level of quality maintained by Company Q was no different, in the eyes of the consumer, than any other manufacturer. To make matters worse, other competitors spent considerably greater amounts of money on advertising, thus creating greater brand equity than Company Q. This brand equity led to a perception by retailers that Company Q competitors were better at creating retail store traffic than Company Q (remember from the Company A example in Chapter 1 that traffic is one of the key value concerns of retailers).

Company Q decided to focus its attention not just on the final consumer of their products but upon the retailers (Company Q refers to them as trade partners) that sell their products. Company Q implemented a series of changes to their supply chains that allows Company Q to guarantee (given certain information provided by the retailers on POS demand and inventory levels) availability of product and on-time delivery to the stores at a much higher percentage of the time than any of their competitors. In fact, Company Q became so proficient at this that they managed to reduce their days sales outstanding (DSO), or the amount of finished product in inventory, while simultaneously raising their in-stock percentage by 5 points. Since a lower DSO means less investment in inventory carrying costs, this positively affects Company Q profitability. Since better availability meant retailers could depend upon Company Q, the retailers could reduce their investment in inventory of Company Q products. Thus, retailers make more profit on Company Q products (same level of sales with less investment in inventory) and, consequently, are more willing to carry Company Q products. Company Q combined this strategy with increased advertising to create greater final consumer brand equity and, thus, overcome the retail store traffic concerns of the retail customers. Company Q market share dramatically increased. In fact, one retail customer simply stopped carrying competitive brands and only stocked Company Q products.

Following SCM Driver Four, Company Q even stopped selling product to some retailers (these retailers were not created as equal as other key retailers) because they would not provide Company Q with the POS information Company Q needed to make this version of substituting information for assets work. Even though these retailers wanted to stock Company Q products, the answer from Company Q executives was, "We cannot make money for us and for you the way you want to do business, so we would rather you did not carry our products." Of course, since the Company Q strategy was making money for both Company Q (by substituting information for their assets) and their retail partners (by substituting information for their retailers' assets), and gaining market share for both Company Q and its trade partner retailers, these nonparticipating retailers suffered an ever decreasing share of this appliance business—and became even less important to Company Q's success.

Company R—Information Creates "Asset Managers"

Company R, also first introduced in Chapter 5, is in a sector of the consumer appliance business that is similar to, but noncompetitive with, Company Q. Company R trains their salespeople (who sell exclusively to retail customers) to see themselves "not as account managers, but as asset managers." This change in orientation is very similar to the Company Q case, where salespeople see their job not as selling product to retailers but rather as selling product through the retailer to the final consumer to achieve profitability for both the retailer and the vendor. (Company R brand equity is such that it does help create considerable retail store traffic.) Company R trains their salespeople to use supply chain information (on demand forecasts, marketing and merchandising plans, new-product introductions, and retailer inventory levels and ordering policies) to help the retailers manage their own inventory levels.

Given the fact that retailers can depend upon Company R to have the product desired in stock, and deliver it quickly, salespeople help retailers change their inventory management decision rules to carry less inventory (substituting information for inventory investment as a source of profitability for the retailers). In addition, salespeople work with retailers to determine what are the fast selling items, which items affect sales of other items, and which items create the most store traffic, and share successful merchandising strategy information across noncompetitive retailers. The result is greater profitability for the retailers (one retailer credits Company R's advice with saving it from bankruptcy) and greater sales for Company R. Further, because from the retailer's perspective, Company R provides not only retail store traffic–creating products but also expertise, retailers are very loyal to this company and work with Company R to sell more of their product, often to the exclusion of competitors.

From Company Q and Company R, we see two manufacturers who are achieving greater profitability (greater sales with lower inventory level investment) and increasing market share, not just from making a quality product but from realizing who are their key customers, what they value (retail store traffic and sales, but also with lower inventory level investments), and (through the use of information to reduce supply chain assets) treating them well.

Radio Frequency Identification

Information availability will continue to change at a rapid pace. As this book is being written, the Massachusetts Institute of Technology's Auto-ID research center is testing radio frequency identification (RFID) chips that can be implanted in most products (Kessler, 2003). The chip contains data about the product and the manufacturer, which can be read by a scanner, so the product can be tracked wherever it is in the supply chain. This information technology could dramatically reduce such supply chain assets as inventory, transportation, and warehousing, not to mention improving customer service levels by being able to locate the product, whether in a warehouse or in the retail store. "Everybody's going to profit from these tags," says Michael Liard, an analyst for Venture Development (Kessler, 2003).

Gillette is already attaching chips to packages of razors sold in Wal-Mart and several British grocery stores. When inventory is low, the chips alert store managers to restock the shelves. Procter & Gamble uses the chips to trace warehouse inventory and lost merchandise for Pantene shampoo and Bounty towels. Prada tags clothing, so in-store salespeople can put together ensembles for customers (when a customer picks out a certain clothing item, scanners tell the salesperson about other colors, styles, and sizes that go with that item and are available in the store).

The trend to substitute information for supply chain assets is not slowing down. If anything, the introduction of RFID indicates that it is increasing.

Summary

Information is becoming increasingly plentiful and less expensive. As a result, the ROI from investing in supply chain information to reduce other forms of supply chain investments (inventory, plants, equipment, people, and storage facilities) is often dramatic and is increasing. As a result, SCM Driver Seven, substitute information for assets, is an increasingly great source of competitive advantage.

Companies often think the easiest solution to any supply chain problem is, "Throw inventory at the problem." In modern supply chains, more inventory is almost always the wrong answer. Using better information to reduce inventory (and other) investments in the supply chain is not always a simple answer, but it is usually the right answer to achieve competitive advantage. The final questions to ask in this chapter are the challenge to implement this SCM Driver in your supply chains:

- What information do you need to reduce other supply chain investments?
- Who in the supply chain has the information you need to accomplish this?
- What is the ROI on obtaining and utilizing that information?
- What are you willing to give the owner of the information in the second question to obtain that ROI?

9

Systems Are Templates
to Be Laid Over Processes

I t is easy to become enamored with the technology implied in Chapter 8, and companies often do. They become convinced that supply chain management is solely an information systems problem. However, no system or computer package exists today that can overcome poorly thought out processes. Processes are the procedures, rules, steps, and personnel involved in accomplishing any task or tasks. Systems are the computer and communications devices, equipment, and software brought to bear to augment accomplishment of those processes.

In business, we often get this backwards and try to define business systems without, first, defining the process the system supports. A common manifestation of this is asking the systems people to develop a system without providing adequate process specifications. We are, then, surprised when the system is ineffective. Of course, it is—systems people are experts at the computer and communications aspects of business, not the underlying processes themselves. What systems personnel need are specifications of

- Where the process starts
- The goal of the process
- The steps to get from the start to the goal
- The people involved at each step
- The information and analytics they need to accomplish their part of the process

Without this information, systems personnel may develop a technically sophisticated system, but there is little likelihood it will accomplish the goals of the process.

Supply chain process design must begin with the process, lay the systems over the designed process, and always take into account the people involved

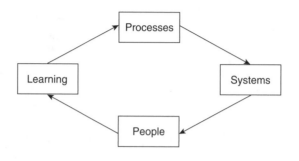

Figure 9.1   Systems Are Not Processes

(Figure 9.1). A global manufacturer of automotive parts decided to install a new demand planning/inventory management process and system. The process and system design steps mentioned above were rigorously followed in the process and system design, development, and implementation stages; and the overall forecasting accuracy on a SKUL (stock keeping unit by location) basis improved from 20% error to 10% error. However, over the first 2 months of implementation of the new system, inventory levels went up 15%! How could a more accurate forecasting system cause higher inventory levels? The answer was the company forgot to consider the people in the implementation. When the inventory managers using the system were interviewed, their answer was, "We've had three new forecasting systems in this company in the last 10 years, and each one has disrupted our inventory system. So, as soon as we heard we were getting a new forecasting system, we stocked up on inventory."

The company forgot to consider the people involved in the process and adequately train them on the new process and system in anticipation of its implementation. However, when the company did train these personnel, inventory levels dropped 10% below the original level (as we would expect from improved accuracy). Further, as the "Learning" box in Figure 9.1 indicates, after an additional 6 months, inventory levels dropped an additional 10%—the users of the system learned from their use of it and, as a result, made suggestions to improve the process and the system.

Company Y—Remember the Process

Systems are templates that should be laid over processes, not the other way around. Company Y purchased a large Enterprise Resource Planning (ERP) package that a software company claimed had been expanded to allow for total supply chain management. Company Y is very promotion driven; that is, sales are highly affected by the level of advertising, trade promotions, and consumer promotions. However, Company Y was having trouble figuring out how to bring promotional lifts into their new supply chain planning package.

When they approached the software company with this problem, the software company's reaction was, "If you're having trouble bringing promotions into the software, you really ought to stop promoting." Sounds laughable, but a true story. What the software company was saying exemplified the approach many software companies take: "If you can make your company and your supply chain run the way our software does, we have a solution for you." This is clearly putting the cart before the horse. The essence of SCM Driver Eight is that the tool should fit the problem, not the other way around.

Software systems should not be purchased in anticipation of process refinement. Many companies have called me and said, "We just purchased XYZ software system. Now we'd like you to come in and help us refine our supply chain processes." My typical answer is, "It's too late." First, decide what is the most effective supply chain process for your markets, your supply chain partners, and your company. Then select a system—whether developed internally, an off-the-shelf package, or a customized external package—that can be fully laid over the top of the process that you have developed. Otherwise you are making your reality, the supply chain, work the way the software does instead of the other way around.

Systems Providers Are Not Entirely to Blame

We see many articles in the popular press about customers of software vendors suing the vendors for systems that do not work, for vendors being unresponsive to customer needs, and for incredibly high costs of getting the software to actually work. These articles are certainly a testimony to the problems software vendors can create, but it is not always entirely the software vendors' fault. To understand this, we have to examine how software vendors make money.

Let's suppose a software company wants to develop and market a distribution requirements planning (DRP) system. They approach a potential client, who also wants a DRP system, and tell them, "We will make you a deal. If you will serve as our beta site to develop our new DRP system, we will customize it to exactly meet your needs. And, to get you to participate, we will not charge you a dime over our development costs." The software vendor is telling the truth and, in fact, develops for the client a DRP package that perfectly matches their needs for exactly the cost of developing the system—what a deal for the customer!

The software vendor then goes to a second customer and tells them, "We will make you a deal. We will sell you the same system we developed for the first company at exactly the same price we charged them. Incidentally, the first customer loves their system (of course, they do—it was developed specifically to fit their processes), and you can call them for a testimonial (which, of course, is a glowing one)."

Sounds like a great deal. The second company is paying the same, no-profit price the first company paid, and the first company is delighted with their DRP package (again, of course, they are—it was customized for their needs). However, there are no development costs for the second customer, so the price to the second customer is almost entirely profit for the software vendor. That is why part of the offer to the second customer includes the statement, "Of course, any customization you may want of the package to fit your company will cost you extra."

As we can see, where most software companies make their money is in getting customers to buy (at a considerable profit) systems that do not necessarily fit their process, and then pay extra to actually get the system to work with their processes. We cannot entirely blame software vendors for doing what makes them money. Rather, we need to understand these economics to make certain systems fit our supply chain processes and not the other way around.

Selecting the Right Software System

To accomplish this goal of making the tool fit the problem (and not the other way around), companies should put software vendors through a more rigorous selection process, not just to determine the quality of their systems but also to determine the appropriateness of their systems for the processes they are to augment. Thus, companies should ask software vendors questions about several key aspects of their supply chain systems before even addressing the company-specific questions that would lead to selecting their systems:

1. The system should serve as a communication vehicle between users of the system.

2. The tool (i.e., the supply chain system) should fit the problem, not the other way around.

3. Complex systems do not have to look that way to the user.

THE SYSTEM AS A COMMUNICATIONS VEHICLE

Mohr and Nevin (1990) described communication as the glue that holds together a supply chain. Communication in supply chains can serve as the process by which persuasive information is transmitted (Frazier & Summers,

1984), participative decision making is fostered (Anderson, Lodish, & Weitz, 1987), programs are coordinated (Gultinan, Rejab, & Roders, 1980), power is exercised (Gaski, 1984), and commitment and loyalty are encouraged. The constant need to improve communications is perhaps the best justification for investing in supply chain information systems.

In one company, there was a long-standing distrust between marketing and operations (production/distribution) regarding each function's demand management efforts. Because of this distrust, there was an almost complete lack of communication between the two functions with regard to demand management efforts. Production personnel at the company maintained that they had no input or access to the demand planning process developed by marketing. Consequently, trying to schedule production/distribution using marketing's sales forecasts was a nightmare because the inaccuracy of marketing's forecast caused problems with suppliers and production scheduling. As a result, operations relied on sales forecasts they generated themselves. Marketing, meanwhile, was concerned because they did not have access and input to production's demand plans. Because the two functions did not have access, electronically or otherwise, to either the other's sales forecasts or the information used to develop the sales forecasts, both were frustrated. Their frustration led to a duplication of effort, with both marketing and production developing independent sales forecasts—which disrupted most supply chain plans.

This example illustrates what are called "system disconnects" and "islands of analysis" (Mentzer & Bienstock, 1998b). *System disconnects* exist when the information needed to manage the supply chain is not electronically available to the managers of the supply chain. When market research information, inventory levels, confirmed orders, EDI input from supply chain members (e.g., suppliers and customers), historical demand, and transportation status information are not available, managers lack the information necessary to do their jobs. No one can accurately manage the supply chain in the absence of information. Conversely, the more information that is available, the better the supply chain will be managed. When the information is available, but not in an electronic form, a considerable amount of error will be built into supply chain processes through manual data entry mistakes. System disconnects can be cured by providing the managers with electronic access to the systems that contain the information necessary to develop and execute informed supply chain plans.

The second systems communication problem is *islands of analysis,* which exist when supply chain managers do not have electronic access to supply chain systems. When managers responsible for supply chain management cannot obtain electronic access to supply chain information, they become frustrated with the inability to interact with supply chain processes. This frustration often

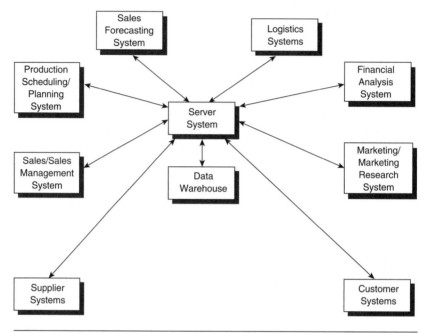

Figure 9.2   Supply Chain Systems Architecture

Adapted from Mentzer and Bienstock (1998a)

results in each functional area independently developing their own supply chain plans for their own use—thus, violating SCM Driver One. In general, these islands of analysis result in duplication of effort, each function operating without access to all the information they need, and no function having input from the other functions.

The cure for both system disconnects and islands of analysis is a connected systems architecture, both internal and external to the company (Figure 9.2). Internally, a connected system architecture means that all the systems used by the functional areas and the management information systems (MIS) area are tied together to a central server system, which has access to a corporate data warehouse. In a data warehouse, all information gathered by MIS is stored in a central location so that all information relevant to supply chains can be easily and electronically accessed. The central server system means that all functional systems can be accessed by all other functional systems through this central server.

An internal system means that anyone involved in developing and/or implementing supply chain plans can electronically access whatever information is needed, whether this information is sales history, order history, market research information, financial plans, production/operations schedules and/or capacity, or inventory levels by location. Use of an internal client-server system also means that anyone involved in developing and/or implementing supply chain plans can electronically provide input to these plans and conduct their own analyses and planning based on the existing supply chain plans. Thus, supply chain managers can electronically obtain information on expected future demand levels and plan operations accordingly.

External architecture means that the corporate system has access to the corporate systems of as many supply chain members as possible. Availability of accurate, timely information concerning the demand a company's customers are facing from *their* customers and the inventory they are presently carrying to meet it increases a company's ability to forecast independent demand and plan derived demand accurately. With this information, more accurate forecasts can be derived, by major customer, thus reducing overall demand planning error and supply chain asset investment. Availability of accurate and timely information from a company's suppliers on the availability of supplier materials for the company's production system improves the demand planning accuracy of a company's suppliers (an improvement which should eventually lower suppliers' costs and, therefore, the prices charged). In effect, the establishment of an external architecture system with suppliers *and* customers affords the company the opportunity to plan demand across the entire supply chain and plan supply chain flows accordingly.

To the degree that the complete architecture illustrated in Figure 9.2 can be achieved, communication between the functional areas will be improved, manual data entries will be minimized, islands of analysis will be eliminated, and overall supply chain management will become a much more informed and accurate process.

THE TOOL SHOULD FIT THE PROBLEM

Supply chain systems exist to serve the participating businesses, not the other way around. This means that any supply chain system should be customized to meet the needs of that particular company and supply chain. If the company wants to plan weekly for logistics needs, with monthly (for marketing), quarterly (for sales), and yearly (for finance) roll-ups, the system should be customized to provide for these planning intervals and horizons. If the company wants to plan for logistics at the SKUL level, for production at the stock keeping unit (SKU), for marketing at the product line, and for finance at the corporate level, with adjustments at any level automatically reconciled at all other levels, the system should again accommodate this. The impact of such systems flexibility on supply chain management is that supply chain plans are available in the time horizon and corporate level that is most useful for the long- and short-term planning needs of all functional areas and at all levels in the supply chain.

COMPLEX SYSTEMS DO NOT HAVE TO LOOK THAT WAY

The job of developing accurate and useful supply chain information can be quite complex. Involved procedures, information gathering, logic, calculations, and managerial input may be necessary to arrive at these plans. These procedures frequently access information from multiple sources and require the performance of hundreds of thousands of calculations. However, none of this complexity needs to be apparent to the user. The job of supply chain managers is to understand the uses and limitations of the systems and to bring their own business and supply chain experience to bear to develop and implement supply chain plans, strategies, and tactics. None of this requires an in-depth understanding of the actual systems functions or the mathematical calculations that may be conducted to bring supply chain plans to the manager. The systems functions are the responsibility of MIS. The mathematical calculations are the responsibility of the developers of supply chain decision support systems. What the manager should see is the results, laid out in a format that is easy to understand and that lends itself to the qualitative analyses the supply chain manager conducts in making decisions.

Company Z—Remember the People

A great example of forgetting the people in the design of supply chain management processes and systems was Company Z, a major manufacturer of agricultural chemicals, and their strategic business unit that sells these agricultural chemicals in Canada. Imagine selling agricultural chemicals in a geographic area where the growing season is only 3 months long. Farmers in Canada typically watch the prices of products on the commodities market from the previous year, weather conditions, and expected rain conditions, and as late as June, make decisions on what products they are going to grow on their farm that year. Based on the products they decide to grow, they need certain insecticides, herbicides, and fertilizers. They make those decisions very quickly and start planting.

As a result, Company Z's total annual demand to customers happens entirely in the month of June. Imagine that as a seasonal cycle. One hundred percent of your sales happen in 1 month. I have often imagined what the consensus forecasting group for that company looks like. Every month they meet and say, "Nothing happened, nothing happened, nothing happened, A WHOLE BUNCH HAPPENED, nothing happened, nothing happened."

To overcome this problem, Company Z realized they could not get farmers to change their behavior patterns, so Company Z decided to develop a supply chain information system to reduce the impact of the problem on their supply chain. Quick response—that was the answer. Company Z decided to give all the farm supply distributors in the country access to an EDI system.

As demand started hitting in various parts of the country in early June, Company Z could immediately find out what that demand was and quickly react to it. The system was developed and put into place. It was tested in the spring of one of the growing years. Company Z management waited anxiously for the orders to start coming in. However, just to make certain the farmers could still be supplied as in the past, Company Z violated SCM Driver Seven (for good reason—as a safety net) and threw inventory at the problem until they were certain the new process and system were running effectively. Company Z inventory staged at various places around the country, but hopefully with the new system in place, Company Z would not have to do this again after the first year.

Suddenly June arrived! Inventory started selling in all kinds of different places, but nobody at the farm supply distributors was entering orders. From the perspective of the new Company Z system, there was no evidence that farmers were actually buying from the farm supply distributors around the country. As a matter of fact, for the entire month of June, *no* orders came across the EDI system!

Finally, when the month was over, Company Z tried to contact many of the farm supply distributors but had trouble getting them to return the phone calls. Finally, they got hold of some of them in late July, and the answer to the question of why they had not used the system was the same from all of them: "In June, we take orders from the farmers, and we ship the chemicals to them as fast as we can. We're taking orders and filling them so fast, we're writing orders down on napkins, scraps of paper, whatever we can get our hands on, and we just throw them into a box. We don't have time to get on that computer of yours and type all this stuff in. We sell like crazy for the whole month of June. When June's over, we have nothing to do so we all take the month of July for vacation. We come back in August, which is the reason you're just now getting us on the phone. We're just back in the office, so sometime in the next couple of weeks we'll sit down and take all these orders we wrote down on napkins and enter them in your system for you."

A great process idea and an EDI system that would instantly tell Company Z where the orders were and, as SCM Driver Seven advocates, substitute information for inventory! Company Z would have been able to pull inventory back to more central locations and drastically lower Canada-wide inventory levels of agricultural chemicals. The only problem was that the process did not work. From the point of view of the farm supply distributors, it was just one more thing to do during their busiest time of the year.

The solution for the next year? The company calculated they would save enough money on inventory to actually pay temporary help and go in and work at the several hundred farm supply distributors. Under the revised process, every night these temporary personnel take all the napkins and scraps of paper and enter the orders into the system. The second year, the revised process and system actually worked. The necessary information was captured on a daily basis as June progressed, and Company Z could watch in real time the trends in sales of various types of chemicals in various locations in Canada. As a result, Company Z could move inventory from central storage areas to match the demand as it was progressing. The result was that the company spent several million dollars paying temporary help to work for their distributors, but reduced the cost of systemwide inventories by over $15 million a year.

Company AA—Systems Should Augment Processes

Company AA uses their supply chain planning software as a communication device for everyone in their company and for their supply chain partners. This global company has a system that allows everyone in the company (and selected supply chain partners) to access the system and, real-time, look at demand plans, look at inventory levels, look at the transportation status of various deliveries, and coordinate all this with the demands from supply chain customers and the inbound materials from supply chain providers. In fact, the term that is used in Company AA is, "Everyone in the company has, at the very least, 'look but don't touch' capabilities." It means they can go in and look at the demand and supply chain plans and delivery status, but they cannot necessarily change them. Only certain people have "look and touch" capability, which means they can actually go in and make adjustments to forecasts, plans, and deliveries. Thus, this system, which was laid over the top of the supply chain processes developed by Company AA and its supply chain partners, serves as a vehicle for communicating between all the partners in the supply chain.

The Nature of E-Commerce
Supply Chain Information Systems

Golicic, Davis, McCarthy, and Mentzer (2002) conducted in-depth interviews with 22 executives at eight companies involved in implementing e-commerce supply chain systems. The results produced numerous themes surrounding e-commerce and supply chain relationship management. The themes specific to the nature of supply chain systems in an e-commerce environment were speed, connectivity, information visibility, market structure, and uncertainty.

SPEED

The speed of e-commerce is composed of two components, the increasing rate of change and the pace of decision making. Regardless of the industry or type of company, electronic business evolves very quickly. The pace at which decisions are made in order to stay ahead of competition has increased. Because e-commerce represents an emerging market, companies are fighting for market share, so they are trying to get to market with their offerings faster than companies competing in the traditional business environment.

Stalk (1988) suggests that a strategic shift toward time-based competitive advantage began in the late 1970s with the flexible manufacturing concept. Faster execution of processes allowed companies to reduce costs, improve quality, and attract the most profitable customers. The speed at which supply chains operate electronically is an attractive aspect of e-commerce. It is business in real time where quick decision making is key. CEOs of e-commerce companies speak of "doing a deal a minute" and being forced to "be on your toes every minute, every second" (Colvin, 1999). Today, the e-commerce environment has intensified the strategic emphasis on speed, enabling further reduction of supply chain flow cycles, increased rate of new product introductions, and increased speed of customer transactions (Greenstein & Feinman, 2000).

CONNECTIVITY

Interaction and market access emerged as the two components of connectivity. Nearly all respondents spoke of the network effect—being interconnected to their suppliers and customers via the Internet. Companies have begun to rely on the "system-to-system connection with strategic suppliers and customers" (Golicic et al., 2002). Executives view e-commerce as a way to open and remove technology barriers among supply chain members and bring everyone in the network closer. The Internet allows companies to communicate and share information across the supply chain.

The second aspect of connectivity, market access, illustrates the ability of companies to access customers they could not reach prior to e-commerce. Some companies spoke of gaining "critical mass" through connectivity—the threshold of network members (suppliers and customers) needed to make their business model successful.

Hamill (1997) asserts that the key to effective use of the Internet is understanding the concept of connectivity. On the Internet, information flows are multidirectional. Compared with the unidirectional, one-to-many communication of traditional business, communication on the Internet has been described as many-to-many (Hoffman, Novak, & Chatterjee, 1995). Connectivity provides a level of interaction that is not as efficiently achieved in the traditional supply chain environment. In addition to providing the opportunity for companies to strengthen relationships with individual customers, the electronic environment also expands the reach of companies as they seek to develop their customer bases. Companies are no longer restricted to markets by their geographic locations. As global access grows, new markets are opening. Thus, the connectivity of e-commerce facilitates the extension of electronic storefronts to any location with online access.

INFORMATION VISIBILITY

E-commerce technology provides information visibility throughout the supply chain. Companies are more responsive to supply chain members' needs due to the visibility of real-time data via the Internet. Information helps supply chain managers plan, execute, and evaluate results with greater precision and speed (Rayport & Sviokla, 1995). Technology that permits complete visibility to this information enables businesses to manage their operations more effectively. Visibility of information across the supply chain, as opposed to information from one supplier or customer, provides for better management of the supply chain as a whole rather than as a set of discrete parts. Companies have transformed this kind of information visibility into competitive advantage (Rayport & Sviokla, 1995), not just for themselves but also for their supply chains. However, visibility can also lead to information overload as companies have access to more information than they are accustomed to managing, potentially resulting in confusion and additional uncertainty in the connected environment.

MARKET STRUCTURES

The fast pace needed to operate in the e-commerce environment and access to new markets have affected traditional market structures. Continuously adapting to the rapid rate of change, companies experience difficulty managing supply chain relationships in dynamic market structures (Golicic et al., 2002). As companies expand into new markets, they begin to work with traditional competitors and compete with suppliers and customers. Companies have to learn to manage the conflict that is created when this occurs. New competitors are materializing—from new intermediaries entering the market to existing supply chain members taking advantage of new opportunities to reach customers. The emergence of the electronic marketspace provides the opportunity for manufacturers to market directly to customers, eliminating the need for traditional channel intermediaries. At the same time, new "cybermediaries" are stepping between trading partners. As e-commerce opens new opportunities for supply chains to consumers, the potential for conflict is magnified (Aldridge, Forcht, & Pierson, 1997). In this new environment, functions and a relative power shift among all members of the value chain—suppliers, manufacturers, retailers, and consumers—blur the boundaries among players in traditional industry structures (Davis & Meyer, 1998; Glazer, 1991; Weiber & Kollmann, 1998).

UNCERTAINTY

The dynamism of markets and the increased information visibility facilitated by the speed and connectivity of e-commerce present an uncertain environment. Companies are making decisions without complete information, making outcomes more uncertain. Dynamism, technological intensity, and change are all characteristics of the e-commerce environment. Achrol and Stern (1988) suggested that dynamic or shifting environments create increased uncertainty for decision makers. In discussing the outcomes of uncertainty, Osborn and Baughn (1990) proposed technological intensity as likely to reflect high uncertainty. Achrol (1997, p. 58) describes how advances in technology have led to increased external uncertainty faced by firms:

> Environments are being disturbed by an increasing pace of technological change, fueled by an explosion in the growth and availability of knowledge. The proliferation of technological and managerial know-how is dismantling economic and political boundaries and slowly but surely moving the world toward a borderless marketplace. The impact of technological change is intensified in global environments that are densely interconnected and interdependent.

E-commerce represents the kind of environment of which Achrol speaks.

E-Commerce Impact on Supply Chain Information Systems

The e-commerce environment affects supply chain relationship management. Golicic et al. (2002) found that relationship management was a prominent theme that emerged from the respondent interviews. As companies deal electronically with more suppliers and customers in a variety of supply chain structures, they find managing relationships to be very important. Even though many of the transactions can be accomplished via the Internet, some companies said they would never move away from providing face-to-face contact with their customers.

Whether it is a partnership or a strategic alliance, companies operating in the e-commerce environment stress relationship management in order to combat uncertainty—by providing stability and obtaining needed resources.

In order to maintain flexibility in this uncertain environment, e-commerce companies support basic operations with a minimal in-house staff and obtain additional resources through relationships with other companies. Many partner with IT (information technology) companies to acquire a technology infrastructure, whereas some partner with consulting firms to provide human resources to achieve scalability for growth.

Successfully competing in dynamic product markets requires resources, capabilities, and strategies that are different from those likely to lead to competitive success in more stable markets (Sanchez, 1993). Higher uncertainty through dynamic market structures and increased information visibility in the e-commerce environment have caused companies to place a stronger emphasis on relationship management in order to secure these resources, capabilities, and strategies. A great deal of research exists that supports a positive relationship between dynamic structures and environments and the formation of relationships such as partnerships (Lambe & Spekman, 1997; Mentzer, Min, & Zacharia, 2000) and alliances (Adler & Scherer, 1999; Cravens, Piercy, & Shipp, 1996; Dahlstrom, McNeilly, & Speh, 1996; Lambe & Spekman, 1997). Achrol (1997) adds that closer relationships between firms offer higher levels of coordination, greater stability, and flexibility. Increased visibility can actually make it more difficult to manage the incredible amounts of information available. Companies, therefore, emphasize relationship management to overcome the uncertainty from information overload.

Firms internalize fewer resources and capabilities in highly uncertain environments with changing markets than in stable markets (Osborn & Baughn, 1990). Firms therefore purposely structure their exchange relationships to reduce uncertainty. Uncertainty is often a determinant for companies deciding whether to obtain or use assets from other organizations or to develop them in-house (Skjoett-Larsen, 1999).

For companies engaged in e-commerce-based supply chain information systems, an emphasis needs to be placed on relationship management in order to deal with the uncertainty, dynamic market structures, and total information visibility that the environment brings. Alliances and partnerships with various providers allow companies to obtain needed resources while maintaining flexibility in the sometimes volatile environment. This may be even more important when the economy shifts; the viability of e-commerce businesses was tested in late 2000 and 2001 due to a downward turn in the economy. Not only did this create even higher levels of uncertainty for companies, but it also put pressure on them to justify their business models. Successful relationship management leads to competitive advantage in the traditional supply chain environment. In e-commerce-based processes and systems, it aids companies in managing their supply chains, which has proven to be critically important not only for success in e-commerce but also for survival. These companies, therefore, need to consider how managing supply chain relationships is incorporated into their supply chain processes.

The infrastructures that e-commerce-based processes build around relationships could affect traditional supply chains. Relationships can create barriers to competition as suppliers and customers rely on those with whom they work on a continual basis. This may make it imperative that traditional supply chains better manage their relationships to not lose suppliers or customers.

Relationship management can enable supply chain partners to more efficiently deal with increased visibility of information afforded by the e-commerce environment. Information overload often leads to uncertainty as firms struggle with decisions regarding which information is important and how to interpret the data. The effective management of information flows among supply chain members is critical to gaining competitive advantage in the e-commerce environment. In the absence of proper management, the flood of information can quickly overwhelm managers operating in this environment. Efforts to collect, organize, and disseminate this information can deplete valuable human and financial resources. Trained in the efficient and effective management of information processes and systems, supply chain managers may prove invaluable in adapting their supply chains to the new information economy.

Summary

E-commerce has created additional uncertainty for the management of supply chains, but the basic principle of SCM Driver Eight remains the same—processes should dictate the nature of systems, not vice versa. Letting the tool define the problem, instead of the other way around, is a formula for disaster. One company that purchased a supply chain planning system without first defining their own processes discovered, after 18 months and $100 million in implementation expenditures, that the system simply would not work with their supply chain, a hard and expensive lesson to learn.

The key to implementing SCM Driver Eight is to always ask the following questions when considering any systems implementation:

- Are the underlying processes fully defined?
- Will this system support these processes, or will the processes have to change to accommodate the system?

10

Not All Products Are Created Equal

Not all products contribute equally to the profitability of a company or a supply chain. In fact, ABC inventory analysis was developed on a variation of this principle—the idea that 80% of the profitability comes from only 20% of the products. Thus, A-class products are the 20% of the product line that contribute most of the profitability. B-class products are the 50% of the product line that are of marginal profitability. C-class products are the remaining 30% that contribute nothing to profitability but support sales of A-class products and, therefore, are kept in stock. Thus, we keep higher availability of A-class products than B-class products, and higher availability of B-class than C-class.

Or so ABC theory goes. The fact is these percentages for different classes are far from accurate, and most companies seldom perform rigorous ABC analysis (simply assuming the supply chain has the right availability of various products).

SCM Driver Nine acknowledges that many supply chains keep in stock a multitude of products that should be discontinued for lack of sales. As one supply executive put it, "We are great at introducing new products but terrible at killing off loser products." This executive works for a company that makes telecommunications products. Analysis of their sales patterns revealed that one product that consumers buy has 2,200 different versions (each version has to be kept in stock in case someone orders it), but the final consumer cannot tell the difference in the features of any of these 2,200 different versions! Thus, this company keeps introducing variations of this product, and spends millions of dollars stocking all the variations in inventory, when the customer could not care less about the variations. SCM Driver Nine is about understanding when we put too much attention into products that do not make money for the company or the supply chain.

Company BB—Too Many Products

Company BB is in the auto aftermarket: that is, they make replacement parts for all the automobiles sold around the world. This is so many products, in so many storage locations, that their inventory management system must keep track of 800,000 SKULs! When we first reviewed their supply chain operations, the first comment to management was, "This is not a big enough company to have this many SKULs—you must have inventory at many locations that never sells." The answer was a predictable lack of understanding of SCM Driver Nine: "No, we must keep all these products in all these locations to meet the needs of our retail partners."

Not bad logic, but also not backed up with any analysis; so we asked for a simple first-cut analysis: "How about running an analysis for us that shows how many of these SKULs have not sold a single unit in the last year?" The response to our research team was, "That's a waste of time. Each of these SKULs is vital." We asked Company BB to humor us and run the analysis.

The results? Over 90,000 SKULs had not sold a single item in the last 12 months! The company had far too much inventory in the C-class: slow-selling or nonselling items.

What resulted was a far more detailed analysis of the sales patterns of each SKU at each location to determine which items were important (more equal) and which could be discontinued at each location (less equal) and only carried at a central stocking location. The result was a 15% decrease in inventory levels, while customer service availability levels went up by 2% (carried more of the right product in stock).

Company R—Too Many Supply Chain Products

Company R, first introduced in Chapters 5 and 8, is in the consumer appliance business, and trains their salespeople (who sell exclusively to retail customers) to see themselves "not as account managers, but as asset managers." This change works with key retail partners but not with all retailers. One retail supply chain through which Company R sells does not work closely with Company R to coordinate supply chain functions. In fact, a Company R executive showed us a report received weekly from this retailer, detailing how much inventory of each Company R product this retailer has in stock. Our reaction was, "This is great. This retailer is finally starting to share supply chain information with you."

The reaction from management was not so sanguine: "You do not understand. This report has inventory information for the 1,300 Company R products this retailer has in stock, but we only sell 670 products to them. The other

630 are products we do not even make any longer, and this retailer still carries them in stock!"

Clearly, the retailer in this supply chain was not conducting ongoing analysis of sell-through by product and subsequently getting rid of the inventory that no longer sold (but still cost money to keep in stock).

Company Q—Getting Rid of Inactive Products

Company Q, also first introduced in Chapter 5 and also in the consumer appliance business (though not competitive with Company R), provides another illustration of SCM Driver Nine. Although (as indicated in Chapter 5) Company Q is quite superior at some aspects of supply chain management, SCM Driver Nine proved a challenge for them. Through supply chain management collaboration with some retailers (SCM Drivers Three, Four, Five, Six, and Seven), Company Q had managed to reduce days sales outstanding (DSO) by 25% over a 2-year period, while maintaining or raising customer service levels—better retailer service with much less inventory—with the goal to reduce DSO by an additional 20% over the next year.

However, Company Q was not good at getting rid of products that were not selling. In fact, an analysis similar to that conducted for Company BB revealed that 27% of Company Q products had not sold a single item in the last 12 months! Although euphemistically called "inactive products," further analysis revealed that eliminating these items from inventory would reduce DSO by 24%, a reduction of 4% more than the reduction goal for the upcoming fiscal year! The effect on customer service levels was nonexistent. (Of course, it was. No one ordered these "inactive" products.)

The solution? All inactive products were moved to one location, with the constant reminder to upper management, "We could close this entire facility if we got rid of the inactive products." The result was upper management required product managers to defend keeping in inventory any item that was not selling (a reversal from the old culture of logistics managers having to defend getting rid of any item), and product managers were not allowed to introduce new products unless they could identify the existing product that it would replace (thus allowing inventory in the replaced item to be phased out). Of course, sometimes truly new innovations were introduced that did not replace existing products, but it was no longer the assumption that this was true for every new-product introduction. Thus, Company Q met their DSO reduction/customer service goals by adding SCM Driver Nine to the pantheon of drivers they already managed so effectively. However, it should be noted that accomplishing this requires close attention to SCM Driver One, in particular, coordinating other supply chain activities with the functions of R&D and new-product development and management.

R&D and New-Product Development and Management

R&D is an important function in most organizations today. Productive R&D is increasingly necessary for business success and value creation (Menke, 1997). The traditional inputs to R&D are people, information, ideas, equipment, facilities, specific requests, and the funds needed to complete various R&D activities (Zacharia, 2000a). However, the need to improve competitive performance has caused companies to search for new and more agile capabilities, including ways to rapidly acquire knowledge and to directly manipulate new tools and technology (Miller, 1995). The need to reduce cycle time translates into a need to know sooner about which new capabilities are possible. R&D has a responsibility for identifying latent customer needs that create business opportunities enabled by technology, developing the architecture for new application systems enabled by technology, and performing field tests with customers to target, develop, and validate capabilities that are enabled by technology (Miller, 1995).

R&D's importance in many firms has grown with increased emphasis on new-product development. For many industries, new-product development is now the single most important factor driving firm success or failure (Schilling & Hill, 1998). As competitive pressures increase in intensity, supply chains need to discover new ways to conceive and deliver innovative products more rapidly, while maintaining quality and reducing product costs.

CROSS-FUNCTIONAL NPD

A lack of communication between the marketing, R&D, and manufacturing functions of a company can be extremely detrimental to the new-product development (NPD) process. Cross-functional miscommunication leads to a poor fit between product attributes and customer requirements. R&D cannot design products that fit customer requirements without input from marketing. By working closely with R&D, manufacturing can ensure that R&D designs products that are relatively easy to manufacture. Ease of manufacturing can lower both unit costs and product defects, which translates into a lower final price, higher quality, and shorter cycle times (Schilling & Hill, 1998).

Strong functional/organizational boundaries can be barriers to speed and efficiency (Davidson, Clamen, & Karol, 1999). This has led to the proliferation of cross-functional/cross-organizational product development teams. The "hand-off" model of moving product development from one function to the next has given way to a team-based approach in which a single team, with support from the respective functions, carries product development from concept through commercialization (Davidson et al., 1999).

R&D and Marketing

Marketers are primarily concerned with identifying and catering to customer needs and competitor threats, whereas R&D personnel are focused on issues of technical feasibility and functional effectiveness (Ruekert & Walker, 1987). Working together, marketing and R&D can bring the organization's capabilities to bear on developing products that deliver benefits that meet or exceed customer needs (Beltramini, 1996). The benefits of such functional coordination include the reduction of development cycle time and closer communication to detect potential problems early in the process and reduce costs (Larson, 1988; O'Dwyer & O'Toole, 1998). Marketing identifies and assesses customer needs, whereas R&D develops the means to meet those needs (O'Dwyer & O'Toole, 1998). R&D also helps develop new technological levels of performance, which enable new customer benefits to be created.

R&D, Marketing, and Manufacturing

Assuming that marketing and R&D work together to develop the final product specifications, the next problem occurs when plans are handed to manufacturing to produce the product. Poor quality and high product costs have always been blamed on inefficient and ineffective manufacturing practices. Recently, the focus has shifted to initial product design as the primary cause of poor quality and, thereby, poor performance in the marketplace. Approximately 40% of all quality problems can be traced back to inferior product design (Raia, 1989). Some of the recent advances in manufacturing, such as lean production, parallel processing, and flexible manufacturing, suggest that manufacturing should be involved earlier in the NPD process and become directly integrated with marketing and R&D in a cross-functional NPD team.

Many practitioners and researchers feel that new-product success rates increase if firms improve the cross-functional integration among the key functions: marketing, production, and R&D (Clark & Fujimoto, 1991; Hutt, Walker, & Frankwick, 1995). Marketing can provide input on the needs of the marketplace, R&D can provide input on the latest technology advances, while manufacturing can provide input on potential cost savings in the production process.

R&D, Marketing, Manufacturing, and Logistics

Assuming marketing, R&D, and manufacturing together develop a new product, other problems arise when trying to deliver the new product. Logistics is the function that is responsible for the inbound procurement, warehousing, inventory control, outbound distribution, and spare parts availability, which can all become very important for the success of a new product (Meyers & Tucker, 1989). Logistics also interfaces with marketing, R&D, and manufacturing within the firm. This suggests that logistics, in the same manner as manufacturing, should be integrated earlier in the NPD process together with marketing and R&D. Logistics interfaces with marketing via customer service and manufacturing with regard to product availability, which permits the unique perspective on more effective intrafirm communication and integration (Cooper & Ellram, 1993). Logistics can also play a vital role in NPD by providing information to reduce the lifetime logistics (distribution and service) costs of the new product and providing input from both the supplier and the customer. Logistics has a role to play in the development of new products that becomes even more critical in industries in which time to market is the distinctive competitive advantage. When individual product life cycle times are short, as in the case of style or fashion goods, logistics processes can make critical contributions to the time it takes a firm to bring a new product to market (LaLonde & Powers, 1993). Logistics can also provide customers with the nurturing service and warranty support a new product needs to ensure commercial success, especially with radical innovation products (Meyers & Tucker, 1989).

Currently in most companies, logistics is not involved with new products until after they are developed. Logistics is usually just asked to distribute the finished product. Anecdotal stories abound about the horrors of not having logistics input earlier in the new-product development process. For example, an automobile manufacturer spent 5 years developing a sports utility vehicle but did not communicate the new vehicle specifications to the logistics group until the vehicles were ready to be delivered. Unfortunately, the changed dimensions of the new sports utility vehicles meant the rail cars typically used could only carry two vehicles whereas in the past they had carried three. This dramatically increased the cost of shipment per vehicle and increased the delivery time—which could have been avoided with early logistics involvement in NPD.

Changes suggested by logistics can translate to marketplace success as they lead to meeting customer needs more effectively. Logistics plays four important roles in NPD, according to Meyers and Tucker (1989): (1) advisor—provide advice about downstream customer participation and product life cycle cost control, (2) liaison—coordinate between NPD teams and external stakeholders, including customers and vendors, (3) problem troubleshooter—capture data, provide analysis and feedback, and (4) knowledge library—provide information on past NPD experiences to NPD teams.

The concept of using integrated product development (IPD) is not new, and there are numerous advantages. IPD leads to reduced development lead times with fewer costly redesigns, better communication, reduction in duplication, cost savings from lower maintenance, more reliable products with fewer recalls, and enhanced customer satisfaction (Dowlatshahi, 1992). By using the four functions discussed (R&D, marketing, manufacturing, and logistics) from the onset, there is greater likelihood that the product will have a market, be technologically advanced, be able to be manufactured, and be procured and distributed efficiently, all leading to greater new-product commercial success. Analyzing performance results of the furniture manufacturing industry in NPD projects, Morash, Dröge, and Vickery (1996a) found that excellence in one functional area was not likely to be the basis for competitive advantage among better performing firms, but rather process integration across functional areas led to competitive advantage.

INTERFIRM R&D

Less than 45% of U.S. manufacturers manage the entire product design process without involvement from major industrial or retail customers (Adrian, 1998). Interfirm R&D partnerships bring several advantages to the participating company. First, R&D costs over the years have become more and more expensive, and a way to reduce the costs of development is to collaborate with both suppliers and customers. Second, by developing alliances or partnerships with major customers and suppliers, cycle time is reduced. When a firm needs to reposition its competitive posture, partnerships can often be a faster approach to NPD than internal development, and can be less costly, less irreversible, and more feasible than mergers (Porter & Fuller, 1986).

For a new product to achieve significant and rapid market penetration, it must match such customer requirements as new features, superior quality, and attractive pricing (Schilling & Hill, 1998). Despite the obvious importance of this imperative, numerous studies have documented the lack of fit between new-product attributes and customer requirements as a major cause of new-product failure (Cooper & Kleinschmidt, 1986; Montoya-Weiss & Calantone, 1994). Companies need to ensure that an adequate market and distribution channel exist for their new products. Collaborating with customers and customers' customers further increases the likelihood of developing viable supply chains.

Many products fail to produce an economic return because they fail to meet customer requirements, especially when financial considerations take precedence over marketing criteria (Schilling & Hill, 1998). One way of improving the fit between a new product and customer requirements is to include customers in the NPD process. By exchanging information effectively with customers, the company helps maximize the product's fit with customer needs.

By tapping into the knowledge base of its suppliers, a firm expands its information resources, and suppliers contribute ideas for product improvement or increased development efficiency. For instance, a supplier may suggest an alternative input (or configuration of inputs) to lower cost. Additionally, by coordinating with suppliers, managers can help ensure that inputs arrive on time and that necessary changes can be made quickly (Asmus & Griffin, 1993; Bonaccorsi & Lipparini, 1994). Firms using supplier interaction are able to produce new products in less time, at a lower cost, and with higher quality (Birou & Fawcett, 1994).

A significant portion of the success of Japanese companies can be attributed to the impact of their relationship with their supply base and the early and extensive involvement of their suppliers in NPD (Clark, 1989). Early supplier involvement in new-product development suggests that suppliers should be involved in pre-launch activities, such as idea generation, idea screening, and product development. In a resource-scarce, dynamic environment, in order to maintain flexibility and benefit from the strengths of suppliers, companies need to build strong, long-term relationships with their suppliers to enable them to bring new products quickly into the marketplace (Gupta & Wilemon, 1990). Supplier involvement in new-product development is typically referred to as early supplier involvement. The goals of early supplier involvement include a reduction in manufacturing costs, improved manufacturing competitiveness, fewer part numbers, and technology transfer (Birou & Fawcett, 1994).

Ellram and Cooper (1990) discussed an example of a company that had their suppliers involved in their new-product design. This enabled the company to utilize a technology that the supplier was still developing. If the company had not had the supplier involved early in the NPD process, the company would have had to wait another 3 years until their next model introduction to incorporate the new technology.

A large percentage of the value-added of a new product is the purchased inputs, and it has the potential to influence directly and substantially not only the cost and quality but also the development time of new products (Birou & Fawcett, 1994). To bring quality new products to market as quickly as possible, manufacturers are streamlining processes and collaborating with supply chain partners (Adrian, 1998).

SUPPLY CHAIN R&D

The focus of R&D in a supply chain management context is beyond the boundaries of the firm, incorporating the focal firm's suppliers' suppliers and customers' customers input early into the new-product team. In a study of the auto industry, Clark (1989) found that integration of the capability between upstream and downstream firms is an important determinant of product development success. This suggests that developing relationships with R&D groups from firms along the supply chain leads to increased NPD success. The information is shared among the partners in the supply chain so there is a benefit to all the members of the supply chain.

Four concepts associated with R&D in a supply chain context include (1) globalization, (2) postponement, (3) speed to market, and (4) flexible NPD.

Globalization

As companies become more supply chain and globally oriented, research and development needs to be managed within a supply chain context. Managing in a global context suggests the relevance of an international innovation network, global management of technology, and the capability to leverage the "best" elements of each location to global benefit (Chiesa, 1996). This implies that companies disperse their R&D facilities in different countries to a much larger extent than in the past (Chiesa, 1996).

Integrated global laboratories become important when the sources of market information, the external sources of technology, and the company's technical resources, skills, and capabilities needed to innovate in a particular product line are geographically dispersed (Chiesa, 1996). This geographical dispersion can result from the company's international expansion or through developing relationships with firms along the supply chain. In other cases, product requirements vary significantly from country to country, local facilities develop specific skills, and as a result, specialized pockets of skills become dispersed geographically (Chiesa, 1996). Many firms have started the process of collaborating with R&D groups with firms along the supply chain, especially those that are multinational in scope and global in focus.

Postponement

The second benefit of utilizing a supply chain R&D focus is postponement. *Postponement* is the concept of designing a product such that it is possible to delay differentiation of the product until customer demand for the specific end product is known (Feitzinger & Lee, 1997; Billington & Amaral, 1999). For example, Hewlett-Packard Company does not insert the power supply (e.g., 110 or 240 volts) in their printers until they reach the customer's country, allowing the company to reduce inventory costs and gain greater flexibility to meet customer demand. Postponement may be more valuable than information sharing in a supply chain, especially under conditions of high demand uncertainty, high cost of a lost sale, and low capacity responsiveness (Billington & Amaral, 1999).

Postponement as a strategy requires R&D to coordinate along the supply chain to develop new-product architecture that allows delayed differentiation to be accomplished inexpensively. Research and development must design the product so that it can be customized at the most efficient point in the supply chain (Feitzinger & Lee, 1997). To practice postponement efficiently requires supply chain–wide coordination among several functions, especially the R&D function, to adopt a modular design. Postponing the final product configuration increases the chances the product more closely fits the needs of the final customer.

Speed to Market

The third benefit of utilizing a supply chain R&D focus is speed to market. In order to be successful at new-product development, a firm must simultaneously meet two critical objectives: maximize fit with customer needs and minimize time to market (Schilling & Hill, 1998). Reducing development time (increasing the speed to market) allows supply chains to continually upgrade their products, incorporating state-of-the-art technology when it becomes available. This enables them to better serve consumer needs, outrun slower competitors, and build brand loyalty. It also enables them to offer a wider range of new products to better serve niches (Schilling & Hill, 1998). Firms late to market are likely to incur opportunity costs, such as reduced market share and loss of margin in their pricing (Liker, Collins, & Hull, 1999).

Flexible NPD

The fourth benefit of utilizing a supply chain focus in R&D is flexible NPD. A flexible product development process allows designers to continue to define and shape products even after implementation has begun (Iansiti & MacCormack, 1997). Having a flexible NPD process enables the supply chain to quickly respond to changing customer needs. By incorporating feedback on changing customer requirements from downstream R&D supply chain members into upstream R&D supply chain members, the likelihood is increased that the new products will meet current and future needs. Flexible new-product development enables companies to incorporate rapidly changing customer requirements and evolving technologies into their designs up until the last possible moment before a product is introduced to the market (Iansiti & MacCormack, 1997). Flexible product development allows upstream R&D designers to sense customer needs, to test alternative technical solutions, and to integrate the acquired knowledge into a coherent product design using an iterative development process.

SUPPLY CHAIN IMPLICATIONS

In the future, it is likely the R&D design teams will also include key suppliers and their suppliers, as well as key customers and their customers, who will work together to develop new products to optimize functioning of the supply chain. Suppliers will have to hire more design staff, be willing to assume more product liability exposure, and adapt to the design technologies and needs of their customers. Planning of R&D will be more collaborative. R&D functions within the supply chain need to adopt a supply chain–wide perspective, which will become more important and necessary in the future, as supply chains continue to be in competition with each other.

Supply chain managers need to consider ways to improve the new-product development process in this era of global competition with short product life cycles. Supply chain managers need to go beyond the boundaries of the firm and consider relationships with their suppliers, suppliers' suppliers, their customers and customers' customers. R&D should be encouraged to work directly with customers and suppliers early in the new-product development process. Managers should also note the benefits of supply chain R&D, such as globalization, postponement, speed to market, and flexible NPD. Forming partnerships and relationships with other members of the supply chain entails risks that need to be considered. Managers need to determine if the benefits of increased efficiency or increased flexibility warrant the costs associated with developing a supply chain R&D focus.

New-product development initiatives need to be coordinated with the phasing out of replaced, obsolete, or slow-moving products. Without such coordination, the NPD process will introduce products that customers want, but supply chain management attention will be drawn away to products that are less profitable for the supply chain.

Company CC—The Dark Side of Too Many Products

Sometimes NPD can overshadow product management. In other words, introducing new products overshadows managing the entire product portfolio, including getting rid of inactive products.

Company CC is in the clothing business. Although proud of their new-product development efforts and how well this function is coordinated with marketing to develop and market products that are customer driven, an analysis of Company CC's inventory revealed that $19 million in inventory—half the overall value of inventory Company CC carried—was obsolete product. In other words, storage had to be provided for $19 million worth of clothes that the company knew no one was ever going to buy.

When you consider the cost of money tied up in this obsolete inventory, the cost of storage (providing a warehouse to hold the inventory), and the cost of risk (after all, there is an annual premium to be paid on the insurance policy that protects this inventory from damage or theft), you have to ask yourself, "Why would Company CC executives keep this inventory around?"

Table 10.1   The Impact of Inactive Inventory Reduction on the Balance Sheet

Prior to Reduction of Inactive Inventory:

Cash	$3,000,000	Accounts Payable	$3,000,000
Accounts Receivable	$3,000,000	Short-Term Debt	$35,000,000
Inventory	$38,000,000	Long-Term Debt	$35,000,000
Other Assets	$50,000,000	Retained Earnings	$21,000,000
Total Assets	$94,000,000	Total Liabilities and RE	$94,000,000

After Reduction of Inactive Inventory:

Cash	$4,000,000	Accounts Payable	$3,000,000
Accounts Receivable	$3,000,000	Short-Term Debt	$35,000,000
Inventory	$19,000,000	Long-Term Debt	$35,000,000
Other Assets	$50,000,000	Retained Earnings	$3,000,000
Total Assets	$76,000,000	Total Liabilities and RE	$76,000,000

The answer is related to SCM Driver Twelve, which we will discuss in Chapter 13—Company CC executives were paid to do the wrong thing. Upper management compensation (bonus) was partially based upon the end result of the income statement, that is, earnings. Thus, this part of compensation should have motivated Company CC management to get rid of the inactive inventory—selling the same amount of products (the sales, or top line, of the income statement) without the cost of carrying the inactive inventory (which would substantially reduce the general selling and administrative lines of the income statement) would significantly increase earnings.

However, the other part of the compensation plan for upper management was the impact of their decisions on the retained earnings line on the balance sheet—generally a good idea, as increasing retained earnings is increasing shareholder value, which is one of the primary jobs of corporate upper management.

Remember, inventory shows up on the balance sheet as an asset. Thus, a $19 million decrease in inventory has to be accounted for somewhere on the balance sheet. Since this was obsolete inventory, management estimated Company CC could only receive $1 million in proceeds from selling it off—proceeds that would be placed in cash. If we look at a simple illustration of this in Table 10.1, we see that the impact of this decision is an $18 million decrease in retained earnings, from $21 million to $3 million, or a drop of 86%!

Clearly, management is not going to want to take any action that reduces shareholder value so substantially. But let's look at this from another point of view. Shareholder value is *already* that low. The first balance sheet in Table 10.1 *looks* better but is actually inaccurate because we are showing inventory worth $38 million when, in fact, half the inventory is composed of obsolete product that is only really worth the true market value of $1 million. By keeping the obsolete inventory in stock, we are not only negatively affecting the income statement every year; we are also artificially inflating the balance sheet. The fact that this method of accounting is within generally accepted accounting practices (GAAP)—after all, GAAP allows inventory to be valued at the cost of producing it—does not change the fact Company CC is spending money every year to carry in stock inventory that has minimal market value (in fact, inventory that no one wants).

Summary

We see from this discussion and examples that not all products are created equal. Some products are more important to customers, some products (particularly those in the NPD process) are more important to the profitability and future of the company and the supply chain, and some products are so unimportant that they should be discontinued.

The key to SCM Driver Nine is constantly focusing management attention on the products that are important, giving less attention to managing and carrying in inventory the marginally important products, and getting rid of the unimportant products.

However, as the examples illustrated, it is a difficult management responsibility to constantly assess the value of products and manage them accordingly. In the example of Company CC, it is often not even in the best interests of management (from a compensation point of view) to do this. Remember though, as with all the SCM Drivers discussed in this book, if it were not difficult to accomplish, it would not be a source of competitive advantage. Anything that is easy to do will be quickly copied by the competition and, thus, will not be a competitive advantage. The challenge to supply chain managers in taking advantage of SCM Driver Nine is to change the motivation and compensation of key executives, both within the company and in supply chain partners, to treat some products as more equal than others.

11

Make Yourself Easy to Do Business With

Perhaps the most popular indicators of marketing effectiveness and competitive advantage are market share and profitability (Dess & Robinson, 1984; Jaworski & Kohli, 1993; Kohli & Jaworski, 1990; Narver & Slater, 1990, 1991; Slater & Narver, 1994). Companies that are able to create value for their customers by satisfying their needs and wants generally increase their market share and their profitability. Profitability is a desirable outcome because it creates shareholder value. When consistently and substantially maintained, it ensures the company's longevity (Groves & Valsamakis, 1998). Thus, an important part of any business, and certainly of any supply chain, is making it easy for customers to do business with us.

Let me use a personal example to initially illustrate this SCM Driver. Years ago, I was trying to buy a new notebook computer, and I called the 800 number (the "customer service hot line" no less) of a popular manufacturer of computers, just to get a question answered. I did not want information faxed to me. I did not want to sign up for their e-mail list. In fact, I did not want any of their preprogrammed options. What I really wanted was to talk to a human being who could answer my question. I wanted very specific answers about a very specific notebook computer model before deciding whether I was going to buy it or not.

I dialed the 800 number for the customer service hot line and was told (by a prerecorded message) that everybody was busy as usual, but I was a very important customer. And I certainly must have been an important customer, because every 30 seconds the pleasant-voiced receptionist's recording came back on and told me how important I was. As a matter of fact, that pleasant voice told me every 30 seconds for the 25 minutes I was on hold how very important I was. (I really came to hate that receptionist's voice!)

Finally, after telling me for 25 minutes that all the representatives were busy, now the system came back and gave me, not a representative but, *options*. (Of course, at this point, I wanted to know why I was kept on hold for 25 minutes to speak to a representative—who was very busy—but then not allowed to speak to a representative.) I then began an odyssey to get to speak to an actual person.

I was told to press 1 if I wanted information on a particular model faxed to me. I didn't want any information faxed. I already had the information in the fax.

I could press 2 if I wanted to be added to their e-mail list. I did not want to be on their e-mail list (I receive too many e-mails already).

I could press 3, . . . well, you get the general idea.

Every time the system gave me options, zero was the option for "other." So, I pressed "other" every time because none of the options they ever gave me was, "Press this number if you would actually like to talk to a living, breathing human being."

I pressed "other" several times until apparently the system figured out that I was not going to cooperate and pick one of their options, and then the system hung up on me! I sat there for a few moments and thought, "Surely I must have done something wrong. Let's try this again."

Sure enough, I was put on hold again for, this time, not quite 25 minutes— only for 21 minutes—and then the system started giving me options, Again, I kept hitting zero. After 21 minutes on hold, and 5 minutes of hitting zero for each option offered, the system once again determined that I was not going to cooperate with the way they wanted us to do business and hung up on me.

The result of the story you can guess—I bought somebody else's notebook computer. This company, although making a fine product at an excellent price with a great service agreement, lost my business and probably the business of many other people because they expected me, the customer, to do business *their* way, instead of the other way around.

Once, when I used this example in a 1998 speech to a large group of executives, representatives from this computer company came up to me after the speech and asked, "Was that our company?" When I told them that it was, but I did not want to use the name of their company in public, their response was, "We know we have this problem, but we're working on fixing it."

Sounds like a company concerned about doing business the way customers want to do business. However, I used the same example in a 2003 speech to a large group of executives, and again a representative from this company came up to me after the speech and asked, "Was that our company?" When I told them that it was, but I did not want to use the name of their company in public, their response was, "We know we have this problem, but we're working on fixing it."

My response was, "Wait a minute. You've known for over 5 years that your customer service hot line hangs up on customers, and you still haven't fixed it?" As you can guess, this company did not have the best trend in market share over those years.

Unfortunately, this principle permeates many supply chains. "That's not the way we do business." "We have standard ways of billing our customers." "There are procedures our customers must follow," is often the mantra of companies who are doing their best to drive their customers to the competition.

Company D—Procedures to Drive Away Customers

Company D, first introduced in Chapter 2, is a North American railroad. Railroads, which have been around since the nineteenth century, are very complex organizations to manage: tens of thousands of miles of track that must be maintained, tens of thousands of engines and railcars that must be maintained and tracked (some cars actually get lost for years), and tens of thousands of employees working over a million-square-mile network of lines and yards that must be managed. Hundreds of trains, going to hundreds of different locations, cannot be on the same track going in opposite directions, or on the same track going at different speeds that might allow them to "catch up" to each other (after all, trains do not have the luxury of passing each other).

This complexity has led most railroads—over the better than 150 years of their existence—to develop very proceduralized ways to doing business. From an operations point of view, this is a good thing. Company D has a procedure to handle just about any imaginable event (including such unlikely events as what to do when a hurricane creates winds so strong that empty railcars are blown off the track).

However, forcing customers to follow strict railroad procedures is not conducive to increasing market share. Several top executives at this company once made the comment, "If we could just get more companies to understand how to do business the railroad way, we could drastically increase our market share." In other words, if potential customers would do business the way we want them to, instead of the way they want to do business, sales would blossom. Unfortunately, this attitude is one of the major reasons why U.S. railroad market shares, for the most part, are steadily declining. Potential customers have found that trucking companies are much more willing than Company D to adjust to the way the customer wants to do business.

One customer of Company D complained that at one of their plants, when Company D backed railcars up to the facility, they regularly hit the building, resulting in considerable damage. Since Company D kept ignoring this customer's complaints, the customer put a large iron "brake" on the track to stop the railcar just short of hitting the building (the railcar hit the brake instead of the building).

Although the brake does a great job of stopping the railcar from hitting the building, it also damages the railcar if the locomotive engineer (an employee of Company D) hits it too hard. As a result, Company D sent their customer a bill for the damage to their railcar—damage a Company D employee caused!

To decrease the incidence of such damage, the customer asked Company D to let them know by phone when the train was ready to back into the facility, so the customer could send one of their employees out to "talk the train back" and have it stop before it hit the brake. The response from Company D was, "It is not our policy to notify customers prior to delivery."

To force Company D to notify the customer of the delivery, the customer started locking the access gate across the rail spur, so Company D could not back the train into the facility without first notifying the customer (which would allow the customer to send out an employee to help the engineer back up the train).

Company D's reaction to this was to simply stop delivering railcars. "If the gate is locked, we've instructed our engineer to go on to the next delivery; and we notify the customer to unlock the gate, and we'll drop off the railcar the next day." Since Company D only guarantees a 14-hour delivery window, the customer is now faced with leaving an employee sitting out at the gate all day, doing nothing but waiting for the train to arrive!

Is this any way to run a railroad? It certainly is if you want to drive away all your business. Precisely what is happening with this customer, who now has as much freight as possible delivered to their facility by truck. Even though the inbound materials could travel more economically by rail, the customer considers the railroad, Company D, just too hard to do business with.

Relationship Marketing

The marketing concept is a business philosophy (cf. Barksdale & Darden, 1971; McNamara, 1972), and a market orientation is the implementation of the marketing concept (Kohli & Jaworski, 1990). Based upon previous conceptualizations of a market orientation (e.g., Drucker, 1954; Felton, 1959; King, 1965; Barksdale & Darden, 1971; McNarama, 1972; McCarthy & Perreault, 1984), Kohli and Jaworski (1990) defined the marketing concept as consisting of three pillars: (1) customer focus, (2) coordinated marketing, and (3) profitability. The marketing concept, as a business philosophy, guides firms to look for customer satisfaction at a profit in a coordinated manner and also guides a firm's behaviors (called relationship marketing) to develop, maintain, and enhance interfirm relationships to satisfy customers (Min, 2000a).

The marketing concept is a necessary component for implementing SCM. As Nabisco executives proposed, "Successful SCM begins and ends with the customer. Satisfying customers must always remain the unswerving objectives of SCM" (Andraski, Wisdo, & Blasgen, 1996).

Kohli and Jaworski (1990) proposed that a market orientation is the implementation of the marketing concept and is composed of three sets of organizationwide activities: (1) generation of market intelligence pertaining to current and future customer needs, (2) dissemination of the intelligence across departments, and (3) responsiveness to market intelligence.

The influences of a market orientation do not stop within the boundaries of the firm but expand to interfirm relationships with customers, suppliers, and distributors. Thus, a market orientation provides an environment in which relationship marketing is nurtured.

Nurturing relationship marketing through a market orientation starts with developing commitment, trust, and cooperative norms between the firms (Berry, 1995; Sheth & Parvatiyar, 1995; Grönroos, 1995). Because a market orientation requires a supplier to devote considerable resources to satisfying distributors' needs, the distributor commits to maintain the relationship with such a devoted supplier (Siguaw, Simpson, & Baker, 1998).

Trust is a willingness to rely on an exchange partner in whom one has confidence. Siguaw et al. (1998) argued that a supplier's market orientation contributes to a distributor's trust through (1) voluntary information and advantage sharing with the distributor, (2) favorable motives and intentions passed on to the distributor, and (3) open communications and responsiveness to customer needs.

Cooperative norms reflect the belief that both parties in a relationship must combine their efforts and cooperate to be successful (Cannon & Perreault, 1997). If a supplier is market oriented and working to satisfy a distributor's needs, the distributor is likely to perceive cooperative norms in the relationship because both parties are working toward the mutual goal of need satisfaction (Siguaw et al., 1998).

THE IMPACT OF RELATIONSHIP MARKETING ON SCM

Grönroos (1990, p. 138) defined the goal of relationship marketing: "Establish, maintain, and enhance relationships with customers and other parties, at a profit, so that the objectives of the parties involved are met. This is achieved by a mutual exchange and fulfillment of promises." Relationship marketing goes beyond repeat purchase behavior and inducement (Sheth & Parvatiyar, 1995).

Min (2000a) claimed that relationship marketing affects SCM, as well as the management of individual firms, by

1. Enhancing interfunctional coordination to satisfy customers with companywide efforts

2. Redefining the responsibilities of each function of a firm

3. Restructuring the organizational system

4. Improving marketing effectiveness of the partner firms by proper marketing resource allocation to the other partners and involvement of the partners in the marketing process

5. Bringing resources outside the firm to satisfy customers who become more demanding in a competitive market

6. Reducing risks in the market

7. Providing financial benefits such as increased revenue and reduced costs

8. Helping build, maintain, and enhance long-term interfirm relationships such as partnerships, strategic alliances, joint ventures, and networks that fit into the goal of SCM

9. Allowing interfirm coordination that is required for the implementation of supply chain management initiatives such as joint inventory, joint cost reduction, and joint planning

With the help of the marketing concept, a market orientation, and relationship marketing, SCM achieves differential advantage for the supply chain and its partners by reducing costs and investments and by improving customer service by making the company easy to do business with.

Understanding Changing Customer Values

Finding ways to retain strategically important customers is crucial to supply chain success. Making yourself easy to do business with involves anticipating and responding to changes in customers' desired value—what customers want from suppliers (Flint, Woodruff, & Gardial, 1997; Woodruff, 1997; Woodruff & Gardial, 1996). Logistics plays a key role in this process in most supply chains. Flint and Mentzer (2000) found that many of customers' changing desires fall along logistical lines, implying that suppliers need to leverage their logistical expertise in order to respond to these changes. Thus, logisticians need to adopt the role of marketing to both internal and external customers from the very initial stages of supply chain relationships. This is due to logisticians' unique ability to see, understand, anticipate, and design solutions for logistics-relevant customer changes that traditional marketers and sales professionals may not recognize.

Customer value has emerged as a crucial concept in business. The business press of the 1990s is replete with advice on how to create customer value (Day,

1990; Gale, 1994; Hamel & Prahalad, 1994; Morrison & Schmid, 1994; Pine, 1993; Slywotzky, 1996). Similarly, the marketing literature contains a growing body of work on customer value (Flint et al., 1997; Woodruff, 1997; Woodruff & Gardial, 1996). Likewise, the logistics literature offers arguments for how and why logistics expertise helps create competitive advantages by influencing customer satisfaction and customer value (Dresner & Xu, 1995; Global Logistics Research Team, 1995; Morash, Dröge, & Vickery, 1996b; Pennsylvania State University, University of Tennessee, and Michigan State University, 1995; Pisharodi & Langley, 1990; Sharma, Grewal, & Levy, 1995). Throughout this literature and elsewhere, it is recognized as an axiom that business is dynamic and customers' desires change. However, the primary ways suggested to deal with changing customer desires are to (1) become extremely flexible, such that responses to change can be rapid (Pine, 1993; Manrodt & Davis, 1992), (2) track macroeconomic and other trends over time (Morrison & Schmid, 1994), or (3) drive changes in what customers desire oneself (Hamel & Prahalad, 1994). A few authors have suggested specific forces, which may drive changes in what customers value and offer tactics such as executive market-based scenario exercises to help predict what customers may value in the future (Flint et al., 1997; Woodruff, 1997; Woodruff & Gardial, 1996). However, all of these approaches lack in-depth understanding of how customers' desires actually change, or suggestions on how to anticipate what those changes will be.

Flint and Mentzer (2000) investigated why and how automobile industry business customers changed what they value from their supply chain relationships and called this phenomenon "changes in customers' desired value." Their first important finding was that customers do change what they value from suppliers, and the suppliers who recognized these emerging needs early were poised to take advantage of the opportunity by offering to become involved in product, system, and distribution design early. As a result, suppliers were able to influence product and logistics service specifications and purchasing managers were able to influence supplier selection. Flint and Mentzer (2000) found that supplier logisticians, as well as marketers, clearly were expected to adopt a responsive, continuous improvement attitude. In essence, customers have moved from merely sending out requests for proposals to building strategic relationships with key suppliers who become extensions of their business and co-design solutions to their problems throughout the life of supplier-customer relationships.

Flint and Mentzer (2000) found that the idea of "customers' desired value change" (CVC) appears to exist in at least five ways: (1) value hierarchy levels, (2) form, (3) rate, (4) magnitude, and (5) volatility. *Changes in value hierarchy level* refers to the finding that customers may change the attributes they desire from suppliers, and/or the resulting consequences. For example, participants described changes in the logistics attributes they desired such as different pallet sizes, different delivery times, and reductions in cycle times. Additionally, participants described changes in consequence desires such as reduction of their inventory costs and improvement in their customer service delivery. Clearly, supplier logisticians (whether members of a production supplier or a third-party firm providing logistics services) ought to be aware of both the changes in desired attributes and desired consequences. Merely responding to a requested attribute change may not effectively address the related desired consequence or broader customer objectives. Unless suppliers dig deep enough, they may waste resources making logistics attribute changes that sub-optimize complex supplier-customer processes and/or fail to most effectively meet customer's changing consequence desires.

The second dimension, *form*, refers to the fact that changes in what customers desire may take several forms. One is simply a change in existence. The desire is added or eliminated. For example, a customer may now want the supplier to hold inventory. A second form change is a change in priority level. For example, a customer may desire on-time delivery now as much as order accuracy, when in the past they merely focused on order accuracy. In short, relative priorities change. This emergent desire may be driven by a customer shift to just-in-time production processes and a resulting reduction of inventory. A third form change is performance level, that is, raising of the bar or increasing expectations of suppliers. Here, customers want to see continuous improvement.

Each of the three forms may have different resource implications for supplier logisticians. For example, changes in existence may require extensive creativity to design a solution that has not been used before. If added to previous desires, it may require additional investment as opposed to a shift in investment. Changes in priority may require a shift in resource allocation from continuous improvement efforts in one area to improvements in a previously neglected area. Finally, changes in desired performance level may require extensive investment in a specific area previously thought to be adequate. Although possibly the easiest to spot, responding to this form of change may be the most costly as it becomes more and more difficult to make incremental improvements in well-performing systems.

The third CVC dimension is *rate* and refers to how quickly changes occur in what customers desire. Some changes are evolutionary, in which supply chain relationships gradually become more involved in each other's operations and along the way gradually increase the expectations of each other. Examples of this include gradually moving toward expecting key suppliers to have warehouse facilities literally across the street from customer operations around the globe or having key suppliers coordinate the delivery of systems of complementary components from several suppliers rather than merely worrying about delivery of their own components. Suppliers become key suppliers because they infiltrate customer operations with people from all areas of functional expertise and are willing to respond to these evolutionary changes on a regular basis.

These suppliers are able to develop the competencies to respond to or influence resource-intensive desire changes.

Other changes are revolutionary, in which changes occur overnight to suppliers and, as a result, come out of the blue. Sometimes this is the result of major internal customer changes, such as key executive management changes, in which the philosophies of new executives differ from those of previous executives. Those suppliers able to react most effectively and rapidly are those who have supplier logisticians involved continuously throughout supply chain relationships in order to quickly recognize even subtle changes in customers' logistics related desires.

The fourth dimension of CVC, *magnitude,* refers to how large the difference is between what was expected previously and what is expected now. For example, customers' desire for delivery of ready-to-install systems as opposed to individual components is another example of a large change in desires. Small changes in logistics desires include changing the size of pallets, changing delivery times, and changing transportation modes. However, responding to what seem to be small changes is still a key to being easy to do business with and is crucial to customer loyalty.

The fifth dimension of CVC is *volatility*—how many desired logistics attributes and/or consequences are changing at once. The more changes taking place simultaneously, the more volatile. While one customer may be asking for a vendor-managed inventory program, another may be asking for that, as well as EDI systems, forecasting assistance, point-of-purchase data tracking assistance, changes in transport modes and packaging, and self-certification because they now must comply with ISO9000 requirements. Being able to respond to multiple changes in logistics desires simultaneously requires far greater resources and expertise than responding to one or two at a time.

Where do changes in customers' desired logistics value come from? Flint and Mentzer (2000) found they were related to the impact of environmental changes and tension those changes created. It is in attempts to reduce this tension that the role suppliers play is recognized and, as such, alters what is valued from those suppliers. Flint and Mentzer (2000) found that changes occurring in at least five areas drive changes in customers' desired value: (1) changing customers' customer demands, (2) changes internal to customer organizations, (3) customers' competitor moves, (4) changes in suppliers' offerings, demands, and/or performance, and (5) changes in the macroenvironment.

Customers' needs are changing in so many ways that uncovering these needs cannot be left only to marketers and sales professionals. Due to the role logistics services are likely to play in responding to changing needs, logisticians ought to be involved from the beginning of customer relationships and throughout. In this way, logisticians are able to help their marketing and sales partners see relevant changes that manifest themselves as threats or opportunities for customer relationships. With greater knowledge of customers' changing logistics needs, logisticians can decide whether they wish to be proactive, and actively influence what customers need, or reactive, and stand prepared to respond when certain value desires are expressed.

Losing Valuable Customers

Since we started this chapter with a personal example, let's end it the same way. A neighbor of mine has three children in their late teens. This means he has five cars under his insurance policy. Although he felt the policy premiums were reasonable, five cars meant he receives a bill twice a year for each car. Thus he is writing checks 10 times a year just for car insurance premiums.

He contacted his insurance provider and asked that he be sent only one bill—the total for all five cars—every six months. The response from his insurance company was, "That is not the way we do business. We bill separately for each car."

So this neighbor started shopping around for another insurance provider, not necessarily to save money, but to add convenience. He found a competitive company that actually charged a little bit more but would send him bills the way he wanted it done.

Paradoxically, when he cancelled his policies, he was bombarded with pleas from his old insurance company (not surprisingly, since he was paying over $6,000 per year for car insurance—remember, three of these cars were driven by teenagers) to not leave, because "Every customer is important to us." Not important enough, apparently, to do business the way the customer wanted to do business.

Summary

Although most companies claim that their customers are "the reason we are in business" and "our sole focus," many companies make it difficult—if not impossible—to do business with them. Understanding what customers value, anticipating when those values change, and making it easy for customers to obtain that value and buy our products and services is not always easy to do, but it is essential for maintaining and growing market share. Since it is not always easy to do, making ourselves easy to do business with is a considerable source of competitive advantage.

To achieve SCM Driver Ten, ask yourselves this final question: "In what ways do we force our customers to do business *our* way instead of *their* way?" The number of ways may surprise you.

12

Do Not Let Tactics Overshadow Strategies

Examples of not understanding this SCM Driver abound in business. Like Company D, which sued a $100 million customer over a $5,000 issue, and Company CC, which kept millions of dollars in inventory that would never sell, companies often create processes and orientations that make executives worry more about today's numbers than the long-term success of the company.

Much of the blame for this can be laid upon the investment community. Wall Street wants to see immediate positive results. Efforts to improve the long-term profitability of the company, at the expense of profits next quarter, are met with skepticism at best. More than likely, such a move would be met by a sell recommendation that would drive down the stock price. Because senior management spends much of its time worrying (appropriately) about shareholder value, their concern is focused on the day-to-day stock price. Thus, publicly traded companies can easily become driven by what Wall Street wants to hear rather than by what is best for the long-term competitive advantage of the company.

Unfortunately, many of the supply chain management strategies discussed in this book fall into the category of investments that do not make the company look good in the next quarter but do pay off in the long run. For instance, Company A (first presented in Chapter 1) implemented a supply chain strategy that made considerable positive gains in market share and profitability over a several-year period.

However, let's look at what happens when we implement the Company A strategy. First, there is a considerable investment in systems, personnel, and training to realize a level of information sharing and collaboration with Retailer B that will make the strategy work. Second, Company A assumes ownership of all Retailer B inventory, an event that shows up on Company A records as negative sales. Both these events have a substantial negative effect on earnings for the first quarter in which the strategy is implemented, a fact that invariably drives down the stock price (after all, Company A is showing a one-quarter decrease in earnings per share). The fact that, long term, this strategy has a considerable positive effect on earnings is not factored into the stock price for the first quarter.

The challenge is to convince Wall Street that these moves are positive. In many ways, implementing what has been discussed in this book is easier for privately held companies. When the CEO of a privately held company is presented with a supply chain strategy that will hurt earnings for one quarter but make considerable improvement in earnings over the long run, he or she does not have to worry about what Wall Street will do to the stock for one quarter. Rather, the CEO simply decides if the return on investment (ROI) is appropriate for the company and makes a decision. Unfortunately, the CEO of a publicly traded company spends much less time on the ROI decision and much more time than their privately-held-company counterparts worrying about what Wall Street will think next week.

We see many examples of this phenomenon in business. Salespeople are pushed to generate additional sales at the end the quarter to make the quarterly numbers, even if such pushing hurts their relationships with customers. We even ran into one company that discovered its salespeople were going to customers at the end of the quarter and asking them to place orders for products they could not use. The reason? The salesperson told the customer, "It would really help me if you placed this order this week so we can make our sales numbers, and you can cancel the order next week."

Of course, what was happening was the company was preoccupied with making the numbers promised to Wall Street. The accounting system recorded the sales in the quarter where they were needed and recorded negative sales (the cancellation) in the next quarter. This tactic met the short-term (this quarter) goals of the company but ignored the negative strategic impacts: the negative sales would have to be made up next quarter, salespeople were spending time meeting the numbers instead of actually building relationships with customers and making real sales, artificial sales followed by cancellations were wreaking havoc on the production scheduling systems, and perhaps most important, everyone involved was encouraged to "massage the numbers" rather than run the supply chain.

Many companies hurt their long-term (strategic) profitability by playing such games. What happens when our customers realize that each quarter, if we are not making our sales numbers, we will drastically reduce our prices to get more sales before the quarter is over? If they are smart, they will wait for the end-of-the-quarter "sale," and then buy enough product at the reduced price to last them for the next 3 months. The result is they have enough inventory to see them through the last quarter of the month, *and* see them through the first

2 months of the next quarter—which will get us to panic and again lower our prices. In fact, customers can work out a mathematical model that includes the amount of the end-of-quarter discounts and their own cost of carrying the extra inventory and determine their optimal forward-buying amount. The result, of course, is that our customers come to expect to never buy at the regular price, and thus force us to give away our margins.

This is good for the tactics of the customer, but what does it do to sales patterns of the supplying company? It creates repeating patterns of demand in which derived demand is very low for the 2 months (causing inventory build-up) when margins (prices) are higher and one month of high derived demand (causing higher production costs) when margins (prices) are lower. Thus, the tactic of making the quarterly numbers is detrimental to the strategic success of the company. In effect, we are encouraging customers to take away our margins and disrupt smooth supply chain operations flows.

Company DD—Losing Sight of Strategic Goals

Remember Company A, the snack food manufacturer that significantly improved market share and profitability by coordinating demand, product, service, and financial flows with Retailer B? Company DD had a very similar opportunity, although their product was very different. Company DD makes automotive parts. Rather than selling snack food to Retailer B, they had the opportunity to accomplish the same SCM Drivers for Retailer B's automotive parts department.

The logic introduced in Chapter 1 was the same for Company DD. In the Company A example, the inventory component of working capital for Retailer B on their Company A business dropped to zero, made possible because no Retailer B dollars are invested in the inventory component of Retailer B's working capital of Company A products. This creates a motivation for Retailer B to sell more of this product, to give it better merchandising, better shelf location, and better store placement because the more of this product Retailer B sells, the more money Retailer B is making on a zero investment in inventory. Because Company A took those 23 days out of the information cycle, their inventory levels through the entire system actually went down, even though now they own the inventory in the Retailer B RDCs and retail stores. Because the demand affecting Company A is no longer lumpy and unexpected, production costs also significantly decreased. More important, when an order actually happens, Company A gets paid 30 days earlier. So Company A working capital systemwide to support Retailer B went from 23 plus 30, or 53 days, down to 15 days. Their total investment in working capital to support Retailer B sales dropped by more than two thirds.

However, the supply chain management processes and systems that were put in place to allow Company A to monitor sales of each of their products real time in each Retailer B store constituted a huge, up-front investment. Further, the reduction in systemwide inventories looked like a short-term drop in sales. (The inventory did not just go away—it had to be sold off, which looked like zero sales, short term.) Thus, Company A's stock price suffered for 2 months because Wall Street did not recognize the long-term advantage these short-term earnings decreases were creating. (Of course, long term, Company A's stock rose from the increased market share and lower costs—i.e., higher margins.)

When faced with the same possible relationship with Retailer B, Company DD procrastinated. "We cannot afford to have our stock price suffer," was the logic. Makes sense tactically—why take a hit to your stock price when you do not have to? But let's look at the strategic implications of this tactically driven procrastination. What if Retailer B decides to enter into a Company A-type of supply chain relationship with *one of Company DD's competitors?* Company DD will lose market share to this competitor. (After all, Retailer B is now making more money selling the products of Company DD's competitor, so it makes sense that they will give these products better store placement.)

In fact, this is precisely what happened. Although Company DD had the capability of doing for the automotive department of Retailer B what Company A had done in the snack food area, they procrastinated so long that Retailer B asked one of their competitors to develop a Company A type of relationship. The result, strategically, for Company DD was that they lost considerable market share with Retailer B (one of their key retailers)—a reasonable tactical decision resulted in a terrible strategic outcome.

Will Wall Street Lead the Way?

The solution to this SCM Driver will eventually come from Wall Street. What happens today when a company announces that it is taking a substantial write-off of nonproductive assets? Even though the company is admitting (tactically) that it has made a mistake, the stock price goes up. This is because Wall Street investors realize the write-off takes managerial attention away from these non-productive assets and focuses attention more appropriately on more profitable endeavors—in other words, Wall Street is rewarding the company (in higher stock prices) for focusing not on nonproductive tactics but rather on potentially more productive strategies.

SCM Driver Eleven will be more fully realized when Wall Street starts rewarding companies for similar supply chain decisions. When Wall Street accepts the argument that we are making decisions that will hurt earnings for the next quarter but will increase market share and decrease supply chain costs in the long run (thus, making us a more profitable company in the long run), companies will be more likely to take advantage of SCM Driver Eleven. To accomplish this, however, supply chain partners need to distinguish between strategic and tactical partnerships.

Strategic Versus Tactical Supply Chain Partnerships

Companies do not pursue partnering relationships with all their supply chain members. The implementation costs (in terms of capital, technology, processes, risk, and people) are too great. Thus, even retailers such as Retailer B that do engage in supply chain partnering do so only with a select group of vendors that have a similar orientation toward supply chain partnering (to the detriment of Company DD). An orientation toward supply chain partnering is the partners' patterns of shared values and beliefs that help individuals in the partner firms understand the functioning of the partnership and, thus, provide partnership behavioral norms (cf. Deshpande & Webster, 1989). This partnering orientation exists on a continuum from strategic to tactical (Mentzer, Min, & Zacharia, 2000).

STRATEGIC PARTNERING ORIENTATION

Strategic partnering is the effort to achieve long-term strategic objectives and, thus, improve or dramatically change a company's competitive position (Hitt, Ireland, & Hoskisson, 1999; Webster, 1992) through the development of new technology, new products, and new markets (Webster, 1992). Johnson (1999) proposed that strategic partnering exists when a firm perceives that (1) its long-term strategy depends on maintaining a good, healthy relationship with its partner, (2) the relationship with its partner is important, and (3) a strong cooperative relationship with its partner is necessary to be competitive in the industry. Ganesan (1994) suggested that retailers with a long-term orientation are concerned with both current benefits (i.e., operational efficiency and effectiveness) and future outcomes (i.e., competitive advantage). A strategic partnering orientation includes exclusivity and nonimitability (Lambert, Emmelhainz, & Gardner, 1996; Varadarajan & Cunningham, 1995). If the competitors of either firm replicate the relationships or similar cooperative arrangements are made between a partner and the major competitor of the other partner, the relationship cannot be strategic.

Partners in a strategic partnering relationship recognize each other as an extension of their own firm (Lambert et al., 1996). Johnson (1999) suggested that a firm's perceptions of strategic partnering include the following: (1) its partner considered a large part of the picture; (2) its own long-term strategy is not its prime concern when it makes plans with its partner; and (3) if its partner went out of business, the firm would have to change its competitive strategy. For example, the trading company Li & Fung performs integrated product development, sourcing, financing, shipping, handling, and logistics for The Limited (Magretta, 1998a). This strategic partnership would not survive if both the trading company and the retailer were not achieving short-term operational advantages and long-term strategic goals. Further, both partners perceive the partnership as exclusive and not easily imitated by the competition.

TACTICAL PARTNERING ORIENTATION

A tactical partnering orientation seeks improvements in operational efficiency and effectiveness. Efficiency minimizes resource use to accomplish specific outcomes, whereas effectiveness is the ability of supply chains to deliver products or services in a manner that is acceptable to end users (Stern, El-Ansary, & Coughlan, 1996). Tactical objectives specify expected performance in terms of delivery speed and consistency, flexibility to handle extraordinary customer service requests, and recognition of malfunctions and recovery from them to serve customers (Bowersox & Closs, 1996). Efficiency is measured by delivery time, product quality, number of short orders, and inventory levels; and effectiveness is measured by service quality and the service needs of the focal firm and the focal firm's customers (Mentzer, 1999).

Tactical decisions involve shorter time spans (Ganesan, 1994; Lambert & Stock, 1993) and fewer organizational resources, and are easier to implement and reverse (Hitt et al., 1999) than strategic decisions. Thus, competitors are more able and likely to match tactical actions than strategic actions (Grimm & Smith, 1997). Finally, each partner does not perceive the other as an extension of its own firm.

Strategic partnering includes an orientation to view the partner as an extension of their own firm, involving the partner in long-term strategic initiatives. Tactical partnering views the partner as a close associate in improving supply chain efficiency and effectiveness in the short term. Strategic initiatives are not shared with tactical partners, but considerable operational coordination still occurs. Transactional relationships are treated on a purchase-by-purchase basis (Frazier, Spekman, & O'Neal, 1988). The relationship between the buyer and the seller does not look beyond the scope of the individual purchase and, thus, does not address the level of operational coordination of tactical partnering nor the strategic coordination of strategic partnering.

PARTNERING IMPLEMENTATION

Partnering orientation (strategic or tactical) is implemented by information sharing, technology utilization, strategic interface teams, organizational issues, joint programs, asset specificity, and establishing joint performance measures.

Information Sharing

The collection, creation, management, and communication of information are critical to the efficiency, effectiveness, and competitive advantage of any supply chain (e.g., Global Logistics Research Team, 1995; Novack, Langley, & Rinehart, 1995; Stern et al., 1996). By providing the supply chain partner with information on the firm's customer demand far in advance of when the product is needed, a lower cost of providing the product and lower incidence of customer service failure due to stockouts results (Mentzer, 1999). The combination of advance shipping notices with POS customer information, connected across supply chain partners through EDI, provides the ability for supply chain partners to coordinate their shipments with retailer demand and plans and reduce supply chain inventories by as much as 40% (Kahn & Mentzer, 1996). Savings of this magnitude have led the Food Marketing Institute (FMI) to advocate efficient consumer response (ECR) systems among its members' supply chains. However, ECR requires considerable information sharing both about the final consumers and about plans to meet demand throughout the retail supply chain.

With the advent of the Internet, this level of information coordination—and its benefits—has increased, especially in the area of Collaborative Planning, Forecasting, and Replenishment (CPFR). For example, Nabisco and Wegmans increased category sales by 13%, increased service levels from 93 to 97%, and decreased inventory days by 18% through a CPFR initiative; Kimberly Clark and Kmart increased in-stock rate from 86.5 to 93.4% and increased retail sales 14% through CPFR; and Wal-Mart and Sara Lee Apparel reduced store-level inventory 14%, increased sales 32%, and increased retail turns 17% through CPFR (VICS, 1998).

Shared information varies from strategic to tactical in nature and from information about logistics activities to general market and customer information (Global Logistics Research Team, 1995). For example, Philips Consumer Electronics experiences different types of shared information in its different partnerships: a major department store shares long-term marketing and logistics strategies as well as short-term plans with Philips, whereas a super appliance store provides only short-term demand forecasts with short notice (Mentzer, Min, et al., 2000). In the latter case, Philips has difficulty developing a long-term marketing and production plan for the partner. Thus, the nature of information shared differs with the orientation of the partners: partners with a strategic partnership orientation share information that is both strategic and tactical, whereas partners with a tactical partnership orientation share only operational information.

Day (1995) indicated that multilevel information sharing between partner firms is useful because employees of both firms realize the benefits of partnering and develop linkages at different levels to ensure smooth operations. Cooper and Ellram (1993) argued that firms in a tactical partnership maintain a single contact for the transaction, whereas strategic supply chains have multiple communication levels. In short, partners in a strategic partnership practice multilevel information sharing, whereas firms in a tactical partnership practice single or limited multilevel information sharing.

Technology Utilization

Strategic partnership success is often based on improving supply chain performance through such technology as EDI, bar coding, scanning, advance shipment notices, and sales forecasting (Mentzer, 1999). Information technology leads to more strategic partnering and greater reliance on time-based strategies, along with more transparent logistics organizational structures and increased emphasis on performance measurement (Bowersox & Daugherty, 1995). Thus, partnering technology highlights the growing importance of supply chain communication and information dissemination (Stern et al., 1996). Strategic partnering utilizes more information technology than tactical partnering in terms of the variety of technologies/databases that link the partners. More important, technology is more standardized and integrated in strategic partnering. Tactical partnering requires technology for more operational applications that are limited in scope and, thus, does not address the breadth of supply chain issues required to implement technology to realize a more strategic orientation.

Strategic Interface Teams

A team approach has been argued as the standard means of making strategic decisions that are complex or large scale (Monczka, Trent, & Handfield, 1998). In implementing a strategic partnering orientation, a firm is so dependent on the partnership that it cannot think of developing strategy without its partner (Johnson, 1999). Therefore, strategic partnering requires each partner to participate in interfirm strategic interface teams. Partners in tactical partnering need similar teams for specific tactical issues, but they are not as encompassing of the entire supply chain.

Organizational Issues

If functional silos with internal organizational barriers exist within both the buyer and supplier, it is unlikely organizational issues in a partnership will be solved (see SCM Driver One). Thus, partners in a strategic partnership establish hierarchies and reporting relationships across partners that address a multitude of supply chain–wide issues. Partners in a tactical partnership depend more upon their own hierarchy and reporting relationships while pursuing joint reporting relationships only for a more limited set of tactical goals.

Joint Programs

Joint programs include reducing supply chain inventories (Cooper, Ellram, Gardner, & Hanks, 1997; Dowst, 1988), new-product development and product portfolio management (Cooper, Lambert, & Pagh, 1997; Drozdowski, 1986; Wasti & Liker, 1997), and design of quality-control and delivery systems (Treleven, 1987). In strategic partnering, partners pursue strategic goals through ongoing, long-term joint programs (Dyer & Ouchi, 1993) that depend upon each partner's unique skills (Wasti & Liker, 1997). For example, Dell Computer treats its suppliers as if they were part of the company; thus, suppliers assign engineers to Dell's design team to launch Dell's new products and fix problems in real time when a customer calls with a problem (Magretta, 1998b). Tactical partners expect joint actions only in limited, operational, short-term areas.

Asset Specificity

Many technology-based partnering assets have little value in other partnerships and cannot be sold at any appreciable price (Mentzer, 1999). The major risk carried by the investing company is the need to recoup its investment, which might lead to opportunistic behavior that ultimately threatens the partnership (Gundlach, Achrol, & Mentzer, 1995). Reciprocal obligations balance risks between buyer and supplier and act as deterrents of opportunistic behavior (Pfeffer & Salancik, 1978). In tactical partnering, asset specificity is relatively limited because partners need few organizational resources to take tactical actions that are easy to implement (Hitt et al., 1999) and those actions are short term (Ganesan, 1994; Lambert & Stock, 1993).

Establish Joint Performance Measures

Because partners in a strategic partnership utilize more joint planning and control through a strategic interface team, it is easier for partners to establish joint objectives and performance measures. Because partnering ties the collaborating companies' forecasting and materials management activities closer together, total system inventories can often be rationalized, improving return on working capital for both partners. This is contrary to traditional agreements in which buyers and sellers focus on the effects of agreements on their own operating revenues, expenses, profits, and growth (Magrath & Hardy, 1994). Thus, partners in a strategic partnership reach agreement on broader performance measures than those in a tactical partnership. These performance measures in a strategic partnership include measures of the total system, whereas those in tactical partnering are more focused on the impact on each firm's performance.

COMPETITIVE ATTAINMENT

Competitive attainment is a continuum from competitive advantage through competitive parity to competitive disadvantage. Each of the positions along the continuum is relative to other competing supply chain partnerships. For example, a retailer may not even consider partnering with a certain vendor, carrying only token components of the vendor's product line on a transactional basis (and not incurring the implementation costs of partnering) but still offering an assortment that provides value in attracting customers because competing retailers offer no better assortment. In this case, competitive parity is achieved without partnering because no competing retailers are pursuing competitive advantage through partnering with vendors in this particular product assortment.

However, Varadarajan and Cunningham (1995) argued that strategic partnerships can achieve competitive advantage through the pooling of skills and resources and classified the advantages into cost leadership and differentiation. *Cost leadership* entails being able to perform supply chain activities at a lower cost than competitors while offering a parity product (Day & Wensley, 1988; Porter, 1980, 1985). *Differentiation* entails being able to offer a product or service that customers perceive as having consistently different and important attributes relative to competitors' offerings (Day & Wensley, 1988; Porter, 1980, 1985).

Competitive advantage from strategic partnering cannot be sustained automatically (Barney, 1991; Day & Wensley, 1988) but must be (1) valuable to customers (Barney, 1991; Day & Wensley, 1988), (2) not perfectly imitable by competition (Barney, 1991; Day & Wensley, 1988), (3) rare among a firm's competitors (Barney, 1991), (4) with no strategically equivalent substitute for the resource (Barney, 1991), (5) hard for the competition to find out how it works (Day & Wensley, 1988), (6) durable and not vulnerable to rapid depreciation or obsolescence competition (Day & Wensley, 1988), and (7) early movers have the power to deter competitors from imitating them (Day & Wensley, 1988). Competitive parity exists when the resource or capability is (1) valuable but not rare, (2) not costly to imitate, and (3) substitutable (Hitt et al., 1999). Competitive parity brings short-term market position advantage, whereas competitive advantage provides long-term advantage because it is difficult for competitors to imitate. Thus, companies that pursue operational efficiency and effectiveness will achieve only competitive parity because competitors can easily imitate them. Because manufacturers and retailers traditionally have seen each other as adversaries, it has been hard for manufacturer-retailer partnering to become strategically oriented (Hitt et al., 1999).

Companies not capable of technology or product leadership, or who are unwilling to incur the implementation costs (in terms of capital, technology, processes, risk, and people) of such relationships, are unlikely to form the close interfirm involvement that is essential in strategic partnering. Because firms in a strategic partnership are interested in accomplishing both current and future goals (Ganesan, 1994), there is a higher chance that strategic partnering creates a relationship that is not easily imitated and, thus, enables each partner to obtain competitive advantage. Firms in a tactical partnership, however, at most achieve competitive parity because they do not pursue long-term, strategic goals that lead to competitive advantage. In the case of strategic partnering, the implementation costs are incurred in hopes of obtaining a superior position over the competition. In the case of tactical partnering, the lesser implementation costs are incurred as a defensive move—to obtain or maintain competitive parity rather then slip into competitive disadvantage.

A competitive disadvantage may occur when a firm chooses not to enter partnerships with other firms in their supply chain while their competitors form partnerships, obtaining lower costs and/or differentiation. For example, small retailers in the Netherlands in strategic partnerships performed better and realized a higher profit than retailers with no partnerships (Reijnders & Verhallen, 1996).

BUSINESS PERFORMANCE

The level of competitive attainment affects both partners' business performance (Mentzer, Min, et al., 2000). Interfirm relationship performance is complex and multidimensional, and includes affective, behavioral, and economic aspects (Johnson & Raven, 1996). The highest level of competitive attainment (competitive advantage) leads to higher levels of partner economic performance, customer satisfaction and loyalty, and relationship effectiveness. Brands with high consumer loyalty face less competitive switching in their target segments, which can lead to higher prices and profitability (Moran, 1984). The same can be said of retailer customer loyalty. Relationship effectiveness is the extent to which both firms are committed to the partnership and find it productive and worthwhile (Bucklin & Sengupta, 1993; Ruekert & Walker, 1987; Van de Ven & Ferry, 1980), the extent to which each partner carries out its responsibilities and commitments, the time and effort expended to build and maintain the relationship, and the level of satisfaction with the relationship (Anderson & Narus, 1990; Ruekert & Walker, 1987; Van de Ven & Ferry, 1980).

Summary

Letting attention to short-term tactics overshadow the accomplishment of long-term strategies can hurt the profitability and competitive viability of a company or a supply chain as a whole. Setting and meeting quarterly goals is no more important than setting and meeting the long-term goals of the supply chain. These goals include the types of relationships to have with various supply chain partners to achieve profitability and competitive advantage.

13

Align Your Supply Chain Strategies and Your Reward Structures

There is a basic principle of organizational behavior (Mentzer & Bienstock, 1998a):

What gets measured gets rewarded,

and

What gets rewarded gets done.

But what happens when we pay our people to do the wrong things? Let's recall what happened to Company CC. Company CC is in the clothing business. Although proud of their new-product development efforts and how well this function is coordinated with marketing to develop and market products that are customer driven, an analysis of Company CC's inventory revealed that $19 million in inventory, half the overall value of inventory Company CC carried, was obsolete product. Why would a company let this happen? Because they rewarded management for doing it. Company CC executives were paid to do the wrong thing! Upper management compensation (bonus) was partially based upon the impact of their decisions on the retained earnings line on the balance sheet, and decreasing inventory caused retained earnings to go down. Remember, inventory shows up on the balance sheet as an asset. Thus, a $19 million decrease in inventory has to be accounted for somewhere on the balance sheet. Clearly, management is not going to want to take any action that reduces shareholder value so substantially.

However, as Table 10.1 illustrated, shareholder value was *already* that low. By keeping the obsolete inventory in stock, Company CC was not only negatively affecting the income statement every year, it was also artificially inflating the balance sheet. The fact that this method of accounting is within GAAP—after all, GAAP allows inventory to be valued at the cost of producing it—does not change the fact that Company CC is spending money every year to carry in stock inventory that has minimal market value (in fact, inventory that no one wants). The point here is that this practice is perpetuated because executives at Company CC were rewarded (in bonuses) for doing it.

The key to this SCM Driver is to reward (and thus motivate) company employees and supply chain partners to act in ways consistent with our supply chain management strategies. Several additional examples of companies that have, and have not, done this follow.

Company EE—Rewarding the Sales Force for Disrupting the Supply Chain

Company EE is a manufacturer of grocery products, but one that experienced extreme fluctuations in derived demand every quarter. Demand from their retail customers invariably followed a pattern of high the first month, high the second month, and low the third month. This pattern created the need for greater production capacity and expenses in the first 2 months, and inventory build-up during the third month. Predictably, this also created operational disruptions for Company EE suppliers.

Company EE executives were at a loss to explain the reason for this quarterly season pattern that seemed to affect all their products. Company EE products were staple items in grocery stores, so there was no logical explanation of why the final consumers would buy in such a strange pattern. In fact, analysis showed that independent demand at the retail level was fairly stable, month to month, throughout the year. Why, then, would all the retail customers order in this pattern? The answer is, they were forced to by the sales force.

The sales force compensation program was a commission on sales, with a bonus for forecasting accuracy. However, the forecast was used to set sales quotas (the sales force knew this), and Company EE wanted to motivate "rigor" in obtaining sales quotas. This last point meant salespeople received a commission on any sales in a given quarter up to the quota, but the commission percentage was cut in half for any dollar sales in the quarter over the quota. In the words of one Company EE executive, "The sales commission structure ensures that salespeople will try to set an accurate quota for themselves. Setting the forecast, and thus the quota, too high means they do not get their forecasting accuracy bonus. Setting the quota too low means they get a lower commission on the higher sales."

Of course, in retrospect, we can see precisely what salespeople were thinking; "If I set the forecast low, I will not be in danger of not hitting the forecast (and the quota), and when I hit the quota, I can simply stop selling." This is precisely what was happening. Company lore was that the salespeople were great forecasters. Of course they were. Each quarter, they intentionally underforecast, obtaining artificially low quotas. The first 2 months of each quarter, the sales force diligently sold Company EE products until quotas were hit and then refused to take any orders from retailers. Why should they take orders? If they simply delayed orders until the first day of the new quarter, they received the higher commission rate, and their "accurate" forecasts from the previous quarter earned them a bonus. In fact, customer value analysis revealed that retailers' major complaint was that it was hard (if not impossible) to obtain Company EE product at the end of the quarter, and final consumers' major complaint about Company EE products was their regular (quarterly) lack of availability. Company EE was paying their salespeople to disrupt their own supply chains and dissatisfy their customers.

Company FF—Rewarding
Operations for Making Low-Quality Products

Company FF is a manufacturer of consumer durables but one that suffered with chronic product quality problems. Company FF just did not seem to be able to make a product that was up to the quality standards of its number one competitor. Although many factors led to this problem, a look at how the two companies (Company FF and their competitor) rewarded their production managers provides an insight into the problem.

Both companies had production plants that were managed by individuals known as production managers. Their responsibility was for all the operations associated with the assembly plant: inbound materials, in-plant materials flow, assembly operations, and personnel. For both these managers, a major portion of their income was an annual bonus. This bonus was based in large part upon how each performed on the following metric:

$$\text{Bonus Metric} = \text{Number of products produced}/\text{Person-hours used}$$

This is a fairly straightforward efficiency metric, one that rewarded maximizing output (products produced) while minimizing input (person-hours). Of course, there were other metrics that affected the bonus that represented the scope of the production managers' jobs (metrics for materials used, storage capacity utilization, inbound and outbound materials flow, etc.), but the metric above was a significant component of the production managers' bonus calculation, so let's concentrate on just this aspect and what it did to the respective supply chains of Company FF and its competitor.

The larger the bonus metric, the larger the production manager's bonus, so the bonus metric tells the production manager, "I am going to be rewarded for sending people home that I do not need (decrease the denominator) and for making product (increase the numerator)." In the Company FF assembly plant, there is a checkpoint at the end of the line, and each product that passes that point adds one unit to the numerator of the bonus metric.

Notice that nothing at this point has been said about the *quality* of the products that pass this checkpoint. In fact, for Company FF, there was no statement about the quality of the products that passed the checkpoint. As long as the Company FF production manager could pull, push, or drag something that remotely looked like a Company FF product past that checkpoint, it counted toward the bonus metric. The Company FF philosophy was, "Once the product is built, we can fix anything wrong with it." Of course, that did not always happen (as evidenced by the high level of product quality complaints from customers), because many problems are harder (if not impossible) to fix once the product is completely built.

Notice also that the Company FF production manager is rewarded for sending key employees home, even if it hurts the quality of the product produced. Since the number of employees working affects the bonus metric but quality does not, the production manager is motivated to send as many people home as possible, as long as it does not affect the *number* of products produced.

The perspective of the production manager was predicable: "I *never* shut off the assembly line. Even if there is a problem in one of our root processes, I am paid to make products. So we will keep the line running, regardless of what it does to quality problems. Any problems can be fixed later."

Now let's turn to the same production manager position at Company FF's major competitor. This manager had the same bonus metric, but the numerator was defined as the number of *perfect products* that passed the checkpoint. In other words, the production manager never received credit for any product that passed the assembly line checkpoint that had *anything wrong*. Even though the problem was fixed prior to shipment, the production manager did not receive credit for making a product that was not perfect.

The manager is now paid to be obsessed with quality. The manager still has the motivation to control personnel expenditures but will not send anyone home who is vital to producing quality products. Also, if there is a problem with any of the root assembly processes, this production manager will immediately shut off the assembly line and fix the problem. After all, this manager gets a bigger bonus if only one perfect product is produced than if 1,000 imperfect products are produced.

The impact of this application of SCM Driver Twelve was profound upon the supply chains of these two companies. Company FF had a widespread (justifiable) reputation for making a shoddy product. Advertising campaigns that

emphasized the commitment of Company FF to quality were viewed by the consuming public as a joke. Their competitor, on the other hand, was widely perceived as a company that simply would not sell a product that was less than perfect. The result was predictable—Company FF steadily lost market share to their competitor.

Again, many factors contributed to the decline of Company FF, but a major contributor was the fact that the production managers were paid to do something that was not aligned with the Company FF strategy of improving product quality. Company FF failed to align their reward structure with their supply chain strategies.

Company GG—Reward Structures and Supply Chain Strategies Aligned

Since the previous examples were largely negative and addressed effects internal to one company, let's now look at an example of applying this SCM Driver across supply chain partners to a positive effect. Much like Company EE, Company GG is a manufacturer of grocery products. A major difference is that Company EE is a publicly traded company, and Company GG is a private company.

Company GG went through an extensive analysis of their supply chain processes to determine how each of the previous eleven SCM Drivers could be applied to their supply chains. The result was an ambitious strategic plan that would take significant advantage of these SCM Drivers and save Company GG an estimated $3 million per year, savings that would directly affect the bottom-line profitability of the company. The only challenge to the strategic plan was that implementation would require significant collaboration with six key Company GG suppliers and three key retailers and major changes in how Company GG managed various aspects of its own internal operations.

The culmination of the planning phase of this strategic plan occurred when the owner of the company met with the executive team to review how the plan would be rolled out over a 2-year horizon. In the middle of this meeting, the owner stopped the proceedings and said, "You know, something has just occurred to me. You're talking about putting $3 million a year in my pocket, and I'm the only one in the room excited about this. So I tell you what: I'm going to create a special, annual million-dollar bonus pool above the existing bonus system. Anyone in this company that we can document played a significant role in this strategic plan being a success gets a share of the special bonus. Now, I define success as driving that $3 million to the bottom line. Any year in which that happens, the special bonus pool exists." He then turned to his three direct reports and instructed them to devise a compensation plan to measure individual impact on the success of the plan and determine how the bonus should be accordingly paid out. Suddenly, everyone in Company GG was interested in supply chain management!

Now when we look at this offer, we see that the owner of Company GG was a very clever man. How do you make certain you clear a hurdle (i.e., $3 million)? You make certain you are far above it. In fact, the first year of implementation, the bottom line impact was not $3 million, it was $3.75 million. Company GG employees were so intent on achieving the $3 million goal, they actually paid for three fourths ($750,000/$1,000,000) of their own bonus. The owner of Company GG clearly knew how to align the reward structure for his employees with his supply chain strategies.

Speaking of supply chain strategies, what happened to those six key suppliers and three key retailers? Company GG executives went to each of the suppliers, explained in full the supply chain strategy and the fact that the supplier was critical to its success, and made the offer that any year in which the supplier fully cooperated with Company GG and Company GG achieved its profit improvement goal, Company GG would not pressure the supplier for price decreases. Further, any savings to Company GG that were a direct result of the supplier efforts would be split fifty-fifty with the supplier. The suppliers were now being paid to help Company GG make its supply chain strategy work. Similar arrangements were made with the retailers.

The result? Company GG had a supply chain that consisted of its six key suppliers and its three key retailers all working in concert (because they were being rewarded for doing so) to make the supply chain strategic plan a success. Not surprisingly, it was.

What We Know About
Supply Chain Performance Measurement

Armitage (1987) and Rhea and Shrock (1987) made an important distinction between supply chain effectiveness determinants (e.g., customer satisfaction) and effectiveness dimensions, such as timeliness and accuracy. Mentzer and Konrad (1991) reviewed the construction and use of performance measures from an efficiency and effectiveness perspective, provided an understanding of how performance measures should be constructed, and described the strengths and weaknesses of their use. They also reviewed existing practices in logistics performance measurement and suggested methods of improvement. Problems they cited in establishing performance measures included lack of resources, incomplete information, comparability, measurement error, evaluation and reward systems which encourage dysfunctional behavior, and underdetermination.

The variables used in a measure might not *entirely* measure (i.e., they underdetermine) all the aspects of actual inputs and outputs. For example,

Table 13.1   The Percentage of Survey Respondents Not Capturing Key Measures
of Supply Chain Activities and Processes

Measure	Percentage Not Capturing
Outbound freight cost	13%
Order fill rate	19%
On-time delivery	21%
Customer complaints	23%
Inbound freight cost	31%
Order cycle time	38%
Forecast accuracy	46%
Invoice accuracy	48%
Equipment downtime	54%

delaying a truck departure until it is filled with multiple shipments may improve the value of the transportation cost measure, but it does not reflect the customer service damage done as a consequence of late delivery. Neither the transportation cost measure nor the on-time delivery measure reveals the ill will of the customer or captures the value of a subsequent lost order. Supply chain measures are fragmented and only partially account for the full performance picture. The underdetermination problem produces an inherently flawed measure, especially when the view of performance is a cross-functional one. Thus, it is important to select performance measurement criteria and establish performance measures carefully. Mentzer and Konrad (1991) stated that good measurements should

- cover all aspects of the process being measured,
- be appropriate for each situation,
- minimize measurement error, and
- be consistent with the management reward system.

Keebler, Manrodt, Durtsche, & Ledyard (1999) reported that measurement of key supply chain activities and processes is not widely done. This study reported that the percentage of survey respondents not capturing key measures was remarkably high. Examples are included in Table 13.1.

Measures for supply chain activities directly affecting a customer are frequently not defined. Less than 60% of the measures were either defined *by* the customer or jointly defined *with* the customer. Keebler et al. (1999) also found the level of measurement *between firms* on key supply chain processes to be very low. Only 59% of the firms were measuring the fulfillment process. Only 22% were actually taking action to coordinate or integrate activities to improve performance based on the fulfillment measurement. Nearly 60% of the firms were *not* measuring sourcing/procurement or planning, forecasting, and scheduling. The failure to achieve agreed-upon definitions of performance and the measures that report that performance is a critical obstacle to achieving SCM Driver Twelve.

ACTIVITY-BASED COSTING

Activity-based costing can take many forms. ABC systems span a continuum from the traditional cost model with a single cost driver to a very elaborate cost system with activities for every conceivable type of work and corresponding activity drivers (Keebler, 2000b). The level of ABC sophistication varies by the proportion of overhead costs and the amount of diversity experienced within the firm.

Activity-based costing represents efforts to create accurate and integrated cost measures to increase the visibility of costs within the supply chain so that cost reduction opportunities can be identified and pursued (Keebler, 2000b). By making use of standard and engineered times and existing rate information, the supply chain activity-based costing approach considers activities across the firms in the supply chain (LaLonde & Pohlen, 1996).

There are two significant constraints. First, those firms that have not implemented ABC cannot provide supply chain–related costs at the activity level. Second, the detailed level of information about process steps and costs of activities that must be shared by the enterprises requires a highly coordinated or integrated partner relationship between them. Such interfirm relationships are difficult and slow to develop. Ultimately, restructuring the supply chain to exploit efficiencies also requires a mechanism capable of identifying and equitably allocating cost benefits between the partners as changes are implemented. Not surprisingly, implementation of ABC lags. Of the 330 firms surveyed by Keebler et al. (1999), 56% indicated they were not planning implementation of activity-based costing, 24% were planning implementation, 9% had ABC implementation under way, and 11% had completed an ABC implementation.

QUALITY

Quality measures in supply chain management range from continuous improvement measures (Fortuin, 1988), quality control systems (Hillman, Mathews, & Huston, 1990), process controls (Novack, 1989), quality programs (Read & Miller, 1991), measurement for strategic planning (Fawcett & Clinton, 1996), strategic performance (Chakravarthy, 1986), outsourcing (Foster, 1998; Aertsen, 1993), design (Stevens, 1989; Perry, 1991), and flow analysis (Scott & Westbrook, 1991; Farris, 1996).

Customer service has become a crucial measure of competitiveness in markets throughout the world. As competition has become more intense, service quality has become a primary determinant for creating overall customer satisfaction. The necessity to achieve service excellence in markets characterized by shrinking margins and tight budgets has created a powerful challenge for supply chain management. The challenge is to balance these operational realities with the need for quality customer service. Service quality can be effectively managed, even when market conditions are difficult and resources are limited, if the organization can focus on a limited number of high-priority logistics service features (Davis, 1998; Harding, 1998; LaLonde & Cooper, 1988; Mentzer, Flint, & Hult, 2001; Rhea & Shrock, 1987).

BENCHMARKING

Most managers want to have a guide to what *to* measure and to compare their own operational performance to that of their competitors, or to a best-in-class model. Most benchmarking is concerned with the *values* of measures and not the numerators and denominators that compose them, leaving the comparability and validity of the values in question (Keebler, 2000b). One notable exception to the emphasis on content rather than process benchmarking is found in the efforts of the Supply Chain Council (Pittiglio Rabin Todd & McGrath, 1994). Started in 1994 by a consulting firm that formed a consortium of many major manufacturers, the emphasis was on developing a standard process model, called the Supply Chain Operations Reference Model, or SCOR (Cohen, 1996). It identified four top-level processes—*plan, source, make,* and *deliver*—and decomposed these into multiple levels of categories and elements. Participating companies must further decompose the model into the activities and tasks particular to their operations. There has been no published evidence of the value of this approach to generating good measurement, and the approach has been faulted on the basis that there is no *one* set of governing standards that define a business model, especially because differentiation is implicit in competitiveness (Mesher, 1997).

DIFFERENCES BETWEEN
ACCOUNTING AND OPERATIONAL MEASURES

The capability to measure actual performance to plan is critical to effective management and control. In the accounting and control system, the plan (budget) can be rolled down and up the organization. It is highly integrated. Top- and low-level managers understand it and the implications for measured deviations from plan. They share a common language. Each has a specific goal. There is alignment.

The operational measurement and control system, where physical measurement takes place, does not share this alignment characteristic with the financial control system. It is not possible for the warehouse manager's measure of cases picked per labor hour, or the fleet manager's measure of deliveries per hour, to be integrated into a CEO's interest in revenue dollars billed today. This poses a dilemma. What should be measured and how? How can the physical measure be integrated with others to provide insight, value, and direction to different levels of management?

PROBLEMS WITH MEASURES

The best measure accomplishes four things:

- captures specific aspects of the activity measures
- provides actionable guidance for management intervention
- allows comparability between it and other measures
- promotes coordination between managers of interdependent upstream and downstream flows of activities (Keebler, 2000b)

Unfortunately, these four measurement criteria cannot be *simultaneously* satisfied. At the operational level, where measures can both capture specific aspects of the activity and provide actionable guidance, the degree of validity and usefulness of the measure is highest. But as measures are consolidated into higher or more strategic levels of reporting, their validity and usefulness diminishes. The reverse is true for the criteria of comparability and coordination. The degree of robustness (generalizability) and integrativeness is greatest at the consolidated or strategic level and lowest at the operational level.

The following is a summary list of problems associated with measures and the implementation of a measurement program (Mentzer & Konrad, 1991; Caplice & Sheffi, 1995; Keebler et al., 1999):

- unavailable information
- lack of resources to collect data
- incomplete/inaccurate information
- comparability
- measurement error
- lack of a customer of the measure
- lack of an owner of the measure
- may not be jointly defined or similarly interpreted
- might not facilitate trust
- conflicting goals/conflicting measures
- misdirected evaluation and reward systems
- might not encourage appropriate behaviors
- underdetermination

- may not be quantitative—soft versus hard
- may be accurate but not useful
- strategic level measures may not be actionable
- operational level measures may not roll-up
- trade-off between validity and robustness
- trade-off between integration and usefulness
- benchmark measures may not be comparable
- may not be easy to understand
- might not be collected economically
- too many versus not enough measures
- efficiency versus effectiveness measures
- measures are always backward looking
- measurement takes time and is hard work

These are some of the issues practitioners must deal with when designing measurement systems for their own departments, functions, firms, and supply chains. With a supply chain orientation necessary to construct supply chain goals, strategies, planning, and governance structures, multifirm dimensionality adds greater complexity and challenge to performance measurement.

MANAGERIAL IMPLICATIONS

Companies still have much ground to cover to design and install measurement systems that will drive improved supply chain performance. Barriers to performance measurement include (Keebler et al., 1999)

- upper management support/leadership,
- clarity of business strategy,
- resource availability to do the work,
- degree of resistance to/acceptance of change,
- skill set of employees,
- organizational culture,
- budget or project approval,
- trust, and
- reward/recognition systems.

It is amazing that the same study found, for firms making progress in performance measurement, that these same reasons were cited as *enablers*. Something must have happened in the successful firms to coordinate and align the multiple forces that motivate and reinforce the work required in creating relevant and meaningful measurement systems. Why do the majority of firms seem to be reactive rather than proactive in measuring performance? What were the catalysts that engaged the more progressive firms? The operational question always seems to be "Who wants to do this anyway?" Lacking a compelling event, and a champion for change, the status quo remains. However, it is the essence of competitive advantage to be the company that shakes up the status quo.

Summary

If performance is important, then measurement is important. Organizations, to a great degree, are not measuring key supply chain processes, activities, or outcomes and, as a result, often have reward systems that are not aligned with their supply chain strategies. Linking measures to supply chain strategies is necessary to ensure alignment and focus. Performance measurement systems should be formally evaluated and managed. Otherwise, the result is a performance measurement system where the interrelations between the measures are not known, duplication is frequent, omissions are undetectable, and many of the misalignments discussed in the examples in this chapter are the result. Measurement is a key competency of successful supply chains.

14

Putting It All Together

W hat have we learned about supply chain management and its ability to drive competitive advantage? To answer that question, let's end where we started, with a review of our first example, Company A, and what this example means in terms of our twelve SCM Drivers.

Revisiting a Previous Example—Company A

Company A is a major manufacturer of snack foods that sells through many outlets, the most prominent of which are the many stores of a mass merchandiser we called Retailer B. Retailer B represents a major percentage of sales for Company A and clearly is an important customer. SCM Driver Four tells us that "Not all customers are created equal," and Company A certainly recognized Retailer B as key to their success. Thus, Company A wanted to look for ways to compete and create value for Retailer B.

Company A realized that Retailer B was driven by the same two values that drive many retailers: traffic and vendor float. Traffic was not something Company A could influence—after all, how many people shop in a particular retail store just for the snack food—so Company A concentrated on improving the vendor float of Retailer B.

What Company A developed was a forecasting and demand planning process to manage the supply chain flow cycles: the flow of the product, the flow of services, the flow of information, the flow of financial resources, and the flow of demand and forecasts (SCM Driver Five). What they discovered was an interesting fact about many supply chains: the average time between a customer buying a Company A product in Retailer B and Company A finding out about it was 23 days! Even with EDI, the traditional, logistics-oriented inventory management system, on average, had a 23-day delay between store sales and Company A notification. This traditional system affected shelf life of the product, average days of inventory that Retailer B carried in its stores and RDCs, inventory levels Company A carried to meet the sudden large order it eventually received from Retailer B, and Company A production costs to meet this "lumpy" demand (i.e., sudden large orders from a major retailer, with no demand from this retailer between the large orders). All of these are supply chain costs that could be reduced through supply chain management.

After examining all these flows, Company A devised an offer for Retailer B that could not be refused. Company A told the retailer, "First of all, we're better at forecasting demand for our products in your stores than you are. Give us real-time, POS demand data (which includes sales of the product, promotions, merchandising activities, co-op ads, etc.), and we'll forecast individual demand. We're so certain we can do this well, we'll offer to directly manage the inventory of each of our stock keeping units (SKUs) in each of your stores (a concept today called VMI, or vendor-managed inventory). We're so sure we can do this well, if we stock out of any of our products, in any of your stores, we'll pay you a per day stock out penalty. Further, we are so sure we can do this well, we won't ask you to pay for any inventory of our product until it sells in your store." What Company A was offering to do was manage (not just forecast) demand (SCM Driver Six).

Now, the offer to Retailer B was obvious. As one supply chain executive in Retailer B put it, "You're offering to put us in the consignment business." Retailer B now has the ability to sell Company A products in all their stores and have no investment in inventory. All the inventory in their regional distribution centers and in their stores belongs to Company A, up to the instant when it sells. When it is rung up on the cash register, and the customer is taking it away, Retailer B now owes the purchase price of that product back to Company A.

The result was an incredibly high vendor float for Retailer B, made possible because no Retailer B dollars were invested in the inventory component of Retailer B's working capital of Company A products. This creates a motivation for Retailer B to sell more of this product, to give it better merchandising, better shelf location, and better store placement because the more of this product Retailer B sells, the more money Retailer B is making on a zero investment in inventory. Behind this statement was a considerable amount of customer value analysis of Retailer B by Company A.

The supply chain management system that was put in place allows Company A to monitor sales of each of their products real time in each Retailer B store. So rather than Retailer B selling the product until it hits a reorder point, then ordering from the regional distribution center, then ordering from the corporate headquarters, and eventually ordering from Company A, Company A can, first, forecast the independent demand (that is, individual customers walking into the store and buying the product) and then plan the derived demand, back through the RDCs, and eventually back to the distribution centers and production facilities at Company A.

Company A was substituting Retailer B information for supply chain assets (SCM Driver Seven)—supply chain–wide inventory and Company A operational costs and financial commitment. With regard to the former of these two, the demand information cycle in this case has been taken from 23 days to 0 days. The effect on Retailer B was obvious. They now have the same (or higher) sales of Company A products, and they have no money invested in inventory. They do not have to forecast or manage Company A products. Any orders that come into the Company A distribution centers, or the Retailer B RDCs, look like Retailer B orders. They look like they came off the Retailer B computer but, in fact, they were initiated by Company A, either to order from Company A and ship to the RDCs or for the RDCs to ship to individual stores. The inventory is entirely managed by the vendor.

The effect on Company A is equally profound but a little less obvious. Because they took those 23 days out of the information cycle (which means they have continuous demand information, real time, rather than the old lumpy occasional demand information), their inventory levels through the entire system actually went down, even though now they own the inventory in the Retailer B RDCs and retail stores. Because the demand affecting Company A is no longer lumpy and unexpected, production costs also significantly decreased. Since Retailer B agreed to instantaneous payment terms, Company A's financial commitment to accounts receivable from Retailer B was drastically reduced. Notice the supply chain synergies that resulted from both companies sticking to their core competencies—Retailer B concentrated on store management, advertising, and merchandising, and Company A concentrated on forecasting and inventory and operations management. Both companies now make more profit on the same level of sales of the same products.

Once again, let's look at the synergistic flows in the supply chain. We have already talked about Retailer B. We talked about the fact that Company A's inventory went down. But what happened to all the flows under the old system? Company A had to carry enough inventory in their own distribution centers to anticipate potential orders coming in, on average, 23 days in the future from Retailer B. Once they received that order, the product had to be moved to Retailer B and eventually would be distributed to various stores. When it hit the Retailer B system, Retailer B then issued a process that would pay Company A in 30 days. The 23-day inventory they carried, plus 30 days accounts receivable, adds up to Company A working capital invested in Retailer B of 53 days. What happened when we took the 23 days out? Now, of course, the whole 23 days of inventory did not go away because there is uncertainty, but under the new system of better, more timely information, Company A now only carries 15 days of inventory. More important, when the order actually happens, they get paid 30 days earlier. So their working capital systemwide to support Retailer B went from 23 plus 30, or 53 days, down to 15 days. Their total investment in working capital to support Retailer B sales dropped by more than two thirds!

What was not mentioned in the previous discussion of this example was how the remaining SCM Drivers also affected the synergistic success (SCM Driver Three) of this supply chain. These results would not have been successful if Company A had not made a commitment to make it easy for Retailer B to do business with them (SCM Driver Ten). Further, Company A had to be willing to ride out the several-month negative impact on sales that resulted from "burning off" the excess supply chain inventory, so a new leaner level of inventory could be reached (i.e., Company A was putting achieving strategic objectives ahead of short-term tactics—SCM Driver Eleven). Considerable analysis went into determining which products that Company A sold through Retailer B made the most profit for both companies, and more managerial attention of both companies was subsequently devoted to managing the availability of these products (SCM Driver Nine). Finally, personnel in marketing, logistics, merchandising, sales, production, product management, procurement, finance, and accounting in both companies were measured, evaluated, and rewarded for making processes and systems in this supply chain partnership work (SCM Drivers One, Eight, and Twelve).

This example illustrates managing the supply chain flows (SCM Driver Five) and having profound effects on the bottom line profitability of not just one company but several companies in the supply chain. Company A now sells more products through the Retailer B supply chain, at considerably greater margins for both. This, of course, leads to a greater willingness on the part of Retailer B to work closely with Company A, which is an ongoing source of competitive advantage for Company A.

Twelve Drivers of SCM Competitive Advantage

The Company A example tells us that competitive advantage can be obtained not just through the products sold but also through the way in which we manage the flows in a supply chain. In fact, our work with many companies like Company A led to the Twelve Drivers of SCM Competitive Advantage that have been discussed extensively throughout this book. Each of these drivers is briefly reviewed here, with a reference back to the Company A example.

COORDINATE THE TRADITIONAL BUSINESS FUNCTIONS

Much of supply chain management involves coordinating all the various business functions. Functional shifting is a term commonly used to refer to two or more companies in a supply chain deciding who best performs a certain function and allowing them to perform this function for the supply chain as a whole.

However, it is a fundamental concept of supply chain management that you cannot coordinate business functions across companies within the supply chain if you cannot do this coordination first within your own company. There is a reason we presented this driver first: the remaining eleven drivers of SCM competitive advantage come to little if this first one cannot be accomplished. To make the Company A example work, both Company A and Retailer B had to realize considerable coordination across the supply chain and within each company of the marketing, logistics, merchandising, sales, production, product management, procurement, finance, and accounting functions.

COLLABORATE WITH SUPPLY CHAIN PARTNERS ON NONCORE COMPETENCY FUNCTIONS

How companies identify and manage their core competencies and out-source noncore competencies was the focus of this SCM Driver of Competitive Advantage. Company A and Retailer B examined their core competencies and noncore competencies and decided which to outsource to, and on which to cooperate with, the other supply chain partner. As a result, Retailer B concentrated on store management, advertising, and merchandising, and Company A concentrated on demand, inventory, and operations management.

LOOK FOR SUPPLY CHAIN SYNERGIES

SCM Drivers One and Two, respectively, encourage companies to coordinate the traditional business functions within the company and across supply chain partners while keeping core competencies under internal control and outsourcing noncore competencies. The result of these two Drivers is that synergistic effects (the whole is greater than the sum of the parts) can result. However, these synergies seldom happen unless they are actively sought, identified, and managed. By managing and coordinating the supply chain, Company A and Retailer B now make more profit on the same level of sales of the same products.

NOT ALL CUSTOMERS ARE CREATED EQUAL

To achieve competitive advantage, companies must realize that some customers are critical to our success, some are less important and should be treated as such, and some are distracting us from serving the first two groups and should not be served at all. Company A realized that Retailer B was "more equal" than other retailers and other customers up and down the supply chain. As a result, Company A management asked several questions about Retailer B:

Who is our customer? (What do we know about the way Retailer B operates?)

How do we reach our customer? (What is the nature of the way we do business with Retailer B?)

How do we reach competitive advantage with our customer? (It was not just the quality of the product Company A manufactured but the ability to manage the supply chain flows that mattered to Retailer B.)

The extensive use of Customer Value Requirements Maps by Company A was critical to understanding what Retailer B valued.

IDENTIFY AND MANAGE THE SUPPLY CHAIN FLOW CYCLES

There are numerous flows in supply chain management. Products and services flow from suppliers through manufacturers through distributors through retailers to final customers. Services that accompany product flows in supply chains also flow both ways. Information about product/service availability, inventory location, transportation options, customer values, and finances—in fact, information about any aspect of supply chain management—flows up and down the supply chain. Although financial flows are ultimately up the supply chain from the final customer to all supply chain participants, the timing of those flows (again, as Company A illustrated) is a critical aspect of supply chain management. Finally, demand for products and services flows up the supply chain, and the ability to forecast, anticipate, and plan for those demand flows has a huge impact on the viability of the supply chain.

Company A sought competitive advantage with Retailer B by managing the flow of the product, the flow of services, the flow of information, the flow of financial resources, and the flow of demand and forecasts.

MANAGE DEMAND (NOT JUST THE FORECAST) IN THE SUPPLY CHAIN

Little attention has been paid to the role of sales forecasting and demand management in the supply chain or how that role might change depending upon the position in the supply chain that a company occupies. From a SCM perspective, the question arises, "Do all members of the supply chain need to forecast demand?" In the case of Company A, the answer was clear. No. The success of Company A is based largely on Company A's use of Retailer B POS independent demand information to forecast independent demand for Retailer B and then derive, from that information, the derived demand that would affect Company A and its suppliers.

As the Company A example illustrated, recognizing the differences between independent and derived demand, recognizing which type of demand affects a particular company, and developing techniques, systems, and processes to deal with that company's particular type of demand can have a profound impact on supply chain costs and customer service levels.

SUBSTITUTE INFORMATION FOR ASSETS

Information technology is changing at an incredible rate. The cost of obtaining that information is also becoming cheaper and cheaper. At the same time, the costs of assets to run a supply chain are not decreasing rapidly. The costs of inventory, plants, equipment, people, and storage facilities, to name a few, are not becoming cheaper. How do we use increasingly available and inexpensive information and information technology to eliminate other, more expensive supply chain assets? Company A invested in a process and supply chain information system that allowed access to key supply chain information 23 days sooner than was previously possible. The result was a dramatic decrease in investment by both Company A and Retailer B in supply chain inventory and an equally dramatic decrease in Company A investment in operations and financial assets to serve Retailer B.

SYSTEMS ARE TEMPLATES TO BE LAID OVER PROCESSES

No system or computer package exists today that can overcome poorly thought out processes. Processes are the procedures, rules, steps, and personnel involved in accomplishing any task or tasks. Systems are the computer and communications devices, equipment, and software brought to bear to augment accomplishment of those processes. Thus, systems are templates to be laid over processes. Company A made no systems decisions until all the process agreements with Retailer B were in place. Then, and only then, were the system templates laid over the supply chain processes.

NOT ALL PRODUCTS ARE CREATED EQUAL

Not all products contribute equally to the profitability of a company or a supply chain. In fact, many supply chains keep in stock a multitude of products that should be discontinued for lack of sales. Considerable analysis went into determining which of the products Company A sold through Retailer B made the most profit for both companies, and then more of the managerial attention of both companies was devoted to managing the availability of these products.

MAKE YOURSELF EASY TO DO BUSINESS WITH

Companies that are able to create value for their customers by satisfying their needs and wants generally increase their market share and their profitability. Thus, an important part of any business, and certainly of any supply chain, is making it easy for customers to do business with us. The results achieved by Company A and Retailer B would not have been possible if Company A had not made a commitment to make it easy for Retailer B to do business with them.

DO NOT LET TACTICS OVERSHADOW STRATEGIES

Letting attention to short-term tactics overshadow the accomplishment of long-term strategies can hurt the profitability and competitive viability of a company or a supply chain as a whole. Setting and meeting quarterly goals is no more important than setting and meeting the long-term goals of the supply chain. These long-term goals include the types of relationships to have with various supply chain partners to achieve profitability and competitive advantage. Company A had to be willing to ride out the several-month negative impact on sales that resulted from burning off the excess supply chain inventory so a new, leaner level of inventory could be reached (i.e., Company A was putting achieving strategic objectives ahead of short-term tactics).

ARE YOUR SUPPLY CHAIN STRATEGIES
AND YOUR REWARD STRUCTURES ALIGNED?

What happens when we pay our people to do the wrong things? The key to this SCM Driver is to reward (and thus motivate) company employees and supply chain partners to act in ways consistent with our supply chain management strategies. The Company A example (and, for that matter, all the positive examples in this book) only worked because personnel in marketing, logistics, merchandising, sales, production, product management, procurement, finance, and accounting in both companies were measured, evaluated, and rewarded for making this supply chain partnership work.

Summary

From the foundations of what has been written before and our experience with numerous companies, twelve Supply Chain Management Drivers of Competitive Advantage were presented in this book. Each was discussed in depth in its own chapter, illustrating its strategic impact by bringing to bear what others have said before and examples of real companies that have succeeded or failed by heeding or ignoring that SCM Driver. The purpose in each case was to stimulate the reader to think about how that particular SCM Driver can be applied in your company and supply chains.

The challenge is now yours. Will the application of these twelve SCM Drivers to your company and supply chain be a future positive or negative example? The answer is up to you, your supply chain partners, and your competitors who are trying to apply the same twelve Supply Chain Management Drivers of Competitive Advantage to achieve a competitive advantage over you.

References

Achrol, R. S. (1997). Changes in the theory of interorganizational relations in marketing: Toward a network paradigm. *Journal of the Academy of Marketing Science, 25* (Winter), 56–71.

Achrol, R. S., & Stern, L. W. (1988). Environmental determinants of decision-making uncertainty in marketing channels. *Journal of Marketing Research, 25* (February), 36–50.

Adler, T. R., & Scherer, R. F. (1999). A multivariate investigation of transaction cost analysis dimensions: Do contract types differ? *Journal of Applied Business Research, 15* (Summer), 65–79.

Adrian, P. (1998). Manufacturers gain from streamlining and integrating product development. *Manufacturing Automation, 8*(2), 3.

Aertsen, F. (1993). Contracting out the physical distribution function: A trade-off between asset specificity and performance measurement. *International Journal of Physical Distribution and Logistics Management, 23*(1), 23–29.

Aiken, M., & Hage, V. (1968). Organizational interdependence and interorganizational structure. *American Sociological Review, 33,* 912–930.

Aldridge, A., Forcht, K., & Pierson, J. (1997). Get linked or get lost: Marketing strategy for the internet. *Internet Research, 7*(3), 161–169.

Andel, T. (1997). Information supply chain: Set and get your goals. *Transportation and Distribution, 38*(2), 33.

Anderson, D., & Lee, H. (1999). Synchronized supply chains: The new frontier. In D. Anderson (Ed.), *Achieving Supply Chain Excellence Through Technology* (pp. 12–21). San Francisco: Montgomery Research.

Anderson, E., Lodish, L. M., & Weitz, B. A. (1987). Resource allocation behavior in conventional channels. *Journal of Marketing Research, 24* (February), 85–97.

Anderson, E., & Weitz, B. (1992). The use of pledges to build and sustain commitment in distribution channels. *Journal of Marketing Research, 29* (February), 18–34.

Anderson, J. C., & Narus, J. A. (1990). A model of distributor firm and manufacturer firm working partnerships. *Journal of Marketing, 54* (January), 42–58.

Anderson, J. C., & Narus, J. A. (1995). Capturing the value of supplementary services. *Harvard Business Review, 73* (January-February), 75–83.

Andraski, J. C., Wisdo, J. P., & Blasgen, R. D. (1996). Dispatches from the front: The Nabisco story. *Supply Chain Management Review,* (Summer), 30-38.

Armitage, H. M. (1987). The use of management accounting techniques to improve productivity analysis in distribution operations. *International Journal of Physical Distribution and Materials Management, 17*(2), 40–50.

Asmus, D., & Griffin, A. (1993). Harnessing the power of your suppliers. *McKinsey Quarterly, 3* (Summer), 63–79.

Aune, K. S., Buller, D. B., & Aune, R. K. (1996). Display rule development in romantic relationships: Emotion management and perceived appropriateness of emotions across relationship stages. *Human Communication Research, 23*(4), 115–145.

Balsmeier, P. W., & Voisin, W. J. (1996). Supply chain management: A time-based strategy. *Industrial Management, 38*(5), 24–27.

Barksdale, H. C., & Darden, B. (1971). Marketer's attitude toward the marketing concept. *Journal of Marketing, 35* (October), 29–36.

Barlow, J. (1994, September 25). What sparks cooperation? *The Houston Chronicle,* 2 Star Edition, Business Section, p. 1.

Barney, J. B. (1991). Firm resources and sustained competitive advantage. *Journal of Management, 17* (March), 99–120.

Barringer, B. R., & Harrison, J. S. (2000). Walking a tightrope: Creating value through interorganizational relationships. *Journal of Management, 26*(3), 367–403.

Beltramini, R. (1996). Concurrent engineering: Information acquisition between high technology marketers and R&D engineers in new product development. *International Journal of Technology Management, 1*(1/2), 58–69.

Berry, L. L. (1995). Relationship marketing of services—Growing interest, emerging perspectives. *Journal of the Academy of Marketing Science, 23* (Fall), 236–245.

Berry, L. L., & Parasuraman, A. (1991). *Marketing Services–Competing Through Quality.* New York: Free Press.

Billington, C., & Amaral, J. (1999). Investing in product design to maximize profitability through postponement. In D. Anderson (Ed.), *Achieving Supply Chain Excellence Through Technology.* San Francisco: Montgomery Research.

Birnbirg, J. G. (1998). Control in interfirm co-operative relationships. *Journal of Management Studies, 34*(4), 421–428.

Birou, L. M., & Fawcett, S. E. (1994). Supplier involvement in integrated product development: A comparison of U.S. and Europe practices. *International Journal of Physical Distribution and Logistics Management, 24*(5), 4–14.

Boddy, D., Macbeth, D., & Wagner, B. (2000). Implementing collaboration between organizations: An empirical study of supply chain partnering. *Journal of Management Studies, 37*(6), 1003–1017.

Bonaccorsi, A., & Lipparini, A. (1994). Strategic partnerships in new product development: An Italian case study. *Journal of Product Innovation Management, 11*(2), 134–145.

Bovet, D., & Sheffi, Y. (1998). The brave new world of supply chain management. *Supply Chain Management Review, 2* (Spring), 14–22.

Bowersox, D. J. (1988). Logistical partnerships. In J. E. McKeon (Ed.), *Partnerships: A Natural Evolution in Logistics.* Cleveland, OH: Logistics Resource Forum.

Bowersox, D. J., & Closs, D. C. (1996). *Logistical Management: The Integrated Supply Chain Process.* New York: McGraw-Hill.

Bowersox, D. J., & Daugherty, P. J. (1995). Logistics paradigms: The impact of information technology. *Journal of Business Logistics, 16*(1), 65–80.

Bowersox, D. J., Mentzer, J. T., & Speh, T. W. (1995). Logistics leverage. *Journal of Business Strategies, 12* (Spring), 36–49.

Bowman, R. J. (1996). Has JIT flopped? *Distribution, 95*(7), 28–32.

Boyle, B. F., Dwyer, R., Robicheaux, R. A., & Simpson, J. T. (1992). Influence strategies in marketing channels: Measures and use in different relationship structures. *Journal of Marketing Research, 29*(4), 462–473.

Buchanan, L. (1992). Vertical trade relationships: The role of dependence and symmetry in attaining organizational goals. *Journal of Marketing Research, 29* (February), 65–75.

Bucklin, L. P., & Sengupta, S. (1993). Organizing successful co-marketing alliances. *Journal of Marketing, 57* (April), 32–46.

Camp, R. C. (1989). *Benchmarking.* Milwaukee, WI: American Society of Quality Control.

Cannon, J. P., & Perreault, W. D., Jr. (1997). *The nature of business relationships.* (Working Paper). Fort Collins: Colorado State University, Department of Marketing.

Caplice, C., & Sheffi, Y. (1995). A review and evaluation of logistics performance measurement systems. *The International Journal of Logistics Management, 6*(1), 61–74.

Carter, J. R., Ferrin, B. G., & Carter, C. R. (1995). The effect of less-than-truckload rates on the purchase order lot size decision. *Transportation Journal, 34*(3), 35–44.

Cespedes, F. V. (1996). *Managing Marketing Linkages.* Upper Saddle River, NJ: Prentice Hall.

Chakravarthy, B. S. (1986). Measuring strategic performance. *Strategic Management Journal, 7*(5), 437–458.

Chiesa, V. (1996). Strategies for global R&D. *Research Technology Management, 39*(5), 19–25.

Christopher, M. L. (1999). Creating the agile supply chain. In D. Anderson (Ed.), *Achieving Supply Chain Excellence Through Technology* (pp. 28–32). San Francisco: Montgomery Research.

Clark, K. B. (1989). Project scope and project performance: The effect of parts strategy and supplier involvement on product development. *Management Science, 35*(10), 1247–1263.

Clark, K. B., & Fujimoto, T. (1991). *Product Development Performance: Strategy, Organization, and Management in the World Auto Industry.* Cambridge, MA: Harvard Business School Press.

Cohen, S. (1996). Supply chain council introduces the supply chain operations reference model. *PRTM Insight, 8*(3). Retrieved March 26, 2000, from www .prtm.com/insight/.

Collins, J. K., Kennedy, J. R., & Francis, R. D. (1976). Insights into a dating partner's expectations of how behavior should ensue during the courtship process. *Journal of Marriage and the Family, 38*(2), 373–378.

Colvin, G. (1999). How to be a great eCEO. *Fortune,* (May 24), 104–110.

Contractor, F. J., & Lorange, P. (1988). Competition vs. cooperation: A benefit/cost framework for choosing between fully-owned investments and cooperative relationships. *Management International Review, 28* (Special Issue), 5–18.

Cooke, J. A. (1999). Auto ID, software drive the supply chain. *Logistics Management Distribution Report, 38*(7), 101–102.

Cooper, M. C., & Ellram, L. R. (1993). Characteristics of supply chain management and the implications for purchasing and logistics strategy. *The International Journal of Logistics Management, 4*(2), 13–24.

Cooper, M. C., Ellram, L. R., Gardner, J. T., & Hanks, A. M. (1997). Meshing multiple alliances. *Journal of Business Logistics, 18*(1), 67–89.

Cooper, M. C., Lambert, D. M., & Pagh, J. D. (1997). Supply chain management: More than a new name for logistics. *The International Journal of Logistics Management, 8*(1), 1–14.

Cooper, R. G., & Kleinschmidt, E. J. (1986). An investigation into the new product process: Steps, deficiencies, and impact. *Journal of Product Innovation Management, 3*(2), 71–85.

Council of Logistics Management. (2003). Retrieved May 15, 2003, from www.clm1.org.

Covin, J. G., & Slevin, D. P. (1991). A conceptual model of entrepreneurship as firm behavior. *Entrepreneurship Theory and Practice, 16*(1), 7–25.

Coyle, J. J., Bardi, E. J., & Langley, C. J., Jr. (1996). *The Management of Business Logistics* (6th ed.). St. Paul, MN: West.

Craig, Z. (1997). The channel challenge. *Informationweek,* June 2, 43–46.

Cravens, D. W., Piercy, N. F., & Shipp, S. H. (1996). New organizational forms for competing in highly dynamic environments: The network paradigm. *British Journal of Management, 7,* 203–218.

Cravens, D. W., Shipp, S. H., & Cravens, K. S. (1993). Analysis of co-operative interorganizational relationships, strategic alliance formation, and strategic alliance effectiveness. *Journal of Strategic Marketing, 1*(1), 55–70.

Dabholkar, P. A., & Neeley, S. M. (1998). Managing interdependency: A taxonomy for business-to-business relationships. *Journal of Business and Industrial Marketing, 13*(6), 439–460.

Dahlstrom, R., McNeilly, K. M., & Speh, T. W. (1996). Buyer-seller relationships in the procurement of logistical services. *Journal of the Academy of Marketing Services, 24* (Spring), 110–124.

Dant, R. P., & Schul, P. L. (1992). Conflict resolution processes in contractual channels of distribution. *Journal of Marketing, 56* (Winter), 38–54.

Das, T. K., & Teng, B. (1998). Between trust and control: Developing confidence in partner cooperation in alliances. *Academy of Management Review, 23*(3), 491–512.

Daugherty, P., Stank, T., & Ellinger, A. (1998). Leveraging logistics/distribution capabilities: The effect of logistics service on market share. *Journal of Business Logistics, 19*(2), 35–51.

Davenport, T. H. (1998). Putting the enterprise into the enterprise system. *Harvard Business Review, 76* (July/August), 121–131.

Davidson, J. M., Clamen, A., & Karol, R. A. (1999). Learning from the best new product developers. *Research and Technology Management, 42*(4), 12–18.

Davis, K. T. (1998). Cash forwarding expands business for university medical products. *Business Credit, 100*(2), 10–12.

Davis, S., & Meyer, C. (1998). *Blur: The Speed of Change in the Connected Economy.* Reading, MA: Addison-Wesley.

Day, G. S. (1990). *Market Driven Strategy.* New York: Free Press.

Day, G. S. (1994). The capabilities of market-driven organizations. *Journal of Marketing, 58*(4), 37–60.

Day, G. S. (1995). Advantageous alliances. *Journal of the Academy of Marketing Science, 23*(4), 297–300.

Day, G. S. (2000). Managing market relationships. *Journal of the Academy of Marketing Science, 28*(1), 24–30.

Day, G. S., & Klein, S. (1987). Cooperative behavior in vertical markets: The influence of transaction costs and competitive strategies. In M. J. Houston (Ed.), *Review of Marketing* (pp. 39–66). Chicago: American Marketing Association.

Day, G. S., & Wensley, R. (1988). Assessing advantage: A framework for diagnosing competitive superiority. *Journal of Marketing, 52* (Spring), 1–19.

Deshpande, R., & Webster, F. E., Jr. (1989). Organizational culture and marketing: Defining the research agenda. *Journal of Marketing, 53* (January), 3–15.

Dess, G. G., & Robinson, R. B., Jr. (1984). Measuring organizational performance in the absence of objective measures: The case of privately-held firm and conglomerate business unit. *Strategic Management Journal, 5* (July-September), 265–273.

Deutsch, M. (1958). Trust and suspicion. *Journal of Conflict Resolution, 2*(4), 265–279.

Dickson, P. H., & Weaver, M. K. (1997). Environmental determinants and individual-level moderators of alliance use: Special research forum on alliances and networks. *Academy of Management Journal, 40*(2), 404.

Dierkx, I., & Cool, K. (1989). Asset stock accumulation and sustainability of competitive advantage. *Management Science, 9* (March), 59–73.

Donlon, J. P., & Galli, J. (1998). Working on the chain gang; includes related articles; panel discussion. *Chief Executive,* (January 11), 54.

Dowlatshahi, S. (1992). Purchasing's role in a concurrent engineering environment. *International Journal of Purchasing and Materials Management, 28* (Winter), 21–25.

Dowst, S. (1988). Quality suppliers: The search goes on. *Purchasing* (January 28), 94A4–12.

Drayer, R. W. (1999). Synchronize for success. *Supply Chain Management Review, 3* (Summer), 60–66.

Dresner, M., & Xu, K. (1995). Customer service, customer satisfaction, and corporate performance in the service sector. *Journal of Business Logistics, 16*(1), 23–40.

Dröge, C. L., & Germain, R. N. (1991). Evaluating logistics management information systems. *International Journal of Physical Distribution and Logistics Management, 21*(7), 22–27.

Drozdowski, T. E. (1986). At BOC they start with the product. *Purchasing* (March 13), 62B5–11.

Drucker, P. F. (1954). *The Practice of Management.* New York: Harper & Row.

Dwyer, F. R., & Oh, S. (1987). Output sector munificence effects on the internal political economy of marketing channels. *Journal of Marketing Research, 25* (November), 347–358.

Dwyer, F. R., Schurr, P. H., & Oh, S. (1987). Developing buyer-seller relationships. *Journal of Marketing, 51* (April), 11–27.

Dwyer, F. R., & Tanner, J. F., Jr. (1999). *Business Marketing: Connecting Strategy, Relationships, and Learning.* Boston: Irwin McGraw-Hill.

Dyer, J. H., & Ouchi, W. G. (1993). Japanese-style partnerships: Giving companies a competitive edge. *Sloan Management Review, 35* (Fall), 51–63.

Ellram, L. M. (1991). Life-cycle patterns in industrial buyer-seller partnerships. *International Journal of Physical Distribution and Logistics Management, 21*(9), 12–21.

Ellram, L. M., & Cooper, M. C. (1990). Supply chain management partnerships, and the shipper-third party relationship. *International Journal of Logistics Management, 1*(2), 1–10.

Emmelhainz, M. (1988). Strategic issues of EDI implementation. *Journal of Business Logistics, 9*(2), 55–70.

Farris, M. T., Jr. (1996). Utilizing inventory flow models with suppliers. *Journal of Business Logistics, 1*(1), 35–61.

Fawcett, S. E., & Clinton, S. R. (1996). Enhancing logistics performance to improve the competitiveness of manufacturing organizations. *Production and Inventory Management Journal, 37*(1), 40–46.

Feitzinger, E., & Lee, H. L. (1997). Mass customization at Hewlett Packard: The power of postponement. *Harvard Business Review, 75* (January/February), 116–121.

Felton, A. P. (1959). Making the marketing concept work. *Harvard Business Review, 37* (July/August), 55–65.

Fliedner, G., & Vokurka, R. J. (1997). Agility: Competitive weapon of the 1990s and beyond. *Production and Inventory Management Journal, 38*(3), 19–24.

Flint, D. J., & Mentzer, J. T. (2000). The logistician as a marketer: Unraveling the logistician's role with respect to changes in customers' desired value. *Journal of Business Logistics, 21*(2), 19–46.

Flint, D. J., Woodruff, R. B., & Gardial, S. F. (1997). Customer value change in industrial marketing relationships: A call for new strategies and research. *Industrial Marketing Management, 26*(2), 163–175.

Fortuin, L. (1988). Performance indicators—Why, where, and how? *European Journal of Operational Research, 34*(1), 1–9.

Foster, T. (1998). You can't manage what you don't measure. *Distribution, 37*(5), 63–68.

Frazier, G. L. (1983). Interorganizational exchange behavior in marketing channels: A broadened perspective. *Journal of Marketing, 47* (Fall), 68–78.

Frazier, G. L., Spekman, R. E., & O'Neal, C. R. (1988). Just-in-time exchange relationships in industrial markets. *Journal of Marketing, 52* (October), 52–67.

Frazier, G. L., & Summers, J. O. (1984). Interfirm influence strategies and their application within distribution channels. *Journal of Marketing, 48* (Summer), 43–55.

Galbraith, J. K. (1977). *Organizational Design.* Reading, MA: Addison-Wesley.

Gale, B. T. (1994). *Managing Customer Value.* New York: Free Press.

Ganesan, S. (1994). Determinants of long-term orientation in buyer-seller relationships. *Journal of Marketing, 58* (April), 1–19.

Garver, M. S., & Mentzer, J. T. (2000). The new role for the sales force in supply chain management. *Supply Chain Management Review, 4* (July/August), 50–56.

Garver, M. S., & Min, S. (2000). The dynamic role of the sales function in supply chain management. In John T. Mentzer (Ed.), *Supply Chain Management* (pp. 101–126). Thousand Oaks, CA: Sage.

Gaski, J. F. (1984). The theory of power and conflict in channels of distribution. *Journal of Marketing, 48* (Summer), 9–29.

Gentry, J. J. (1996). The role of carriers in buyer-supplier strategic partnerships: A supply chain management approach. *Journal of Business Logistics, 17*(2), 35–55.

Gill, P., & Abend, J. (1996). Wal-Mart: The supply chain heavyweight champ. *Supply Chain Management Review, 1* (Summer), 8–16.

Glazer, R. (1991). Marketing in an information-intensive environment: Strategic implications of knowledge as an asset. *Journal of Marketing, 55* (October), 1–19.

Global Logistics Research Team at Michigan State University. (1995). *World Class Logistics: The Challenge of Managing Continuous Change.* Oak Brook, IL: Council of Logistics Management.

Golicic, S. L., Davis, D. F., McCarthy, T. M., & Mentzer, J. T. (2002). The impact of e-commerce on supply chain relationships. *International Journal of Physical Distribution and Logistics Management, 32*(10), 851–871.

Golicic, S. L., Foggin, J. H., & Mentzer, J. T. (2003). Relationship intensity and its role in interorganizational relationship structure. *Journal of Business Logistics, 24*(1), 57–76.

Grandori, A., & Soda, G. (1995). Inter-firm networks: Antecedents, mechanisms and forms. *Organization Studies, 16*(2), 183.

Granovetter, M. (1973). The strength of weak ties. *American Journal of Sociology, 78*(6), 1360–1380.

Granovetter, M. (1985). Economic action and social structure: The problems of embeddedness. *American Journal of Sociology, 91* (November), 481–510.

Greenstein, M., & Feinman, T. M. (2000). *Electronic Commerce: Security, Risk Management and Control.* Boston: Irwin McGraw-Hill.

Grimm, C. M., & Smith, K. G. (1997). *Strategy as Action: Industry Rivalry and Coordination.* Cincinnati, OH: Southwestern College Publishing.

Grönroos, C. (1990). *Service Management and Marketing.* Lexington, MA: Lexington Books.

Grönroos, C. (1995). Relationship marketing: The strategy continuum. *Journal of the Academy of Marketing Science, 23* (Fall), 252–254.

Groves, G., & Valsamakis, V. (1998). Supplier-customer relationships and company performance. *International Journal of Logistics Management, 9* (No. 2), 51–64.

Gruen, T. W. (1997). Relationship marketing: The route to marketing efficiency and effectiveness. *Business Horizons, 6*(40), 32.

Guerrero, L. K., & Andersen, P. A. (1994). Patterns of matching and initiation: Touch behavior and touch avoidance across romantic relationship stages. *Journal of Nonverbal Behavior, 18*(2), 137–153.

Gulati, R. (1995). Does familiarity breed trust? The implication of repeated ties for contractual choice in alliances. *Academy of Management Journal, 38*(1), 85–112.

Gulati, R. (1998). Alliances and networks. *Strategic Management Journal, 19* (April), 293–317.

Gultinan, J. P., Rejab, I. B., & Roders, W. C. (1980). Factors influencing coordination in a franchise channel. *Journal of Retailing, 56* (Fall), 41–58.

Gundlach, G. T., Achrol, R. S., & Mentzer, J. T. (1995). The structure of commitment in exchange. *Journal of Marketing, 59* (January), 78–92.

Gupta, A. K., & Wilemon, D. L. (1990). Accelerating the development of technology-based new products. *California Management Review, 32* (Winter), 24–44.

Gustin, C. M., Daugherty, P. J., & Stank, T. P. (1995). The effects of information availability on logistics integration. *Journal of Business Logistics, 16*(1), 1–21.

Hamel, G., & Prahalad, C. K. (1994). *Competing for the Future.* Boston: Harvard Business School Press.

Hamill, J. (1997). The Internet and international marketing. *International Marketing Review, 14* (May), 300–323.

Harding, F. E. (1998). Logistics service provider quality: Private measurement, evaluation, and improvement. *Journal of Business Logistics, 19*(1), 103–120.

Harland, C. M. (1996). Supply chain management: Relationships, chains and networks. *British Journal of Management, 7* (March), S63–S80.

Harrington, T. C., Lambert, D. M., & Christopher, M. (1991). A methodology for measuring vendor performance. *Journal of Business Logistics, 12*(1), 83–104.

Heide, J. B. (1994). Interorganizational governance in marketing channels. *Journal of Marketing, 58* (January), 71–85.

Heide, J. B., & John, G. (1988). The role of dependence balancing in safeguarding transaction-specific assets in conventional channel. *Journal of Marketing, 52* (January), 20–35.

Heide, J. B., & Miner, A. S. (1992). The shadow of the future: Effects of anticipated interaction and frequency of contact on buyer-seller cooperation; includes appendix. *Academy of Management Journal, 35*(2), 265.

Hillman, W. T., Mathews, M., & Huston, R. C. (1990). Assessing buyer/planner performance in the supply network. *International Journal of Physical Distribution and Logistics Management, 20*(2), 16–21.

Hitt, M. A., Ireland, D. R., & Hoskisson, R. E. (1999). *Strategic Management.* Cincinnati, OH: Southwestern College Publishing.

Hodge, B. J., Anthony, W. P., & Gales, L. M. (1996). *Organizational Theory: A Strategic Approach* (5th ed.). Upper Saddle River, NJ: Prentice Hall.

Hoffman, D. L., Novak, T. P., & Chatterjee, P. (1995). Commercial scenarios for the Web: Opportunities and challenges. *Journal of Computer-Mediated Communication, 1* (December).

Hofstede, G. (1980). Motivation, leadership, and organization: Do American theories apply abroad? *Organizational Dynamics, 9*(1), 42–63.

Hofstede, G. (1984). The cultural relativity of the quality of life concept. *Academy of Management Review, 9,* 389-398.

Holmlund, M., & Kock, S. (1993). Buyer dominated relationships in a supply chain—A case study of four small-sized suppliers. *International Small Business Journal, 15* (October-December), 26–40.

Hoyt, J., & Huq, F. (2000). From arms-length to collaborative relationships in the supply chain. *International Journal of Physical Distribution and Logistics Management, 30*(9), 750–764.

Hui, C. H. (1988). Measurement of individualism/collectivism. *Journal of Research in Personality, 23,* 17–36.

Hui, C. H., & Triandis, H. C. (1986). Individualism/collectivism and psychological needs: Their relationships in two cultures. *Journal of Cross-Cultural Psychology, 17*(2), 225–248.

Hui, C. H., & Villareal, M. J. (1989). Individualism/collectivism and psychological needs. *Journal of Cross-Cultural Psychology, 20*(3), 310–323.

Hutt, M. D., Walker, B. A., & Frankwick, G. L. (1995). Hurdle the cross-functional barriers to strategic change. *Sloan Management Review, 36*(3), 22–30.

Hyman, P. (1996). Maximizing the cross-functional experience. *Electronic Buyers' News,* (April 8).

Iansiti, M., & MacCormack, A. (1997). Developing products on Internet time. *Harvard Business Review, 75* (September/October), 108–117.

Innis, D., & LaLonde, B. (1994). Customer service: The key to customer satisfaction, customer loyalty and market share. *Journal of Business Logistics, 15*(1), 1–27.

Jaworski, B. J., & Kohli, A. K. (1993). Market orientation: Antecedents and consequences. *Journal of Marketing, 57* (July), 53–70.

Johnson, J. L. (1999). Strategic integration in industrial distribution channels: Managing the interfirm relationship as a strategic asset. *Journal of the Academy of Marketing Science, 27*(1), 4–18.

Johnson, J. L., & Raven, P. V. (1996). Relationship quality satisfaction and performance in export marketing channels. *Journal of Marketing Channels, 5*(3/4), 19–48.

Kahn, K. B., & Mentzer, J. T. (1996). EDI and EDI alliances: Implications for the sales forecasting function. *Journal of Marketing Theory and Practice, 4*(2), 72–78.

Kahn, K. B., & Mentzer, J. T. (1998). Marketing's integration with other departments. *Journal of Business Research, 42*(1), 53–62.

Kalwani, M. U., & Narayandas, N. (1995). Long-term manufacturer-supplier relationships: Do they pay off for supplier firms? *Journal of Marketing, 59* (January), 1–16.

Keebler, J. S. (2000a). Financial issues in supply chain management. In J. T. Mentzer (Ed.), *Supply Chain Management* (pp. 321–346). Thousand Oaks, CA: Sage.

Keebler, J. S. (2000b). Measuring performance in supply chain management. In J. T. Mentzer (Ed.), *Supply Chain Management* (pp. 411–436). Thousand Oaks, CA: Sage.

Keebler, J. S., Manrodt, K. B., Durtsche, D. A., & Ledyard, D. M. (1999). *Keeping Score: Measuring the Business Value of Logistics in the Supply Chain*. Oak Brook, IL: Council of Logistics Management.

Kessler, M. (2003). Several consumer products to get "tagged." *USA Today,* (January 28), p. B-1.

King, R. L. (1965). The marketing concept. In D. Schartz (Ed.), *Science in Marketing*. New York: John Wiley & Sons.

Kohli, A. K., & Jaworski, B. J. (1990). Market orientation: The construct, research propositions, and managerial implications. *Journal of Marketing, 54* (April), 1–18.

Korsgaard, M. A., Schweiger, D. M., & Sapienza, H. J. (1995). Building commitment, attachment, and trust in strategic decision-making teams: The role of procedural justice. *Academy of Management Journal, 38*(1), 60–84.

Kotler, P. (1997). *Marketing Management* (9th ed.). Englewood Cliffs, NJ: Prentice Hall.

Krapfel, R. E., & Mentzer, J. T. (1982). Shippers' transportation choice processes under deregulation. *Industrial Marketing Management, 11,* 117–124.

Kumar, N., Scheer, L. K., & Steenkamp, J. E. M. (1995). The effects of supplier fairness on vulnerable resellers. *Journal of Marketing Research, 32* (February), 54–65.

LaLonde, Bernard J. (1997). Supply chain management: Myth or reality? *Supply Chain Management Review, 1* (Spring), 6–7.

LaLonde, B. J., & Cooper, M. C. (1988). *Partnerships in Providing Customer Service: A Third Party Perspective*. Oak Brook, IL: Council of Logistics Management.

LaLonde, B. J., & Pohlen, T. L. (1996). Issues in supply chain costing. *The International Journal of Logistics Management, 7*(1), 1–12.

LaLonde, B. J., & Powers, R. F. (1993). Disintegration and reintegration: Logistics of the 21st century. *International Journal of Logistics Management, 4*(2), 1–12.

Lambe, C. J., & Spekman, R. E. (1997). Alliances and technological change. *Journal of Product Innovation Management, 14*(2), 102–116.

Lambert, D. M., Emmelhainz, M. A., & Gardner, J. T. (1996). Developing and implementing supply chain partnerships. *International Journal of Logistics Management, 7*(2), 1–17.

Lambert, D. M., & Stock, J. R. (1993). *Strategic Logistics Management* (3rd ed.). Homewood, IL: Dow Jones and Irwin.

Landeros, R., & Monczka, R. M. (1989). Cooperative buyer-seller relationships and a firm's competitive posture. *Journal of Purchasing and Materials Management, 25*(3), 9–18.

Langfield-Smith, K., & Greenwood, M. R. (1998). Developing co-operative buyer-seller relationships: A case study of Toyota. *Journal of Management Studies, 35*(3), 331–353.

Larson, C. (1988). Team tactics can cut development costs. *Journal of Business Strategy, 9*(5), 22–25.

Larson, P. D. (1994). An empirical study of inter-organizational functional integration and total costs. *Journal of Business Logistics, 15*(1), 153–169.

Larson, P. D., & Lusch, R. F. (1990). Quick response retail technology: Integration and performance measurement. *The International Review of Retail, Distribution and Consumer Research, 30,* 111–118.

Larzelere, R. E., & Huston, T. L. (1980). The dyadic trust scale: Toward understanding interpersonal trust in close relationships. *Journal of Marriage and the Family, 42* (August), 595–604.

Lewis, I., & Talalayevsky, A. (1997). Logistics and information technology: A coordination perspective. *Journal of Business Logistics, 18*(1), 141–157.

Liker, J. K., Collins, P. D., & Hull, F. M. (1999). Flexibility and standardization: Test of a contingency model of product design-manufacturing integration. *Journal of Product Innovation Management, 16,* 248–267.

Lorange, P., Roos, J., & Bronn, P. S. (1992). Building successful strategic alliances. *Long Range Planning, 25*(5), 10–17.

Lusch, R. F., & Brown, J. (1996). Interdependency, contracting, and relational behavior in marketing channels. *Journal of Marketing, 60* (October), 19–38.

Lyles, M. A., & Salk, J. E. (1996). Knowledge acquisition from foreign parents in international joint ventures: An empirical examination in Hungarian context. *Journal of International Business Studies, 27* (Special Issue), 877–903.

Magrath, A. J., & Hardy, K. G. (1994). Building customer partnerships: Strengthening the foundation for customer relations in business-to-business relationships. *Business Horizons, 37*(1), 24.

Magretta, J. (1998a). The power of virtual integration: An interview with Dell Computer's Michael Dell. *Harvard Business Review,* (March-April), 73–84.

Magretta, J. (1998b). Fast, global, and entrepreneurial: Supply chain management, Hong Kong style, an interview with Victor Fung. *Harvard Business Review,* (September-October), 103–114.

Mallen, B. (1963). A theory of retailer-supplier conflict, control, and cooperation. *Journal of Retailing, 39* (Summer), 24–32.

Malone, T. W., & Rockart, J. F. (1991). Computers, networks and the corporation. *Scientific American, 265*(3), 128.

Manrodt, K. B., & Davis, F. W. (1992). The evolution of service response logistics. *International Journal of Physical Distribution and Logistics Management, 22*(9), 3–10.

McCall, G. J. (1970). The social organization of relationships. In G. J. McCall, M. M. McCall, N. K. Denzin, G. D. Suttles, & S. B. Kurth, (Eds.), *Social Relationships.* Chicago: Aldine.

McCarthy, E. J., & Perreault, W. D., Jr. (1984). *Basic Marketing* (8th ed.). Homewood, IL: Irwin.

McNamara, C. P. (1972). The present status of the marketing concept. *Journal of Marketing, 36* (January), 50–57.

Menke, M. M. (1997). Essentials of R&D strategic excellence. *Research Technology Management, 40*(5), 40–41.

Mentzer, J. T. (1999). The impact of forecasting improvement on return on shareholder value. *Journal of Business Forecasting,* (Fall), 8–12.

Mentzer, J. T. (2000). *Supply Chain Management.* Thousand Oaks, CA: Sage.

Mentzer, J. T., & Bienstock, C. C. (1998a). *Sales Forecasting Management.* Thousand Oaks, CA: Sage.

Mentzer, J. T., & Bienstock, C. C. (1998b). The seven principles of sales-forecasting systems. *Supply Chain Management Review,* (Fall), 76–83.

Mentzer, J. T., Bienstock, C. C., & Kahn, K. B. (1999). Benchmarking sales forecasting management. *Business Horizons, 42* (May-June), 48–56.

Mentzer, J. T., DeWitt, W., Keebler, J. S., Min, S., Nix, N. W., Smith, C. D., & Zacharia, Z. G. (2001). Defining supply chain management. *Journal of Business Logistics, 22*(2), 1–26.

Mentzer, J. T., Flint, D. J., & Hult, G. T. M. (2001). Logistics service quality as a segment-customized process. *Journal of Marketing, 65* (October), 82–104.

Mentzer, J. T., Foggin, J. H., & Golicic, S. L. (2000). Collaboration: The enablers, impediments, and benefits. *Supply Chain Management Review, 4* (September/October), 52–58.

Mentzer, J. T., & Konrad, B. P. (1991). An efficiency/effectiveness approach to logistics performance analysis. *Journal of Business Logistics, 12*(1), 33–62.

Mentzer, J. T., & Krapfel, R. E., Jr. (1981a). Reactions of private motor carriers to toto and compensated intercorporate hauling rights. *Transportation Journal, 20* (Spring), 66–72.

Mentzer, J. T., & Krapfel, R. E. (1981b). Reactions of shippers to deregulation of the motor carrier industry. *Journal of Business Logistics, 2*(2), 32–47.

Mentzer, J. T., Min, S., & Zacharia, Z. G. (2000). The nature of interfirm partnering in supply chain management. *Journal of Retailing, 76*(4), 1–20.

Mentzer, J. T., & Moon, M. A. (2003). Conducting a sales forecasting audit—response to the commentaries. *International Journal of Forecasting, 19*(1), 27–42.

Mentzer, J. T., Moon, M. A., Kent, J. L., & Smith, C. D. (1997). The need for a forecasting champion. *Journal of Business Forecasting, 16* (Fall), 3–8.

Mentzer, J. T., & Schroeter, J. (1993). Multiple forecasting system at Brake Parts, Inc. *Journal of Business Forecasting, 12* (Fall), 5–9.

Mentzer, J. T., & Williams, L. R. (2001). The role of logistics leverage in marketing strategy. *Journal of Marketing Channels, 8*(3/4), 29–48.

Mesher, A. (1997). Danger: Common reference models for supply chain. *Integrated Logistics Strategies, TopVIEW,* (December 3), Gartner Group.

Meyer, J. P., Allen, N. J., & Smith, C. A. (1993). Commitment to organizations and occupations: Extension and test of a three-component conceptualization. *Journal of Applied Psychology, 78*(4), 528–551.

Meyers, P. W., & Tucker, F. G. (1989). Defining roles for logistics during routine and radical technological innovation. *Journal of the Academy of Marketing Science, 17*(1), 73–82.

Miller, W. L. (1995). A broader mission for R&D: Part one. *Research Technology Management, 38*(6), 24–36.

Min, S. (2000a). The role of marketing in supply chain management. In J. T. Mentzer (Ed.), *Supply Chain Management* (pp. 355–370). Thousand Oaks, CA: Sage.

Min, S. (2000b). Inter-functional coordination in supply chain management. In J. T. Mentzer (Ed.), *Supply Chain Management* (pp. 371–390). Thousand Oaks, CA: Sage.

Min, S. (2000c). Inter-corporate cooperation in supply chain management. In J. T. Mentzer (Ed.), *Supply Chain Management* (pp. 391–410). Thousand Oaks, CA: Sage.

Min, S., & Keebler, J. S. (2000). The role of logistics in supply chain management. In J. T. Mentzer (Ed.), *Supply Chain Management* (pp. 237–288). Thousand Oaks, CA: Sage.

Min, S., & Mentzer, J. T. (2000). The role of marketing in supply chain management. *International Journal of Physical Distribution and Logistics Management, 30*(9, 10), 765–787.

Minahan, T. (1998). Enterprise resource planning: Strategies not included. *Purchasing, 125*(1), 112–113.

Mintzberg, H. (1996). Reading 6.2: The structuring of organizations. In H. Mintzberg & J. B. Quinn (Eds.), *The Strategic Process: Concepts, Contexts, Cases* (3rd ed.). Upper Saddle River, NJ: Prentice Hall.

Mohr, J., & Nevin, J. R. (1990). Communications strategies in marketing channels: A theoretical perspective. *Journal of Marketing, 54* (October), 36–51.

Monczka, R. M., Trent, R., & Handfield, R. (1998). *Purchasing and Supply Chain Management.* Cincinnati, OH: Southwestern College Publishing.

Montoya-Weiss, M. M., & Calantone, R. (1994). Determinants of new product performance: A review and meta-analysis. *Journal of Product Innovation Management, 11*(5), 397–417.

Moon, M. A., & Mentzer, J. T. (1999). Improving salesforce forecasting. *Journal of Business Forecasting, 18*(2), 7–12.

Moon, M. A., Mentzer, J. T., & Smith, C. D. (2003). Conducting a sales forecasting audit. *International Journal of Forecasting, 19*(1), 5–25.

Moon, M. A., Mentzer, J. T., & Thomas, D. E., Jr. (2000). Customer demand planning at lucent technologies: A case study in continuous improvement through sales forecast auditing. *Industrial Marketing Management, 29* (January), 19–26.

Moorman, C., Deshpande, R., & Zaltman, G. (1993). Factors affecting trust in market research relationships. *Journal of Marketing, 57* (January), 81–101.

Moran, W. T. (1984). Research on discrete consumption markets can guide resource shifts. *Marketing News,* (May 15), 4.

Morash, E. A., Dröge, C. L., & Vickery, S. K. (1996a). Boundary spanning interfaces between logistics, production, marketing and new product development. *International Journal of Physical Distribution and Logistics Management, 26*(8), 43–62.

Morash, E. A., Dröge, C. L., & Vickery, S. K. (1996b). Strategic logistics capabilities for competitive advantage and firm success. *Journal of Business Logistics, 17*(1), 1–22.

Morgan, J. (1995). Best sales reps have ideas and a desire to succeed. *Purchasing,* (November 9), 45–49.

Morgan, R., & Hunt, S. (1994). The commitment—Trust theory of relationship marketing. *Journal of Marketing, 58* (Summer), 20–38.

Morrison, I., & Schmid, G. (1994). *Future Tense: The Business Realities for the Next Ten Years.* New York: William Morrow.

Murphy, J. V. (2002a). Forecasting tool lowers Coke bottler's inventory. *Global Logistics & Supply Chain Strategies, 6* (November), 41–44.

Murphy, J. V. (2002b). Smaller companies also benefit from collaboration with partners. *Global Logistics & Supply Chain Strategies, 6* (November), 45–47.

Narus, J. A., & Anderson, J. C. (1996). Rethinking distribution: Adaptive channels. *Harvard Business Review, 74* (July/August), 112–120.

Narver, J. C., & Slater, S. F. (1990). The effect of a market orientation on business profitability. *Journal of Marketing, 54* (October), 20–35.

Narver, J. C., & Slater, S. F. (1991, October). Becoming more market oriented: An exploratory study of the programmatic and market-back approaches. *Marketing Science Institute Working Paper* (Report No. 91–128). Boston: Marketing Science Institute.

Nevin, J. R. (1995). Relationship marketing and distribution channels: Exploring fundamental issues. *Journal of the Academy of Marketing Science, 23*(4), 327–334.

Nix, N. W. (2000a). Supply chain management in the global environment. In J. T. Mentzer (Ed.), *Supply Chain Management* (pp. 27–60). Thousand Oaks, CA: Sage.

Nix, N. W. (2000b). The consequences of supply chain management: Creating value, satisfaction, and differential advantage. In J. T. Mentzer (Ed.), *Supply Chain Management* (pp. 61–76). Thousand Oaks, CA: Sage.

Nix, N. W. (2000c). Purchasing in a supply chain context. In J. T. Mentzer (Ed.), *Supply Chain Management* (pp. 205–236). Thousand Oaks, CA: Sage.

Nix, N. W. (2000d). Customer service in a supply chain management context. In J. T. Mentzer (Ed.), *Supply Chain Management* (pp. 347–370). Thousand Oaks, CA: Sage.

Nooteboom, B., Berger, H., & Noorderhaven, N. G. (1997). Effects of trust and governance on relational risk. *Academy of Management Journal, 40*(2), 308–338.

Novack, R. A. (1989). Quality and control in logistics: A process model. *International Journal of Physical Distribution and Materials Management, 19*(11), 1–44.

Novack, R. A., Langley, C. J., Jr., & Rinehart, L. M. (1995). *Creating Logistics Value: Themes for the Future.* Oak Brook, IL: Council of Logistics Management.

O'Dwyer, M., & O'Toole, T. (1998). Marketing—R&D interface contexts in new product development. *Irish Marketing Review, 11*(1), 59–68.

Osborn, R. N., & Baughn, C. C. (1990). Forms of interorganizational governance for multiple alliances. *Academy of Management Journal, 33*(3), 503–519.

Pagell, M., Das, A., Curkovic, S., & Easton, L. (1996). Motivating the purchasing professional. *International Journal of Purchasing and Materials Management, 32*(3), 27–34.

Palich, L. E., & Bagby, D. R. (1995). Using cognitive theory to explain entrepreneurial risk-taking: Challenging conventional wisdom. *Journal of Business Venturing, 10*(6), 425–438.

Parasuraman, A., Zeithaml, V. A., & Berry, L. L. (1988). SERVQUAL: A multiple-item scale for measuring consumer perceptions of service quality. *Journal of Retailing, 64*(1), 12–37.

Parker, K. (2000). Surviving in a Web-based world. *Supply Chain Management Review, 4*(1), 93–94.

Pennsylvania State University, University of Tennessee, and Michigan State University. (1995). *Creating Logistics Value: Themes for the Future.* Oak Brook, IL: Council of Logistics Management.

Perry, J. H. (1991). Emerging economic and technological futures: Implications for design and management of logistics systems in the 1990s. *Journal of Business Logistics, 12*(2), 1–16.

Peters, J. E. (1996). For logistics success, command three fronts. *U.S. Distribution Journal, 223*(7), 14. Retrieved April 21, 2000, from *Dow Jones Interactive Publications Library,* http://nrstg2p.djnr.com/.

Pfeffer, J., & Salancik, G. R. (1978). *The External Control of Organizations: A Resource Dependence Perspective.* New York: Harper & Row.

Pine, B. J., Jr. (1993). *Mass Customization: The New Frontier in Business Competition.* Boston: Harvard Business School Press.

Pisharodi, M., & Langley, C. J., Jr. (1990). A perceptual process model of customer service based on cybernetic/control theory. *Journal of Business Logistics, 11*(1), 26–48.

Pittiglio Rabin Todd & McGrath. (1994). Integrated supply chain performance measurement: A multi-industry consortium recommendation. *Conference Proceedings* (pp. 1–16). Oak Brook, IL: Council of Logistics Management.

Porter, M. (1980). *Competitive Strategy: Techniques for Analyzing Industries and Competitors.* New York: Free Press.

Porter, M. (1985). *Competitive Advantage: Creating and Sustaining Superior Performance.* New York: Free Press.

Porter, M., & Fuller, M. B. (1986). *Coalitions and Global Strategy.* In M. E. Porter (Ed.), *Competition in Global Industries* (pp. 315–344). Boston: Harvard Business School Press.

Pruitt, D. G. (1981). *Negotiation Behavior.* New York: Academic Press.

Raia, E. (1989). Quality in design. *Purchasing, 106*(6), 58–65.

Rayport, J. F., & Sviokla, J. J. (1995). Exploiting the virtual value chain. *Harvard Business Review,* (November-December), 75–85.

Read, W. F., & Miller, M. S. (1991). The state of quality in logistics. *International Journal of Physical Distribution and Logistics Management, 21*(6), 32–47.

Reijnders, W. J. M., & Verhallen, T. M. M. (1996). Strategic alliances among small retailing firms: Empirical evidence for the Netherlands. *Journal of Small Business Management, 34*(1), 36–45.

Remple, J. K., Holmes, J. G., & Zanna, M. P. (1985). Trust in close relationships. *Journal of Personality and Social Psychology, 49*(1), 95–112.

Rhea, M. J., & Shrock, D. L. (1987). Measuring the effectiveness of physical distribution customer service programs. *Journal of Business Logistics, 8*(1), 31–45.

Richeson, L., Lackey, C. W., & Starner, J. W., Jr. (1995). The effect of communication on the linkage between manufacturers and suppliers in a just-in-time environment. *International Journal of Purchasing and Materials Management, 31*(1), 21–28.

Rindfleisch, A., & Moorman, C. (2001). The acquisition and utilization of information in new product alliances: A strength of ties perspective. *Journal of Marketing, 65*(2), 1–18.

Rinehart, L. M., Eckert, J. A., Hanfield, R. B., Page, T. J., & Atkin, T. (2002). Structuring supplier-customer relationships (working paper). Knoxville: The University of Tennessee.

Rogers, D. L., & Whetten, D. A. (1982). *Interorganizational Coordination: Theory, Research, and Implementation.* Des Moines: Iowa University Press.

Rogers, D. S., Daugherty, P. J., & Stank, T. P. (1992). Enhancing service responsiveness: The strategic potential of EDI. *International Journal of Physical Distribution and Logistics Management, 22*(8), 15–20.

Rogers, D. S., Dawe, R. L., & Guerra, P. (1991). Information technology: Logistics innovations for the 1990's. *Proceedings of the 1991 Council of Logistics Management Annual Conference,* Oak Brook, IL, 245–261.

Ruekert, R. W., & Walker, O. C., Jr. (1987). Interactions between marketing and R&D departments in implementing different business strategies. *Strategic Management Journal, 8*(3), 223–248.

Salmond, D., & Spekman, R. (1986). Collaboration as a mode of managing long-term buyer-seller relationships. *AMA Educator's Proceedings,* Chicago, 162–166.

Sanchez, R. (1993). strategic flexibility, firm organization, and managerial work in dynamic markets: A strategic-options perspective. *Advances in Strategic Management, 9,* 251–291.

Santoro, M. D. (2000). Success breeds success: The linkage between relationship intensity and tangible outcomes in industry-university collaborative ventures. *The Journal of High Technology Management Research, 11*(2), 255–273.

Schewe, C. D., & Smith, R. M. (1983). *Marketing Concepts and Applications.* New York: McGraw-Hill.

Schilling, M. A., & Hill, C. W. L. (1998). Managing the new product development process: Strategic imperatives. *Academy of Management Executive, 12*(3), 67–81.

Schonberger, R. J., & El-Ansary, A. (1984). Just-in-time purchasing can improve quality. *Journal of Purchasing and Materials Management, 20* (Spring), 1–7.

Schulz, D. P. (1985). Just-in-time systems. *Stores, 67* (April), 28–31.

Schultz, R. (1984). The implication of forecasting models. *Journal of Forecasting, 3*(1), 43–55.

Schurr, P. H., & Ozanne, J. L. (1985). Influences on exchange processes: Buyer perceptions of a seller's trustworthiness and bargaining toughness. *Journal of Consumer Research, 11* (March), 939–953.

Schwalbe, R. J. (1998). SMART 2001: Supply chain management, Siemens style. *Supply Chain Management Review, 2* (Fall), 69–75.

Scott, C., & Westbrook, R. (1991). New strategic tools for supply chain management. *International Journal of Physical Distribution and Logistics Management, 21*(1), 23–33.

Sengupta, S., & Turnbull, J. (1996). Seamless optimization of the entire supply chain. *IIE Solutions, 28*(10), 28–33.

Sharma, A., Grewal, D., & Levy, M. (1995). The customer satisfaction/logistics interface. *Journal of Business Logistics, 16*(2), 1–22.

Sheombar, H. S. (1992). EDI-induced redesign of co-ordination in logistics. *International Journal of Physical Distribution and Logistics Management, 22*(8), 4–14.

Sheth, J. N., & Parvatiyar, A. (1995). Relationship marketing in consumer markets: Antecedents and consequences. *Journal of the Academy of Marketing Science, 23* (Fall), 255–271.

Siguaw, J. A., Simpson, P. M., & Baker, T. L. (1998). Effects of supplier market orientation on distributor market orientation and the channel relationship: The distributor perspective. *Journal of Marketing, 62* (Summer), 99–111.

Sinkula, J. M. (1994). Market information processing and organizational learning. *Journal of Marketing, 58* (January), 35–45.

Skjoett-Larsen, T. (1999). Third party logistics—from an interorganizational point of view. *International Journal of Physical Distribution and Logistics Management, 30*(2), 112–127.

Slater, S. F., & Narver, J. C. (1994). Does competitive environment moderate the market orientation-performance relationship? *Journal of Marketing, 58* (January), 46–55.

Slywotzky, A. J. (1996). *Value Migration: How to Think Several Moves Ahead of the Competition.* Boston: Harvard Business School Press.

Smith, C. D. (2000). Improving supply chain sales forecasting. In J. T. Mentzer (Ed.), *Supply Chain Management* (pp. 155–182). Thousand Oaks, CA: Sage.

Spekman, R. E., Kamauff, J. W., Jr., & Myhr, N. (1998). An empirical investigation into supply chain management: A perspective on partnerships. *International Journal of Physical Distribution and Logistics Management, 28*(8), 630–650.

Stahl, M. J. (1994). *Management: Total Quality in a Global Environment.* Cambridge, MA: Blackwell.

Stahl, M. J. (Ed.). (1999). *Perspectives in Total Quality.* Boston: Blackwell.

Stalk, G. (1988). Time—The next source of competitive advantage. *Harvard Business Review,* (July-August), 41–51.

Stalk, G., Evans, P., & Shulman, L. (1992). Competing on capabilities: The new rules of corporate strategy. *Harvard Business Review,* (March-April), 57–69.

Stallkamp, T. (1998). Chrysler's leap of faith: Redefining the supplier relationship. *Supply Chain Management Review,* (Summer), 16–23.

Stern, L. W. (1971). Antitrust implications of a sociological interpretation of competition, conflict, and cooperation in the market place. *The Antitrust Bulletin, 16* (Fall), 509–530.

Stern, L. W., El-Ansary, A. I., & Coughlan, A. T. (1996). *Marketing Channels.* Upper Saddle River, NJ: Prentice Hall.

Stern, L. W., & Reve, T. (1980). Distribution channels as political economies: A framework for comparative analysis. *Journal of Marketing, 44* (Summer), 52–64.

Stevens, G. C. (1989). Integrating the supply chain. *International Journal of Physical Distribution and Materials Management, 19*(8), 3–8.

Treleven, M. (1987). Single sourcing: A management tool for the quality supplier. *Journal of Purchasing and Materials Management, 23* (Spring), 19–24.

Tyndall, G. (2000). The global supply chain challenge. *Supply Chain Management Review, 3*(4), 13–15.

Van de Ven, A. H., & Ferry, D. L. (1980). *Measuring and Assessing Organizations.* New York: John Wiley & Sons.

Varadarajan, P. R., & Cunningham, M. H. (1995). Strategic alliances: A synthesis of conceptual foundation. *Journal of the Academy of Marketing Science, 23*(4), 282–296.

VICS. (1998). Collaborative planning, forecasting, and replenishment. Retrieved May 1998 from Collaborative Planning, Forecasting, and Replenishment Web site: www.cpfr.org.

Walton, S. V., & Marucheck, A. S. (1997). The relationship between EDI and supplier reliability. *International Journal of Purchasing and Materials Management, 33* (Summer), 30–35.

Wasti, S. N., & Liker, J. K. (1997). Risky business or competitive power? Supplier involvement in Japanese product design. *Journal of Product Innovation Management, 14*(5), 337–355.

Webster, F. E., Jr. (1992). The changing role of marketing in the corporation. *Journal of Marketing, 56* (October), 1–17.

Weiber, R., & Kollmann, T. (1998). Competitive advantages in virtual markets—Perspectives of "information-based marketing" in cyberspace. *European Journal of Marketing, 32* (July/August), 603–615.

Williams, L. R. (1994). Understanding distribution channels: An interorganizational study of EDI adoption. *Journal of Business Logistics, 15*(2), 173–204.

Williamson, O. E. (1985). *The Economic Institutions of Capitalism.* New York: Free Press.

Willis, C., Klimek, M., & Hardcastle, N. (1998). How winners do it. *Forbes,* (August 24). Retrieved March 26, 2000, from www.forbes.com/asap/98/0824/088.htm.

Wind, Y., & Mahajan, V. (1997). Issues and opportunities in new product development: An introduction to a special issue. *Journal of Marketing Research, 34* (February), 1–12.

Witt, C. E. (1998). Crossdocking: Concepts demand choice. *Material Handling Engineering, 53*(7), 449.

Womack, J. P., Jones, D. T., & Roos, D. (1990). *The Machine That Changed the World: Based on the Massachusetts Institute of Technology 5-Million Dollar 5-Year Study on the Future of the Automobile.* New York: Rawson.

Woodruff, R. B. (1997). Customer value: The next source for competitive advantage. *Journal of the Academy of Marketing Science, 25*(2), 139–153.

Woodruff, R. B., & Gardial, S. F. (1996). *Know Your Customer: New Approaches to Understanding Customer Value and Satisfaction.* Cambridge, MA: Blackwell Business.

Woods, L. (1991). The myths and realities of customer service. *Electronic Business, 17,* 156–158.

Zacharia, Z. G. (2000a). Research and development in supply chain management. In J. T. Mentzer (Ed.), *Supply Chain Management* (pp. 127–154). Thousand Oaks, CA: Sage.

Zacharia, Z. G. (2000b). The evolution and growth of production in supply chain management. In J. T. Mentzer (Ed.), *Supply Chain Management* (pp. 183–204). Thousand Oaks, CA: Sage.

Zacharia, Z. G. (2000c). The evolution and growth of information systems in supply chain management. In J. T. Mentzer (Ed.), *Supply Chain Management* (pp. 183–204). Thousand Oaks, CA: Sage.

Zuckerman, A. (1998). The human side of information technology. *Supply Chain Management Review, 2*(1), 80–86.

Index

About the Author

John T. Mentzer (Tom) is the Harry J. and Vivienne R. Bruce Excellence Chair of Business in the Department of Marketing and Logistics at the University of Tennessee. He is Executive Director of the Supply Chain Management Forum and Director of the Supply Chain Management Certification program, both at the University of Tennessee. He has served as a consultant for numerous companies in the area of supply chain management, taught supply chain management courses for over 25 years, conducted numerous supply chain management executive seminars, and published five books and more than 180 articles and papers in the areas of supply chain management, marketing, and logistics.